KU-547-371

The Sociology of Gender

An Introduction to Theory and Research

Amy S. Wharton

LIVERPOOL JOHN MOORES UNIVERSITY
Aldham Roberts L.R.C.
TEL. 051 231 3701/3634

Blackwell
Publishing

© 2005 by Amy S. Wharton

BLACKWELL PUBLISHING
350 Main Street, Malden, MA 02148-5020, USA
9600 Garsington Road, Oxford OX4 2DQ, UK
550 Swanston Street, Carlton, Victoria 3053, Australia

The right of Amy S. Wharton to be identified as the Author of this Work has been asserted in accordance with the UK Copyright, Designs, and Patents Act 1988.

All rights reserved. No part of this publication may be reproduced, stored in a retrieval system, or transmitted, in any form or by any means, electronic, mechanical, photocopying, recording or otherwise, except as permitted by the UK Copyright, Designs, and Patents Act 1988, without the prior permission of the publisher.

First published 2005 by Blackwell Publishing Ltd

2   2005

Library of Congress Cataloging-in-Publication Data

Wharton, Amy S.
   The sociology of gender : an introduction to theory and research / Amy S. Wharton.
      p. cm.
Includes bibliographical references and index.
      ISBN 1-4051-0124-5 (hardback : alk. paper) – ISBN 1-4051-0125-3 (pbk. : alk. paper)
1. Gender identity.   2. Sex differences.   3. Sex role.   4. Equality.
I. Title.

   HQ1075.W48 2004
   305.3–dc22

                                                                2003024688

ISBN-13: 978-1-4051-0124-0 (hardback : alk. paper) – ISBN-13: 978-1-4051-0125-7 (pbk. : alk. paper)

A catalogue record for this title is available from the British Library.

Set in 10 on 12 pt Sabon
by SNP Best-set Typesetter Ltd, Hong Kong
Printed and bound in the United Kingdom
by TJ International, Padstow, Cornwall

The publisher's policy is to use permanent paper from mills that operate a sustainable forestry policy, and which has been manufactured from pulp processed using acid-free and elementary chlorine-free practices. Furthermore, the publisher ensures that the text paper and cover board used have met acceptable environmental accreditation standards.

For further information on Blackwell Publishing, visit our website:
www.blackwellpublishing.com

Contents

Figures and Tables

FIGURES

TABLES

Preface

I have been a student of gender for almost 30 years, starting with my days as an undergraduate sociology student at the University of Oregon. Since that time I have had the opportunity to introduce the sociological study of gender to many undergraduate and graduate students. Most have been as eager as I to explore the role of gender in their lives and the larger world. This eagerness may partly reflect intellectual curiosity. I believe it also speaks to the simple fact that gender is a pervasive, yet somewhat mysterious, feature of social life that we all – at some level – seek to understand.

Sociologists and other social scientists have had *a lot* to say about gender over the past three decades. My main objective in this book is to provide a relatively concise, theoretically sophisticated introduction to this body of work. Unlike some sociology of gender textbooks, my approach is not encyclopedic: I do not try to cover every area of social life or every issue where gender is at play. Instead, I aim to provide students with some ways to think about gender – how it operates and how sociologists have tried to conceive of its expression and effects.

Like any other group of social scientists, gender scholars bring diverse conceptual, theoretical, and methodological perspectives to their work. Often, these differences give rise to provocative debates. This book does not shy away from these controversies. Engaging with these debates leaves us better equipped to articulate and defend our own views.

Early on in the book, I introduce the idea of gender as operating at the individual, interactional, and institutional levels, and I rely on this framework throughout the text. Ultimately, I want my readers to understand that gender is a multilevel system that cannot be understood by looking solely at individuals. In addition, through its impact on identities, social relations, and institutions, gender is intricately connected to many social processes.

The most important of these, as I show, is social inequality. By exploring the contours of the gender system, this book thus also provides tools for understanding gender inequality.

A.S.W.

Acknowledgments

There are many people who, directly or indirectly, contributed to this book. First, I want to thank my students and my teachers. At different times and in different ways, they have profoundly shaped my thinking about gender and sociology. My biggest debt, by far, is to Joan Acker, from whom I took my first class in the sociology of gender as an undergraduate and from whom I have continued to learn for my entire career.

I would also like to acknowledge the colleagues who have had a hand in this book, including Julia McQuillan, Jean Potuchek, and especially Serina Beauparlant. At Blackwell Publishing, I should like to thank the editorial staff of Susan Rabinowitz and Ken Provencher, and the production assistance of Valery Rose and Caroline Richards.

Finally, I acknowledge the loving support of my extended and immediate family. I dedicate this book to Melinda and Lucie, who are everything to me.

The author and publisher gratefully acknowledge the following for permission to reproduce copyright material:

Harbour Fraser Hodder, "What's in a Name?," *Harvard Magazine* (July–August 2000), pp. 21–2. Reprinted by permission of the author.

David P. Barash, "Evolution, Males, and Violence," *The Chronicle of Higher Education* (May 24, 2002). Reprinted by permission of the author.

Suzanne J. Kessler, "Ambiguous Genitalia and the Construction of Gender," extracts from her "The Medical Construction of Gender," *Signs* 16: 3–26 (1990). Reprinted by permission of the publisher and author. © 1990 by The University of Chicago. All rights reserved.

A. H. Eagly, extracts from "The Science and Politics of Comparing Men and Women," *American Psychologist*, March 1995, 50: 155–6. Copyright © 1995 by the American Psychological Association. Reprinted by permission.

Robert Goldman and Stephen Papson, " 'If you let me play': Nike Ads and Gender," an extract from their "Transcending Difference? Representing Women in Nike's World," chapter 6 of *Nike Culture*, pp. 132–5 (Thousand Oaks, CA: Sage Publications, 1998). Reprinted by permission of the publisher.

Candace West and Don Zimmerman, "Resources for Doing Gender," an extract from their "Doing Gender," *Gender & Society* (1987), pp. 125–51 (with some notes). © 1987 by Sociologists for Women in Society. Reprinted by permission of the publisher.

Ruth Milkman, "Constructing Jobs as Women's Work in World War II," extracts from her *Gender at Work: The Dynamics of Job Segregation by Sex During World War II*, pp. 49–50, 61 (University of Illinois Press, 1987). Reprinted by permission of the publisher.

Laura Den Dulk, "Work–Family Arrangements in Four Countries," extracts from her "Work–Family Arrangements in Organizations: An International Comparison," in Tanya van der Lippe and Liset van Dijk (eds.), *Women's Employment in a Comparative Perspective*, pp. 6–7, 69–72 (New York: Aldine de Gruyter, 2001). Reprinted by permission of Tanya van der Lippe and Liset van Dijk. Copyright © 2001 by Walter de Gruyter, Inc., New York.

Sandra Lipsitz Bem, "Raising Gender-Aschematic Children," extract from her "Gender Schema Theory and Its Implications for Child Development: Raising Gender-aschematic Children in a Gender-schematic Society," *Signs*, 8: 598–616 (1983). Reprinted by permission of the publisher and author. © 1983 by The University of Chicago. All rights reserved.

Patricia Hill Collins, "The Meaning of Motherhood in Black Culture," extract from *Black Feminist Thought: Knowledge, Consciousness, and the Politics of Empowerment* (Boston, MA: Unwin Hyman, 1990). Reproduced by permission of the publisher.

Michelle J. Budig and Paula England, "The Wage Penalty for Motherhood," extract from their "The Wage Penalty for Motherhood," *American Sociological Review* 66: 204–25 (2001). Reprinted by permission of the publisher and authors.

Arlie Russell Hochschild, "Women as Emotion Managers," extracts from her *The Managed Heart: The Commercialization of Human Feeling*, 20th anniversary edition, pp. 164–70 (Berkeley, CA: University of California

Press, 1983). Copyright © 1983 The Regents of the University of California Press. Reprinted by permission of the publisher.

Christine L. Williams, "Hegemonic Masculinity in Female Occupations," extracts from her *Still a Man's World: Men Who Do Women's Work*, pp. 123–41 (Berkeley, CA: University of California Press, 1995). Copyright © 1995 The Regents of the University of California Press. Reprinted by permission of the publisher.

Allan G. Johnson, "Privilege as Paradox," extracts from his *Privilege, Power, and Difference*, pp. 34–8 (Mountain View, CA: Mayfield Publishing Company, 2001). Reprinted by permission of The McGraw-Hill Companies.

Barbara J. Risman, "Gender Vertigo," extracts from her *Gender Vertigo*, chapter 7, pp. 157–62 (New Haven, CT: Yale University Press, 1998). Reprinted by permission of the publisher.

Every effort has been made to trace all copyright holders, but if any has been inadvertently overlooked, the publisher will be pleased to make the necessary arrangement at the first opportunity.

1

Introduction to the Sociology of Gender

CHAPTER OBJECTIVES

- Provide an overview of the book's general aims
- Explain how sociologists approach the study of social life and gender
- Define "gender" and identify the three frameworks sociologists use to examine this concept
- Discuss some of the ways that gender shapes individuals, social interaction, and institutions

Last summer at a family gathering, my mother asked what I would be working on during my sabbatical. "Gender," I responded. "You mean gender bias?" she asked helpfully. "No, gender," I said. There ensued an awkward silence, then my sixteen-year-old nephew quipped, "There are men and there are women. What more is there to say? Short book."

Mary Hawkesworth, "Confounding Gender"

INTRODUCTION

I identify with the narrator in this story. Like her, I have often found myself having to explain my interest in the topic of gender. Many people share – at least implicitly, anyway – the teenage nephew's belief that gender is something unproblematic, self-evident, and uncontested. Is there anything more to say?

My belief that there is, indeed, more to say on the topic of gender is the motivation for this book. In it, I hope to achieve two goals: First, I aim to convince readers that understanding gender requires us to go beyond the obvious and to reconsider issues we may think are self-evident and already well understood. Challenging the taken-for-granted is one essential component of the sociological perspective. In fact, sociologists argue that what people view as unproblematic and accept as "the way things are" may be most in need of close, systematic scrutiny. A second goal of the book is to demonstrate the ways that gender matters in social life. Though complex and ever-changing, the social world is ordered and, at some level, knowable. As a principle of social relations and organization, gender is one of the forces that contributes to this patterning of social life. By understanding gender, we understand more about the social world.

Meeting these goals is more challenging than ever before. Virtually all of the social sciences have produced a staggering amount of empirical research on gender. As this research has proliferated, so, too, have the number of theoretical and conceptual approaches to the study of gender. In fact, as Acker (1992a: 565) notes: "Although the term [gender] is widely used, there is no common understanding of its meaning, even among feminist scholars."

This multiplicity of views and perspectives does not have to result in chaos and confusion. The field's conceptual and theoretical diversity can be a source of enrichment rather than fragmentation. In order to receive the benefits of this diversity, however, students of gender must be skilled at communicating across perspectives, identifying points of overlap, convergence, and opposition. Demonstrating how this navigation among perspectives can be accomplished, while at the same time doing justice to the range and variety of theory and research on gender, presents challenges I hope to meet in the following pages.

SOCIOLOGICAL VANTAGE POINTS

There are many ways to gather information and produce knowledge, including knowledge about gender. This book, however, is premised on my belief that sociology (and the social sciences) offers the most useful vantage points from which this topic can be understood. Sociology does not provide the *only* access to the social world, of course. Fiction, music, and art, for example, all may provide people with meaningful insights about their lives. The power of sociological knowledge, however, stems from what Collins (1998: 10) calls the field's "intellectual social location." As a scientific discipline, sociology values systematic, theoretically informed analyses of the empirical world. While personal narratives and experiences are undeniably important, relying exclusively on these sources of information may lead to the "fundamental attribution error" – the tendency to explain behavior by invoking personal dispositions while ignoring the roles of social structure and context (Aries 1996; Ross 1977). Only by moving away from the purely subjective can we understand the broader social forces that shape our lives. Sociologists employ a wide variety of quantitative and qualitative methods in gathering the information that forms the basis of our empirical claims. We use these methods as means to ensure that data are gathered and analyzed systematically, with the aim of explaining and extending knowledge.

Though embracing the assumptions and methods of science as it has traditionally been conceived, sociologists have – out of necessity – also broadened these traditions. We recognize that the social world we study is complex and that this demands multiple forms of knowledge gathering, some of which may be unique to the social (as opposed to the other) sciences. Models of science that work well for those studying the natural or physical world are not always applicable or desirable for studying the social world. As numerous social scientists have pointed out, humans – unlike other species – have tremendous capacities for reflection, creativity, and agency. People are not programmable machines nor are they prisoners of their instincts. As a result, sociologists must contend with the fact that all people know something of the circumstances in which they act and thereby possess a degree of "sociological competence" (Lemert 1997: x). As sociologists, we are at our best when we can communicate with and learn from those we study. The sociological enterprise is further strengthened by its practitioners' capacities to critically reflect on the circumstances through which their knowledge is produced. The ability to engage in self-reflection and critique one's assumptions, methods, and conceptual orientations contributes vitally to the growth of sociological knowledge.

There are several, more specific characteristics of sociological knowledge – including knowledge about gender. Most importantly, this knowledge emanates from diverse theoretical perspectives and methodologies. Because they focus attention on different aspects of the social world and ask different kinds of questions, the interplay of diverse perspectives and methods helps facilitate the production of knowledge. I believe that the most useful sociological knowledge is produced collectively, through dialogue and debate, rather than in self-contained isolation. Sociological knowledge is not complete, seamless, or monolithic, however. Rather, like all knowledge grounded in the practices of science, this knowledge is incomplete, contingent, and often inconsistent.

These disciplinary characteristics have shaped what we know about gender and how we have come to know it. What follows thus draws on these characteristics. In my view, the tools of social science and sociology, in particular – while not flawless or complete – have been and continue to be the most useful in providing people with the means to challenge the taken-for-granted, to understand their own lives and the world around them, and create possibilities for change.

A Brief History of the Sociological Study of Gender

Beginnings

I took my first course on gender as an undergraduate at the University of Oregon in 1975. As I recall, the course had only been in existence for a few years. "Gender" appeared nowhere in the course title: It was called "The Sociology of Women." My experience of being introduced to the study of *gender* through the sociology of *women* was fairly typical for sociology students of my generation. The study of gender in sociology grew out of the second wave of the women's movement. One expression of this movement in colleges and universities was its criticism of academic disciplines, like sociology, for ignoring women. Women were rarely the subjects of research, and activities heavily dominated by women (e.g., housework) received little attention. To cite just one example: Blau and Duncan's 1967 "classic" study of careers, *The American Occupational Structure*, based its conclusions on a sample of 20,000 men. The relevance of these conclusions to women's occupational careers was questionable. Critics thus claimed that sociology reflected a "male bias," generating knowledge most applicable to men's lives rather than to the lives of women and to society defined more broadly.

The challenge for sociology at that time was best captured in the question posed by the late sociologist Jessie Bernard (1973: 781): "Can [sociology] become a science of society rather than a science of male society?" Reforming sociology was seen to require adding women to the sociological mix. What Smith (1974) called the "add women and stir approach" led to the sociological focus on women that guided my early coursework on gender described above. Courses on the sociology of women thus were seen as helping to counterbalance the rest of sociology, which was still viewed as essentially about men.

While the term "gender" gradually began to enter the sociological literature, the legacy of the "add women and stir" approach lingered until very recently. For example, gender scholars for many years devoted considerably more attention to women – and topics related to femininity – than to men and topics related to masculinity. In addition, much more was written about differences between women and men than was written about *variations among women* and *among men*. Perhaps more fundamental was the persistent, often implicit, assumption that sociology as a discipline could accommodate new knowledge about gender without having to rethink some of its own key assumptions about the social world. Each of these tendencies has been challenged in recent years.

Recent conceptual developments

The sociology of women has gradually given way to a sociology of gender. On one level, this change is reflected in a growing literature on men and masculinity (Connell 1995; Kimmel and Messner 1989). Although men have long been of interest to sociologists, this recent literature focuses on men as gendered rather than generic beings. This development, in turn, has been accompanied by the recognition that gender itself is *relational*: Understanding what women are or can be thus requires attention to what men are or can be.

Another important development involves the growing recognition of variations among men and among women, resulting in increased attention to masculini*ties* and feminini*ties*. The acknowledgment of multiple rather than singular expressions of gender has been accompanied by a recognition that some forms of masculinity or femininity are more socially valued than others. In this view, relations between particular kinds of masculinity (or particular kinds of femininity) are understood as relations of domination and subordination. For example, while there may be many ways to be men in American society at the end of the twentieth century, "hegemonic masculinity" denotes that which is most "culturally exalted" (Connell 1995: 77). In addition, this formulation recognizes that "masculinities [and femininities] come into existence at particular times and places and are always subject to change" (Connell 1995: 185).

A related development in the sociology of gender is the field's increased concern with the relations between gender and other bases of distinction and stratification, such as age, race or ethnicity, sexual orientation, or social class. This literature challenges the notion that women (or men) represent a homogeneous category, whose members share common interests and experiences. Theory and research exploring the intersections between race, class, and gender, for example, have proliferated exponentially (Andersen and Collins 1995). This research have been especially valuable in demonstrating the ways that these categories – acting together – shape how people experience the world. Hence, while gender, race and ethnicity, and social class are analytically separate, as aspects of lived experience, they are highly intertwined.

Ironically, some postmodern observers of these developments suggest that this diversity within and among genders makes our ability to conceive of – and draw any conclusions about – something called "gender" extremely problematic. Taken to its extreme, "[w]hat remains is a universe . . . in which the way men and women see the world is purely as *particular* individuals, shaped by the unique configurations that form that particularity" (Bordo 1990: 151, emphasis in original). This position of "gender skepticism" raises the possibility that gender is a convenient fiction, a product of language rather than social relations and organization.

Gender skeptics make provocative claims. We particularly should heed their caution about the dangers of overgeneralization. Overgeneralization occurs when one assumes that conclusions based on one group of women or men can be automatically extended to all women or all men. As we saw earlier, a similar kind of critique was what led sociologists to examine women in their own right in the first place. Nevertheless, it is important not to throw the baby out with the bathwater. Gender remains a central organizing principle of modern life: "In virtually every culture, gender difference is a pivotal way in which humans identify themselves as persons, organize social relations, and symbolize meaningful natural and social events and processes" (Harding 1986: 18).

This claim forms the basis for another kind of intellectual project – that of transforming sociological knowledge. These theorists and researchers argue that it is insufficient to simply add knowledge about gender to existing sociological literatures. Their project instead has involved a rethinking of taken-for-granted sociological concepts and ideas, with the aim of refashioning these literatures. Purportedly gender-neutral practices and institutions, such as law, work, and formal organization have received new scrutiny from scholars interested in gender. These scholars' efforts have helped move the sociology of gender from the margins to the center of sociological thought. In turn, they have contributed to the growing recognition that gender scholarship has something to offer the sociological mainstream.

WHAT IS GENDER?

What is gender? Gender used to be seen as the "psychological, social, and cultural aspects of maleness and femaleness" (Kessler and McKenna 1978: 7) – in other words, it represented the characteristics taken on by males and females as they encountered social life and culture through socialization. While a start, this conception of gender is much too narrow. As we will see, even those who believe that there are some important biological or genetic differences between women and men agree that the natural (i.e., biological, physiological, or genetic) and the social cannot be cleanly separated. Scientists of all kinds are discovering that these are not discrete realms. A second problem with this conception of gender is its tendency to assume that gender is an exclusively individual characteristic. In this view, gender is seen as sets of traits or behavioral dispositions that people come to possess based on their assignment to a particular sex category. As I hope to show throughout this book, this view is far too limiting in the kinds of questions it makes possible and the kinds of knowledge it can generate.

A working definition of gender

To get started I offer readers "a working definition of gender." This definition will be clarified and refined as the book unfolds. Following Ridgeway and Smith-Lovin (1999: 192), I view gender as a "system of social practices"; this system creates and maintains gender distinctions and it "organizes relations of inequality on the basis of [these distinctions]." In this view, gender involves the creation of both differences *and* inequalities. But which social practices are most important in creating gender distinctions and inequalities, and how do these practices operate? The book's primary aim is to examine alternative answers to these questions. In the process, readers will be introduced to the range and diversity of sociological understandings of gender.

Three features of this definition are important to keep in mind. First, gender is as much a process as a fixed state. This implies that gender is being continually produced and reproduced. Stated differently, we could say that gender is enacted or "done," not merely expressed. Understanding the mechanisms through which this occurs thus is an important objective. Second, gender is not simply a characteristic of individuals, but occurs at all levels of the social structure. This is contained in the idea of gender as a "system" of practices that are far-reaching, interlocked, and that exist independently of individuals. Gender thus is a multilevel phenomenon (Risman 1998). This insight enables us to explore how social processes, such as interaction, and social institutions, such as work, embody and reproduce gender. Third, this definition of gender refers to its importance in organizing relations of inequality. Whether gender differentiation must necessarily lead to gender inequality is a subject of debate that we will take up in the next chapter. For now, however, the important point is that, as a principle of social organization, gender is one critical dimension upon which social resources are distributed.

THREE FRAMEWORKS FOR UNDERSTANDING GENDER

Corresponding to the definition of gender supplied above, three broad frameworks will be used to organize the material presented in this book.

These frameworks correspond generally to where the "sociological action" is with respect to the social practices that produce gender: For some, this action resides in individuals – their personalities, traits, emotions, etc. This "individualist" approach will be introduced in Chapter 2. The social practice most closely associated with this framework is socialization. For others, gender is created through social interaction and is inherently contextual in its impact. This implies that gender cannot be reduced to an identity or set of personality traits. Still others argue that gender is embedded in the structures and practices of organizations and social institutions, which appear on the surface to be gender-neutral. I refer to these latter two approaches as "contextual," as they locate the forces producing gender outside the person. These approaches will be introduced in Chapter 3.

Each framework focuses attention on different aspects of the social world. As a result, each asks different kinds of questions and draws different kinds of conclusions. I envision these frameworks as being somewhat like lenses in that each brings certain issues into sharp focus, while others remain outside the field of vision and are ignored or overlooked. A particular framework thus may enable its users to perceive something they may not have noticed using another framework. At the same time as frameworks enable perception, however, they also limit what is seen by excluding other issues from view.

The fact that all frameworks are necessarily partial and selective is the basis for gender scholars' growing awareness that one alone is insufficient for understanding a topic as complex as gender. Fundamentally, gender is a multilevel system whose effects can be seen at all levels of social life. This does not mean that the frameworks we will be using fit together like pieces of a single puzzle, with the truth revealed in the whole. As we will see, pieces of one framework may be compatible with pieces of another, though this is not necessarily the case. Moving between frameworks or combining them in creative ways requires intellectual effort. What we can do here is examine the different angles of vision sociologists have used to address gender, explore the knowledge each has produced and the questions each leaves unanswered, and develop ways to navigate between perspectives.

The three frameworks for understanding gender to be used in this book include individualist, interactional, and institutional approaches. While each framework contains within it a range of viewpoints, I believe that the differences between frameworks are more salient than differences among perspectives within each framework. For example, although each framework contains some recent and some more classic perspectives on gender, the frameworks generally tended to emerge at different historical moments. As such, some have been used more extensively than others. Individualist approaches to gender have been used extensively by gender scholars throughout the social sciences and have most in common with lay understandings of gender. Included among individualist perspectives are theories drawn from psychology as well as from sociology. More recently, many theorists and researchers have moved toward a more relational understanding of gender, turning their attention to social interaction and social relations. Interactionists tend to draw on perspectives like ethnomethodology that focus on social situations. "Gendered institutions" is the most recent framework to emerge and thus is somewhat less theoretically developed than the others. Those with an institutional orientation often draw from more "macrostructural" sociological traditions.

Is one perspective more "true" than another? While specific claims made by proponents of each perspective may be empirically tested and more (or less) supported by the evidence, the perspectives themselves cannot be judged as "true" or "false." Rather, as perspectives on a multilevel phenomenon, they should be viewed as providing guidelines for analysis and investigation. Perspectives tell us what we should most carefully attend to and what we can downplay or ignore. The perspectives covered in this chapter emphasize different domains of social life and each alerts students of gender to the ways that gender operates in that domain. Throughout the book I will refer to these perspectives as they become relevant when we discuss particular aspects of gender. Some perspectives will be more relevant for some issues than others. Sometimes more than one perspective will be relevant. I believe that one perspective alone is insufficient to cover contemporary gender scholarship.

GENDER MATTERS

Why study gender? One of this book's major premises is that gender matters in social life – it is one of the organizing principles of the social world: it organizes our identities and self-concepts, structures our interactions, and is one basis upon which power and resources are allocated. Moreover, gender is a tenacious and pervasive force, its existence extending across space and time. Understanding how and, to some extent, why gender matters are issues to be taken up in the following chapters. To preview this discussion, however, we can draw on the three gender frameworks described above.

First, gender matters because it shapes the identities and behavioral dispositions of individuals. Researchers disagree over the means by which these gendered characteristics are acquired and precisely how they become a part of the person, but they agree that gender enters into how people see themselves, the ways they behave, and how they view others. While modern life enables people to have many identities, gender identity may be among the most influential in shaping the standards people hold for themselves.

Second, gender matters in the ways that it shapes social interaction. Identities, of course, are products of and sustained through interactions with others. Social interaction thus is an important setting in which gender emerges and is enacted. Social interaction also seems to require sex categorization. As Ridgeway (1997: 219) observes: "It is striking that people are nearly incapable of interacting with one another when they cannot guess the other's sex." That the identification of someone as female or male facilitates social interaction testifies to this category's power in social life.

Finally, gender also organizes social institutions. By "social institution," I mean the "rules" that constitute some area of social life (Jepperson 1991). Social institutions thus include large, formally organized, public sectors of society, such as education, religion, sports, the legal system, and work, and they include the more personal, less formally organized areas of life such as marriage, parenthood, and family. While social institutions may vary in the degree to which they are "gendered," many institutions cannot be understood without attention to the ways they embody and hence reinforce gender meanings.

As this discussion implies, gender gives shape and meaning to individuals, social relations, and institutions. We cannot fully understand the social world without attending to gender. But the opposite is equally true: We cannot understand gender without understanding the social world. As social life unfolds, gender is produced; as gender is produced, social life unfolds.

WHO'S TO BLAME? UNDERSTANDING GENDER INEQUALITY

One inadvertent consequence of an individualist view of gender is that women and men are often portrayed as either villains or victims – oppressing, exploiting, or defending against each other. While inequality does not just happen, how it happens is more complex than this. Just as gender must be viewed not simply as a property of individuals, so too, gender inequality must be understood as the product of a more complex set of social forces. These may include the actions of individuals, but they are also to be found in the expectations that guide our interactions, the composition of our social groups, and the structures and practices of the institutions we move through in our daily lives. These forces are subject to human intervention and change, but are not always visible, known, or understood. Their invisibility is one source of their power over us. They are subtle, may be unconscious, and are reproduced often without conscious intent or design. As we learn how gender operates, however, we will be better equipped to challenge it and remake the world more self-consciously and in ways that we desire.

CHAPTER SUMMARY

This chapter introduced some of the guiding themes of this book. They include my belief that gender is an important principle of social life and relations, and my contention that sociological vantage points represent the most useful way to understand these issues. The sociological study of gender is relatively young. Recent developments in this field include greater attention to men and masculinity, attention to variations within and between gender categories, and a desire to rethink important sociological concepts and ideas from a gender perspective. This chapter also introduced a "working definition of gender" and introduced the three frameworks that will be used to discuss why and how gender matters in social life.

FURTHER READING

Bernard, Jessie. 1973. "My Four Revolutions: An Autobiographical History of the ASA." *American Journal of Society* 78: 773–91.

Collins, Patricia Hill. 1998. "On Book Exhibits and New Complexities: Reflections on Sociology as Science." *Contemporary Sociology* 27: 7–11.

Smith, Dorothy. 1974. "Women's Perspective as a Radical Critique of Sociology." *Sociological Inquiry* 44: 7–13.

Stacey, Judith and Thorne, Barrie. 1985. "The Missing Feminist Revolution in Sociology." *Social Problems* 32: 301–16.

A CLOSER LOOK

Reading 1: What's in a Name?

Harbour Fraser Hodder

By now *firemen*, *policemen*, and *mailmen* sound like cultural relics from the 1950s next to the no-nonsense *firefighters*, *police officers*, and *mail carriers* who people our streets today. The once universal *he* has given way to *he or she* and the androgynous *they*. But what about first names, which rank among the most important markers of gender? Have androgynous names multiplied along with equal rights? Lowell Professor of Sociology

"What's in a Name?," reprinted from *Harvard Magazine*, July–August 2000, pp. 21–2.

Stanley Lieberson heard this question so often that he set out to analyze the names of almost 11 million babies born in Illinois between 1916 and 1989 – plus additional data from 1995 – with graduate students Susan Dumais and Shyon Baumann. (Their study, published in the *American Journal of Sociology*, confines itself to white births because of the enormous increase in newly invented names among black children from the 1960s onward.)

"I expected it to be a simple answer, that more and more children were being given androgynous names – end of story," says Lieberson, author of *A Matter of Taste: How Names, Fashions, and Culture Change* (Yale University Press). Instead, the use of androgynous names like "Dale," "Jackie," "Merle," and "Robin" remains rare, and has barely increased in 80 years. Only 1 to 2 percent, approximately, of all the children studied had unquestionably androgynous names (those whose populations included at least a third from either gender).

The authors note that "for the average girl (or boy) less than 3 percent of the children with her (his) name are of opposite sex" – reflecting the fact that, over time, name androgyny tends not to persist. A given moniker usually resolves itself into a predominantly male or female choice. A name like "Robin," for example, might become popular for both sexes, then drop out of favor for one sex – usually boys – and so lose its androgynous character. To explain these findings, Lieberson turned in a surprising direction, to a model that Thomas Schelling used to describe the process of racial segregation in housing. "The great insight provided by the Schelling model is to show how easily a racially mixed area can lose its equilibrium and become a highly segregated black area," write Lieberson and his coauthors. He adds, "The language in residential segregation is that a 'tipping point' is reached, generally from white to black – enough black move in, and the rest of the whites just sort of get out." Lieberson compares androgynous names to "neighborhoods" that are "occupied" by girls and body. If the population skews far enough toward one gender, the other sex stops moving in.

This process is not symmetrical: parents are more likely to choose androgynous names for daughters. The 1995 Illinois data showed that for college-educated parents, 8 percent of the daughters – but only 3 percent of sons – received one of 45 common androgynous names. "To some degree the androgyny is appealing," says Lieberson. "But this can also give it a negative value for their sons and a positive value for their daughters." The researchers explain this asymmetry using the well-known sociological concept of *status contamination*: "The advantaged have a greater incentive to avoid having their status confused with the disadvantaged," they write. If boys (like whites) are relatively advantaged compared with girls (or blacks), these privileged groups will systematically "leave the neighborhood" when customary markers of status disappear – as they do when names lose their sexual specificity.

Consider "Kim," a name that was popular for both sexes in the 1950s. In Illinois, male Kims increased steadily in the early '50s, until 153 boys and 90 girls received the name in 1953. The following year, movie star Kim Novak became a top box-office attraction. That year saw the start of a drastic upsurge in girls named "Kim": by 1957 there were 453 female Kims – but only 76 boys. "Isn't that a mind-blower?" interjects Lieberson, who is particularly fond of this graph. "You know it's not chance, because just the year of her debut, *phew*!" and his thumb shoots up. "For males," he adds, "use of the name did go up slightly for a year, continuing the earlier trend, but then it really dropped off."

The appearance of someone like Kim Novak in the cultural consciousness "accelerates and maybe alters the trend," Lieberson explains. The Novak phenomenon "really killed the name 'Kim' for boys," he says, adding with a laugh, "You don't want to name your son after a screen goddess."

References

Lieberson, Stanley. 2000. *A Matter of Taste: How Names, Fashion, and Culture Change.* New Haven, CT: Yale University Press.

Lieberson, Stanley, Dumais, Susan, and Baumann, Shyon. 2000. "The Instability of Androgynous Names: The Symbolic Maintenance of Gender Boundaries." *American Journal of Sociology* 105: 1249–87.

What has been the fate of androgynous names? What does this say about the significance of gender distinctions in daily life?

Part I

Conceptual Approaches

2

The Gendered Person

CHAPTER OBJECTIVES

- Define key terms and understand the debates over their use
- Critically evaluate psychological research on sex differences
- Critically evaluate research on the biological and genetic contributions to the study of sex differences
- Critically evaluate sociological views of gender as an individual attribute

What is gender? For many, answering this question requires attention to personalities, minds, bodies, and all the other characteristics that comprise individuals. In this view, gender is reflected in who people are or how they behave; it is something that individuals possess as a part of themselves and that accompanies them as they move through life. This "something" may be understood in terms of masculinity or femininity, or it may be defined more specifically in terms of particular qualities or characteristics. In all instances, however, gender is understood as something that resides in the individual. This way of thinking about gender – what I call the individualist perspective – is probably the most widely shared of the three frameworks we will be discussing in this book. In this chapter, we will critically examine this approach, looking at some of the many ways that sociologists and psychologists have applied this framework.

We begin this discussion with an important issue of terminology. As you have probably noticed, I have used the terms "gender" and "sex" frequently in the preceding pages. There is no firm consensus on the appropriate use of these two terms among gender scholars. Some reject the term "sex" altogether and refer only to "gender." Others use the terms almost interchangeably, while still others employ both concepts and recognize a clear distinction between them. These differences in usage are not merely semantic; rather, they reflect more fundamental differences in perspective and theoretical orientation. Understanding the sociological meaning of sex and its relationship to gender is our first order of business in this chapter.

In the second part of the chapter I will explore the "gendered person" in more detail by looking at some of the ways that gender has been conceptualized by sociologists (and psychologists). Despite the fact that all treat gender as a characteristic of individuals, there is tremendous diversity among their approaches to this issue.

SEX AND GENDER

Sex and sex category

In conversation people often refer to men or women as the "opposite sex." The term "opposite sex" implies that men and women belong to completely separate categories. Are women and men truly opposites? In fact, human males and females share many characteristics, especially biological characteristics. For example, both normally have 23 pairs of chromosomes and they are warm-blooded: In other respects, however, male and female bodies differ. These distinguishing characteristics, which include chromosomal differences, external and internal sexual structures, hormonal production, and other physiological differences, and secondary sex characteristics, signify **sex**.

The claim that sex marks a distinction between two physically and genetically discrete categories of people is called **sexual dimorphism**. Many view sexual dimorphism in humans as a biological fact; they believe that sexual differentiation creates two "structurally distinguishable" categories of humans (Breedlove 1994: 390). Others are more skeptical, arguing that social rather than biological forces produce two sexes in humans. This disagreement, which I will return to below, is an important area of debate among gender scholars.

In addition to the concept of sex, sociologists also use terms such as **sex assignment** or **sex category**. These concepts describe the processes through which social meanings are attached to biological sex. Sex assignment refers to the process – occurring at birth or even prenatally – by which people are identified as male or female (their sex category). Sex assignment is guided, at least in part, by socially agreed upon criteria for identifying sex, such as external genitalia. In most cases, sex assignment is a straightforward matter. Yet this is not always the case. Researchers estimate that in as many as 2 percent of all live births, infants cannot be easily categorized as male and female (Blackless et al. 2000). In these cases, the sex chromosomes, external genitalia, and/or the internal reproductive system do not fit the standard for males or females. These individuals are called **intersexuals**.

Lessons from the intersexed

Intersexuals have been a subject of fascination and debate throughout recorded history (Kessler 1998). More than any other group, however, the medical profession has defined the issue of intersexuality and societal responses to it. Not surprisingly, as medical technology has become more sophisticated, intersexuality has come to be defined as a condition requiring medical intervention – as a "correctable birth defect" (Kessler 1998: 5). In these cases, doctors perform complicated surgery designed to provide an infant with "normal" genitals – that is, with genitals that match a particular sex category.

In recent years, some intersexuals have begun to speak out against this practice of surgically altering children born with ambiguous genitalia. In 1992, Cheryl Chase, an intersex woman, founded an organization called the Intersex Society of North America (ISNA). This group's primary goal is to reduce, if not eliminate, genital surgery on intersex infants. Instead, members of INSA believe that surgery should be a choice made when the intersexed person is old enough to give informed consent. In 1996, members of INSA demonstrated at the American Academy of Pediatrics annual meeting in Boston, advocating "an avoidance of unnecessary genital surgery, family counseling with regard to the child's future medical needs and options, complete disclosure of medical files, referral of the adolescent to peer support, and the fully informed consent of the intersexual youth to any and all medical procedures" (Turner 1999: 457). INSA also advocates for people's right to remain intersexed and to gain social acceptance for this status. Members of ISNA thus reject the belief that everyone must fall into one of two sex categories, and they envision a society where genital variation is accepted.

INSA's goals may sound unrealistic. The fact that it is difficult to imagine a world where genitals no longer anchor people's understanding of male and female underscores the close ties between genitals and gender in people's taken-for-granted reality. Hawkesworth (1997: 649) calls this taken-for-granted reality "the 'natural attitude' toward gender." The "natural attitude" comprises a set of beliefs that on the surface appear

LIVERPOOL JOHN MOORES UNIVERSITY
LEARNING SERVICES

"obvious" and thus not open to examination or questioning. Among these "unquestionable axioms" are: "the beliefs that there are two and only two genders; gender is invariant; genitals are the essential signs of gender; the male/female dichotomy is natural; being masculine or feminine is not a matter of choice; all individuals can (and must) be classified as masculine or feminine" (Hawkesworth 1997: 649; Garfinkel 1967). By raising the possibility that genitals are not definitive evidence of one's maleness or femaleness, intersexuals are challenging "the natural attitude."

Sex or gender?

INSA and research on intersexuals have helped reveal the social processes that shape assignment to and (in the case of many intersexuals) construction of a sex category. These efforts can be seen as part of a broader attempt to understand the links between sex and gender. Most now agree that the biological or genetic aspects of maleness and femaleness cannot be understood as fully separate and distinct from the social processes and practices that give meaning to these characteristics. As Hoyenga and Hoyenga (1993: 6) explain: "We are the products of both our biologies and our past and present environments, simultaneously and inseparably; we are bodies as well as minds at one and the same time."

This view – that biology and society interact to shape human behavior – may not seem controversial, but researchers disagree over exactly how this interaction should be understood. Is sex the biological and genetic substrate from which gender distinctions emerge, or do gender distinctions lead us to perceive two, easily distinguishable sexes? Is sexual dimorphism itself a social construction?

The two positions in this discussion represent fairly distinct conceptions of the body (Connell 1995) and hence a disagreement over the *degree to which they see sex as socially constructed*. At one end of the spectrum are those who believe that gender is not grounded in any biological or genetic reality (Lorber 1994). In this view, the body "is a more or less neutral surface or landscape on which a social symbolism is imprinted" (Connell 1995: 46). Accordingly, sexual dimorphism, from this perspective, is less an objective reality than a socially constructed distinction. In Kessler and McKenna's words, "Scientists construct dimorphism where there is continuity . . . Biological, psychological, and social differences do not lead to our seeing two genders. Our seeing of two genders leads to the 'discovery' of biological, psychological, and social differences" (1978: 163). In other words, first we have social understandings of what men and women are, or should be, and then we perceive sex differences.

Kessler and McKenna (1978) suggest that, while assignment to a sex category occurs first at birth (or perhaps even prenatally), people continue to categorize one another as males or females throughout life. This continual process of categorization (or, in their words, "attribution") is the means through which gender distinctions emerge and are reproduced. As these authors explain, however, adults typically lack the kind of information about others' bodies that is used to assign sex category at birth. In particular, since clothing usually hides people's genitals from the view of others, people rely on other "markers" to assign a sex category. These markers may include physical characteristics, such as hair, body type, or voice, or they may include aspects of dress, mannerisms, or behavior.

What count as markers of sex category depend heavily on cultural circumstances and thus vary widely across time, place, and social group. For example, long hair on men became more common among some segments of American society during the 1960s than it had been previously. Since many men on college campuses during that time had long hair, this attribute was not a reliable marker of sex category in those settings in the way that it had been in the 1950s. Matters of appropriate hair length for women and men – as well as views about appropriate clothing or decoration – are clearly governed by social norms, rather than biological or genetic factors. That these and other related characteristics are used to assign a person to a sex category thus underscores the idea that assignment to sex categories relies heavily on social criteria. Moreover, as the hair length example shows, social understandings about gender also enter into these judgments. As views on what are acceptable ways to express oneself as a male or female change, so too do markers of sex category.

These processes are further complicated by Kessler and McKenna's observation that, regardless of what criteria are invoked to assign sex category, there is none that works in every circumstance to distinguish males from females. As these authors explain: "If we ask by what criteria a person might classify someone as being either male or female, the answers appear so self-evident as to make the question trivial. But consider a list of items that differentiate males from females. There are none that always and without exception are true of only one gender. No behavioral characteristic (e.g., crying or physical aggression) is always present or never present for one gender. Neither can physical characteristics – either visible (e.g., beards), unexposed (e.g., genitals), or normally unexamined (e.g., gonads) – always differentiate the genders" (Kessler and McKenna 1978: 1–2). Returning to the example of hair length, it is obvious that, even in the 1950s, one could not use long hair as a marker of the female sex.

These claims imply that sex distinctions are not based on any fully "objective" characteristics of human beings; rather, they are themselves social constructions (Kessler and McKenna 1978). Further, this means that it is impossible to conceive of sex apart from gender. Rather than sex being the basis for gender distinctions, as some claim, this view argues that gender is the basis for distinctions based on sex.

From this perspective, the fact that most people *believe* in the existence of two, objectively identifiable and, hence, "real" sex categories is what requires explanation. Researchers like Kessler and McKenna want to explain how sex distinctions take on their self-evident quality and why belief in these distinctions is so "incorrigible," as they put it, and thus resistant to change (Garfinkel 1967: 122–8). Kessler and McKenna's perspective may be difficult to grasp, since a belief in objectively real sex categories is a widely shared view in Western thought. Ironically, however, the very taken-for-grantedness of this belief fuels Kessler and McKenna's interest in understanding how such a widely shared view emerges in daily life.

If gender meanings have their roots in the social world, as this position implies, then social, rather than biological or genetic, processes are the key to understanding gender. These social processes might include individually focused practices, such as socialization (examined later in this chapter) or they could include social practices operating at other levels of analysis, such as those occurring within groups or organizations (see Chapter 3).

On the other side of this debate are sociologists who emphasize the ways in which biology sets limits on what societal influences can achieve (Rossi 1977; Udry 2000). Sometimes referred to as **biosocial** perspectives, these views treat sex as objectively, identifiable "real" distinctions between males and females that are rooted in human physiology, anatomy, and genetics. These distinctions become the raw material from which gender is constructed. Sociologists who embrace this view would not necessarily deny that assignment to sex categories reflects socially agreed-upon rules, nor would they deny that gender shapes what counts as a marker of sex category. However, these sociologists draw a clear distinction between sex and gender, arguing that sex limits the construction of gender. As we will see later in this chapter, this position is most compatible with an individualist framework.

I present these views to show that differences in how sociologists define sex and gender reflect more than debates over terminology. Underlying these disagreements are fundamental differences in the kinds of questions researchers ask and the kinds of knowledge they hope to gain. For example, the biosocial perspective is most strongly identified with research seeking to identify biological, genetic, or evolutionary contributions to male and female behaviors and characteristics. We will discuss this research later in this chapter. Those agreeing with Kessler and McKenna, on the other hand, tend to reject this line of research, which they see as taking for granted precisely what is most in need of explanation: people's belief in the existence of two, discrete sex categories.

Like most sociologists, I believe that the biological and the social worlds are interdependent and mutually influential. The biological or genetic aspects of maleness and femaleness cannot be understood as fully separate and distinct from the social processes and practices that give meaning to these characteristics. It is thus impossible to neatly separate the realm of sex from that of gender when we are trying to explain any aspect of social life. These views are somewhat closer to Kessler and McKenna's than the biosocial accounts. Accordingly, I will use the term "gender," rather than "sex" or "sex category" most often throughout the book. When discussing a particular theory or body of work that uses sex instead of gender, however, I will adopt the terminology used by the proponents of that perspective. As discussed in Chapter 1, the term gender refers to a system of social practices that constitute women and men as different and unequal.

THE GENDERED PERSON

While sociologists may disagree over how they understand the relations between sex and gender, they agree that individuals are one site where gender can be examined. Individualist views of gender include a wide variety of sociological and psychological perspectives. Though they differ from one another in some important respects, these perspectives share the view that gender is an attribute – or characteristic – of people. To see gender in operation, according to individualist perspectives, we must focus our attention primarily on individuals, rather than on social situations or institutions.

One further assumption of this framework is its implicit belief that average differences *between* women and men as groups are greater than the differences *within* each sex category. This is not a claim that all women are alike or all men are alike. Instead, the argument is that sex imposes limits or constraints on gender. The constraints imposed by sex come primarily from the different reproductive roles of women and men. Hence, those who view gender as an attribute of individuals tend to believe that there are some differences between the sexes that are relatively stable across situations.

Because individualist approaches see differences between women as a group and men as a group as greater than differences within each category, researchers working within this framework generally pay less attention to differences *among* women (or men) with respect to race, ethnicity, sexual orientation, social class, and so on than do researchers adopting other frameworks (although this tendency has changed substantially in recent years). These researchers believe that sex distinctions are the most powerful organizers of human capabilities and behavior.

The individualist orientation will become clearer as we consider two kinds of perspectives that fall within this framework. The first perspective is one that views gender as a set of individual *traits, abilities, or behavioral dispositions* and attempts to understand how women and men differ in those areas. The second set of approaches explores how women and men become gendered, focusing on the social (or, for some, biosocial) processes that produce gender.

GENDER AS TRAITS, ABILITIES, OR BEHAVIORAL DISPOSITIONS

Are women more empathetic than men? Do men tend to take more risks than women? These are the kinds of questions that motivate researchers who share this view of gender. The kinds of characteristics that have been examined using this individualist perspective are as broad and diverse as can be found among humans. Much of this literature is comparative, in that emphasis is placed on identifying differences between women and men. This tradition emerged before the term "gender" had entered academic discourse; hence, researchers almost exclusively used the term "sex" instead. Even today, many psychologists and sociologists who embrace this perspective use sex rather than gender to describe the nature of the traits and dispositions they describe. Hence, the focus of this research tradition can be broadly described as "sex differences."

Sex difference research

Given its focus on individual characteristics, it is not surprising that sex difference research has been especially popular among psychologists, who are generally more interested than sociologists in individual attributes. Maccoby and Jacklin's (1974) treatise, *The Psychology of Sex Differences*, is widely regarded as the classic work in this area. In encyclopedic fashion, these authors reviewed and synthesized the existing literature on sex differences in temperament, cognition, and social behavior – no small feat, even in 1974. Examples of sex differences discussed by Maccoby and Jacklin include various intellectual capabilities, such as verbal and math skills, and social behaviors, such as aggressiveness. Ironically, however, one of this book's most important conclusions was that differences between women and men were fewer and of less magnitude than many had assumed.

The women's movement was the impetus for many of these initial studies (Eagly 1995). Researchers were especially interested in challenging negative cultural stereotypes about women, and they believed that their empirical research would help serve this goal by demonstrating the essential similarities between men's and women's personalities and behavioral dispositions. In this respect, sex difference researchers were putting into practice Bernard's (1973) belief that scientific research on women and sex differences would help eliminate damaging stereotypes and cultural views that assumed women were inferior to men. Maccoby and Jacklin's (1974) work set into motion a tradition of sex difference research that continues today. Literally hundreds of personality characteristics, capabilities, and behavioral orientations have been examined as researchers seek to identify differences (and, to a lesser extent, similarities) between women and men. For example, as mentioned above, researchers often study cultural stereotypes, such as nurturing interest and ability among women, or aggression among men (Eagly and Crowley 1986; Eagly and Steffen 1986). Studies have also explored sex differences in personality traits, such as assertiveness and self-esteem; in cognitive abilities, such as language use; in attitudes, such as those related to sexuality; and in many other areas (Cohn 1991; Deaux 1985; Feingold 1993, 1994; Oliver and Hyde 1993; Voyer et al. 1995).

What is the significance of these sex differences? To answer this question, we have to examine two related issues: (a) the magnitude or size of sex differences; and (b) the consistency of these differences across samples, time periods, and situations. These are important issues because there are virtually no traits or behaviors that reliably distinguish all men from all women. Hence, whenever sex differences are found, they represent *average* differences between the sexes, not categorical distinctions. That men and women differ, on average, implies that their responses are, to some degree, overlapping. Understanding the degree of overlap allows researchers to determine whether a particular sex difference is large or small, relative to other kinds of differences between individuals.

Size of sex differences

Not surprisingly, there is considerable debate about what constitutes a large or small sex difference. One way to approach this, however, is to think about the degree of overlap in the scores of the two sexes (Eagly 1995). When 85 percent or more of the scores of women and men overlap, it is considered a small average difference. When 65 percent of the scores overlap, it is considered a medium average difference. When only 53 percent of the scores overlap, it is considered a large average difference. Note that even when large differences between the sexes exist, a majority (53 percent) of women's and men's scores overlap. In fact, for many of the characteristics examined by sex difference researchers, women and men are much more similar than different.

Questions about the size of particular sex differences are difficult to address and resolve, yet they are extremely important. When researchers fail to address issues of size, they help perpetuate one of two kinds of bias (Hare-Mustin and Marecek 1988). The "alpha bias" is the tendency to exaggerate sex differences, thus creating the impression that women and men are, as the saying goes, "opposites," when in fact even the most robust sex differences are still average differences, not categorical ones. On the other hand, when relatively large sex differences are minimized or dismissed, researchers display the "beta bias." In this instance, researchers treat all sex differences as if they are trivial. Both kinds of bias can be avoided by careful attention to issues of magnitude.

Consistency of sex differences

The *consistency* of sex differences refers to their relative stability across different samples (such as samples differing by age, race or ethnicity, or social class), time periods, or social contexts. To determine the consistency of a sex difference, researchers must synthesize and integrate results from many studies to find out if sex differences reported in one sample, time period, or setting are found in others. Researchers' ability to address these kinds of questions was improved in the late 1970s with the development of more quantitatively sophisticated means of synthesizing research findings. These techniques, referred to as meta-analysis, have enabled researchers to systematically assess the magnitude and consistency of a wide variety of sex differences.

Voyer et al.'s (1995) study of sex differences in spatial-visual abilities is an example of a meta-analytic approach to sex differences. Spatial abilities are normally examined through tests that involve the mental rotation of objects. Voyer et al.'s meta-analysis was based on examination of 286 published studies of sex differences in spatial abilities conducted between 1970 and 1990. Consistent with other research, most studies did show a significant sex difference favoring males, though some variations between tests were found. In addition, this research showed that the size of sex differences in spatial abilities varied across studies and has declined in recent years.

Like magnitude, consistency is, to some extent, a relative matter. As the previous example illustrates, studies of a particular sex difference are rarely perfectly consistent; the same magnitude and even the direction (e.g., favoring females, favoring males, or no difference) of effect may vary from study to study. Given this, researchers sometimes assess whether a particular sex difference is more or less consistent across samples than are other kinds of personality or behavioral differences. Because there are many factors that make perfectly consistent results unattainable in the social sciences, researchers must be able to identify the reasons results vary, disentangling those having to do with sex difference from those having to do with other factors. Determining the degree of consistency is important because researchers can then link a particular trait or behavioral disposition with a particular sex, rather than with another social category, setting, or time period. If sex explains some aspect of human personality or behavior, then we would expect this association to persist across studies. Improvements in the sex difference research methods have helped fuel new debates about the existence and persistence of sex differences. Alice Eagly (1995) summarizes these debates in her reassessment of Maccoby and Jacklin's work (and the broader tradition of sex difference research that it spawned). Eagly (1995) argues that some of the sex differences that Maccoby and Jacklin could not substantiate appear to be more robust than believed. She argues that sex difference research in the areas of cognitive abilities, as well as research in personality and social interaction, yield some sex differences that require explanation. Eagly's claims have been disputed by others, however, and her views continue to be a subject of debate (Hyde and Plant 1995). Note that the focus of sex difference research is largely descriptive. That is, researchers are interested in determining whether a difference exists and describing that difference. Though descriptive research can be useful, its value is limited in certain respects. Researchers' interest in describing how women and men differ has led to an enormous amount of research, but it has produced fewer attempts to integrate and synthesize these findings. With the exception of a few differences that have been studied extensively, there is little cumulative scientific knowledge about the ways that women and men differ.

Sex differences and gender inequality

What is at stake in these debates about sex differences? Underlying these debates are broader issues of gender inequality. As discussed earlier, a great deal of sex difference research has been motivated by the hope that findings would dispel cultural stereotypes about women, and in some cases, men. If research showed that the two groups were not really very different, according to this logic, it would be more difficult for societies to defend gender inequality. History provides some support for this argument. Unequal treatment has often been justified by supposed biological or genetic differences between women and men. Women in particular have been excluded from such domains as politics and employment on the basis of their differences from men. Sex differences are not the only differences that societies have used as a basis for exclusion and unequal treatment, of course. Racial and ethnic inequalities have also been justified on the basis of supposed biological or genetic differences between groups. It is always a good idea to be wary when social arrangements are justified by arguments about differences between groups.

A focus on sex differences may be problematic for other reasons as well. Hollander and Howard (2000: 340) argue that a focus on group differences "may act as self-fulfilling prophecies, predisposing researchers to overlook group similarities and to exaggerate or even elicit information that confirms their preconceptions." This makes it all too easy for researchers to confirm gender stereotypes. According to these authors, sex difference research is also problematic because it "often obscures the fact that different almost always means unequal" (Hollander and Howard 2000: 340). Differences, they argue, are almost never just differences, but instead reflect imbalances of power.

In response, some suggest that denying differences is no more compatible with equality than acknowledging them, and they dispute the claim that differences must necessarily be seen as deficiencies on the part of one group. As Eagly observes, "the sex differences that scientists have documented do not tell a simple tale of female inferiority" (1995: 155). Eagly and others argue that equality is best served by having accurate knowledge about women and men. Differences do not imply inequality any more than similarity guarantees equal treatment. This view has received increasing support in recent years as researchers have developed more complex ways to understand the relations between gender difference and gender inequality.

BECOMING GENDERED

Think back for a minute to your childhood and try to remember becoming aware of gender for the first time. Do you recall your first memories of perceiving yourself or others around you as female or male? If these memories are too distant, have a conversation with a preschool-age child about gender. See if you can learn how this child views the differences between girls and boys, and try to identify some of the meanings she or he associates with her or his own gender. If you take these suggestions, you will undoubtedly discover that gender – their own as well as others' – is a meaningful concept to children. By age three or so, most can identify themselves as female or male and associate particular qualities or characteristics with each gender.

How do children come to understand themselves as female or male? How is it that people take on characteristics seen as socially appropriate for their gender? From an individualist perspective, there are two general answers to these questions. One explanation suggests that women and men are "hard-wired" for certain characteristics during their prenatal and perhaps even postnatal development. A second explanation says that these differences result from people's efforts to comply with social roles.

Biological and genetic contributions to sex differences

Whether there are biological or genetic contributions to the behavior of males and females is a subject of heated debate. Although researchers disagree on some points, many acknowledge that some sex differences may have biological or genetic contributions. At the same time, however, most sociologists (and many other scientists who study sex differences) insist that the impact of these biological or genetic contributions depends upon the environment or culture in which they emerge. In other words, accepting the possibility that biological or genetic factors may influence human personality and behavior does not imply that personality and behavior can be reduced to these factors. Understanding how biology, genetics, and culture interact to shape personality and behavior, rather than examining each factor separately, is perhaps the best way to proceed as we explore these issues.

Research seeking to identify possible biological or genetic contributions to male and female behavior is certain to continue; we learn more and more about human biology, genetics, and evolution every day. Interest in precisely how sex differences may develop focuses on two general areas: epigenetic and evolutionary. Epigenetic research on sex differences is based on the notion that "both genes and environment, acting together at all times, determine the structure and function of brain cells and thus the behavior of the organism" (Hoyenga and Hoyenga 1993: 20). Studies from this perspective have examined prenatal sex hormones and their role in "priming" (i.e., predisposing) females and males to respond differently outside the womb (Hoyenga and Hoyenga 1993; Maccoby 1998). An epigenetic perspective also guides research on sex differences in perinatal (i.e., postnatal) hormones and brain organization.

Udry's (2000) research on the relationship between girls' exposure to prenatal androgens (i.e., male sex hormones) and their receptiveness to being socialized in a traditionally feminine way is a good example of an epigenetic approach. Udry's sample consisted of 163 white women ranging in age from 27 to 30. Because the women's mothers had supplied prenatal blood samples, Udry had a measure of the women's exposure to prenatal androgens. He also collected data on the women's gender socialization as children and their gendered adult behaviors, which he defined as having "feminine interests" (e.g., a concern with their physical appearance), characteristics of their job and home lives (e.g., marriage, children, and division of household labor), and their scores on personality measures of masculinity and femininity.

Udry found that women's level of exposure to prenatal androgens conditioned the relationship between their gender socialization as children and their gendered adult behaviors. For instance, women exposed to high doses of prenatal androgens were less receptive to traditional female socialization than girls who did not have high prenatal androgen exposure. In contrast, among women exposed to low doses of prenatal androgens, traditional female socialization had a strong effect on women's adult gendered behaviors. These findings imply that gender socialization may be, to some extent, conditioned by sex hormones.

Udry's (2000) research has been strongly criticized. Critics argue that his research is insufficiently attentive to the role of social forces in shaping behavior (Kennelly et al. 2001) and that he reduces gender to sex differences "or sex-dimorphism itself" (Risman 2000: 607). In short, they suggest that his biosocial model of gender places too much emphasis on the biological component of behavior.

Evolutionary psychology – a relatively new field that explores links between psychology and genetic inheritance – may also yield knowledge about sex differences. Evolutionary psychologists believe that "males and females will be the same or similar in all those domains in which the sexes have faced the same or similar adaptive problems" (Buss 1995: 164). From this perspective, sex differences stem from differences in the adaptive problems each sex confronts during evolution. Evolutionary psychologists reject what they see as a "false dichotomy between biology and environment," arguing instead that humans develop through their attempts to effectively respond to their surroundings.

In which domains do women and men face different adaptive problems? Evolutionary psychologists argue that sexual selection is the key domain in which women and men confront different kinds of challenges. Sexual selection refers to "the causal process of the evolution of characteristics on the basis of reproductive advantage, as opposed to survival advantage" (Buss 1995: 165). Sexual selection occurs primarily through inter- and intrasex competition by both sexes. However, because of women's reproductive role, as well as other biological and physiological sex differences, evolutionary psychologists suggest that each sex faces unique sexual selection challenges. How each sex confronts these sex-specific challenges leads to sex differences in sexuality and mating.

Evolutionary psychologists have received their share of criticism. Many evolutionary biologists, as well as others in the natural sciences, have criticized evolutionary psychologists for ignoring the tremendous variability and flexibility in human and animal societies (Angier 1999). Learning and experience are also important factors in human and animal behavior, and these, too, have been downplayed by evolutionary psychologists. Anthropologists and sociologists suggest that the sex differences evolutionary psychologists attempt to explain could just as easily be explained by social processes. These debates are likely to continue, underscoring the difficulty of disentangling genetic effects from the many other forces shaping human social life.

Of all individualist researchers, those with an epigenetic or evolutionary perspective make the most direct connections between biological sex, personality, and behavior. As a result, it is not surprising that this research has been criticized for having a simplistic or superficial conception of social influences. Social influences figure more highly in the perspectives of other researchers, however. This group sees a somewhat looser connection between sex and gender than those adopting an epigenetic or evolutionary psychological approach. For this latter group, sex category sets into motion sex-specific processes of socialization. The socialization process transforms the "raw material" of biological sex into gender-differentiated personalities and behaviors. We turn to these approaches next.

Gender socialization

What is the process through which people learn how to be feminine and masculine? How do society's messages about what are appropriate behaviors for women and men get transmitted to its members? More importantly, we might ask how it is that societal members come to use gender as a basis for organizing and assimilating information (Bem 1983). Answers to these questions are supplied by various theories of gender socialization.

Socialization refers to the processes through which individuals take on gendered qualities and characteristics and acquire a sense of self. In addition, through socialization people learn what their society expects of them as males or females. Even if these expectations are not realized fully, people learn that they will at some level be held accountable to them; that is, they will be assessed in part on the basis of whether they are "appropriately" masculine or feminine.

Gender socialization is a two-sided process. On one side is the *target* of socialization, such as a newborn, who encounters the social world through interactions with parents and caretakers. Through these encounters children not only experience other people and the outside world, but also become aware of themselves. The fact that information about gender is so essential to understanding and interacting with a newborn reveals just how deeply implicated gender is in the process of becoming human and developing a self. On the other side of the socialization process are the *agents* of socialization – the individuals, groups, and organizations who pass on cultural information. As we will see in Chapter 5, parents are perhaps the most important agent of socialization because they are the most powerful people in children's lives.

There are three major theories of socialization (Bem 1983; Stockard and Johnson 1992). Two theories, **social learning** and **cognitive development**, are general learning theories that are also applicable to learning about gender, while the third perspective – **identification theory** – was developed specifically to explain gender socialization and, in particular, the acquisition of gender identity.

Social learning

Social learning theory asserts that gender roles are learned through the reinforcements – positive and negative – children receive for engaging in gender-appropriate and gender-inappropriate behavior (Mischel 1970). This perspective also acknowledges that learning takes place through observation and modeling (Bandura and Walters 1963). According to social learning theorists, reinforcements, whether experienced directly in the form of rewards and punishments or vicariously through observation, are the primary means through which children take on gender-appropriate behaviors. Differential treatment of female and male children by parents and other socializing agents creates gender differences in behavior. It is important to note that parents' responses to their children do not have to be conscious or intentional to have consequences. Indeed, parents' actions can be reinforcing regardless of intent or awareness.

The mechanisms of social learning can be easily illustrated. Imagine the responses of a parent to a three-year-old boy who falls down and begins to cry. The boy may be immediately picked up and comforted, he may simply be told to "be a big boy and stop crying," or perhaps he is simply ignored. Social learning theorists would argue that the child's future reactions to similar situations will be influenced by which of the above responses he receives. The child who is picked up and consoled may continue to display his feelings of pain and displeasure through tears, while boys who are scolded or ignored will gradually learn that crying or similar emotional expressions should not be expressed in these situations. If parents of boys tend to respond one way and parents of girls tend to respond in another, social learning theorists would say that a gender-typed behavior has been created. A **gender-typed behavior**, then, is one that elicits different responses depending upon whether the person engaging in the behavior is female or male. Can you identify any other gender-typed behaviors?

Although reinforcement may be one mechanism through which gender roles are acquired, this theory does not fully explain this process (Bem 1983; Stockard and Johnson 1992). For example, evidence suggests that children, especially boys, may persist in gender-appropriate behaviors even when they are not reinforced for these activities, or even when they are negatively reinforced (Maccoby 1992; Stockard and Johnson 1992). More generally, research suggests that children are more actively involved in their own socialization than social learning theorists acknowledge (Maccoby 1992). Regarding social learning theory, Bem notes: "This view of the passive child is inconsistent with the common observation that children themselves frequently construct and enforce their own version of society's gender rules" (1983: 600). To simplify somewhat, we can say that social learning theory tends to view children (and other targets of socialization) as lumps of clay that are molded by their environments. This approach reflects a view of the socialization process "from the outside." A cognitive perspective on gender socialization offers a different view.

Cognitive approaches

How is *being* male or female expressed in people's *understandings* of themselves as masculine or feminine? Cognitive psychological approaches answer this question by examining how people internalize gender meanings from the outside world and then use those meanings to construct an identity consistent with them. This approach thus examines the connections between sex category membership and the meanings people attach to that membership (Bem 1993; Howard 2000). These meanings, in turn, are assumed to guide and help explain individual behavior.

Most closely associated with psychologists Lawrence Kohlberg (1966) and Sandra Bem (1983, 1993), cognitive theory embraces a much more active view of children than proponents of social learning. Rather than focusing on the environment's role in molding children's behavior, cognitive theorists focus on the ways that children actively seek to understand themselves and their worlds. This approach thus provides a look at socialization from the "inside out" – that is, from the perspective of the child and his or her thought processes.

Kohlberg's (1966) cognitive theory is based on the claim that gender learning can be explained using the principles of cognitive development (see also Piaget 1932). In this view, learning about gender occurs as part of a more general psychological process of cognitive maturation. According to this perspective, once children have labeled themselves as female or male, and recognize this as stable over time and situations, they are motivated to seek out gender-appropriate behaviors. In addition, children attach greater value to these behaviors and experience them as more positively reinforcing than gender-inappropriate behaviors. With age, children's abilities to interpret gender cues become more sophisticated and flexible, a pattern cognitive development theorists argue parallels intellectual development more generally.

While some are sympathetic to elements of this approach, others are skeptical of its claim that gender learning takes place only after children have labeled themselves as female or male. In addition, Bem (1983, 1993) argues that Kohlberg fails to sufficiently explain why and how children come to employ gender, rather than some other characteristic, as a cognitive organizing principle. These concerns have led to another kind of cognitive perspective, Bem's **gender schema theory**.

Bem (1983, 1993) argues that in cultures like American society where gender distinctions are strongly reinforced, children learn to use gender to make sense of their experience and process new information. Through this process people acquire traits and personalities that are consistent with their understandings of themselves as male or female. They develop **gender schemas**, cognitive structures (or lenses) that help people assimilate and organize perception. As Bem observes, "The gendered personality is more than a particular collection of masculine or feminine traits; it is also a way of looking at reality that produces and reproduces those traits during a lifetime of self-construction" (1993: 154). In this view, the larger social world provides the "raw material" from which gender identities are constructed and these identities, in turn, guide perception and action.

Two other aspects of Bem's gender schema perspective are worth noting. The first is Bem's (1993) contention that gender schemas in late twentieth-century American society emphasize **gender polarization** – the belief that what is acceptable or appropriate for females is not acceptable or appropriate for males (and vice versa) and that anyone who deviates from these standards of appropriate femaleness and maleness is unnatural or immoral. Bem argues that these notions become part of children's internalized gender schemas, thus leading them to think of the other gender as the "opposite sex."

Another feature of gender schemas in American society, according to Bem (1993), is that they are **androcentric**. Androcentrism refers to a belief that males and masculinity are superior to females and femininity, and that males and masculinity are the standard or the norm. Not only do children internalize gender schemas that define males and females as inherently different, but they also internalize a sense that maleness and masculinity are more desirable and highly valued. For example, children may learn to associate dolls with girls and trucks with boys, but they will also learn that boys who play with dolls should be ridiculed while girls who play with trucks should be admired. In Bem's view, androcentrism damages both females *and* males. Regarding its effects on men, Bem says that androcentrism

> so thoroughly devalues whatever thoughts, feelings, and behaviors are culturally defined as feminine that crossing the gender boundary has a more negative cultural meaning for men than it has for women – which means, in turn, that male gender-boundary-crossers are much more culturally stigmatized than female gender-boundary-crossers. At the same time, androcentrism pro-

vides such an unreachable definition of what a real man is supposed to be
that only a few men can even begin to meet it. (Bem 1993: 149–50)

Bem's research suggests children use gender schemas because these categories are helpful in making sense of the social world. Extending this logic
would lead us to predict that children would be more likely to attend to
some social categories than others, and that these differences would be
related to the category's usefulness in distinguishing between different kinds
of people. Hirschfeld's (1996) research on preschoolers' awareness of social
categories is consistent with this argument. He found that gender was
salient in children's understanding and recall of visual and verbal narratives, but its relevance relative to other social categories, such as occupation and race, varied. Children use social categories like gender not simply
because they are easily observed, but rather because they are curious about
the social world and the kinds of people within it.

In sum, cognitive perspectives, such as those associated with Kohlberg
and Bem, view children as, in important respects, socializing themselves.
They imply that gender distinctions become very significant to children –
as they are to adults – and that gender is therefore used to organize and
process information from the environment. Moreover, for Bem, gender
socialization not only involves learning about what is expected of one as
male or female, but also the process of becoming gender schematic (i.e., of
using gender schemas to process, organize, and interpret information). As
she notes, "a gendered personality is both a product and a process. It is
both a particular collection of masculine or feminine traits and a way of
constructing reality that itself constructs those traits" (Bem 1993: 152).
Because children are motivated to become "competent" members of their
culture, they will learn to use the tools their culture provides (and values)
to regulate their own behavior and interpret the world around them.

Although social learning and cognitive approaches are very different in
some respects, they should not be seen as mutually exclusive perspectives.
Rather, as I have stressed, social learning theory attends more to the ways
that parents and others respond to children, while cognitive theories focus
on children's efforts to make sense of the world around them. Both are
important; we can only understand socialization if we examine the
parent–child relationship itself, rather than focusing only on the parents'
behavior or on the child's (Maccoby 1992).

The psychoanalytic perspective

Identification theory, the third major theory of socialization, differs from
the previous two perspectives in significant ways. First, unlike social learning and cognitive development approaches, identification theory is explic-

itly concerned with gender, gender identity, and sexuality (Stockard and Johnson 1992). More important, however, this perspective disagrees that gender-appropriate behavior is learned through reinforcement or imitation, or reflects an intent to behave in a particular way. Instead, drawing from the ideas of Freud and his followers, identification theorists assert that at least some aspects of gender result from unconscious psychological processes (Chodorow 1978; Johnson 1988; Williams 1989).

The most influential version of psychoanalytic theory among sociologists of gender is the perspective developed by Nancy Chodorow in her 1978 classic, *The Reproduction of Mothering*, and refined in her later writings. Chodorow's perspective focuses on how women and men develop a personal sense of what it means to be female or male. According to Chodorow, gender identity is formed during early childhood as children develop emotional attachments to a same-sex parent or adult. In cultures like the USA, where women have primary responsibility for infant care, children of both sexes typically form their earliest emotional attachments to their mother – a woman. This attachment is important, given infants' extreme dependence on their mothers for the satisfaction of all their needs. For psychoanalytic theorists, infants' relations with mothers are emotionally significant and deeply meaningful, feelings that may be incorporated into the child's unconscious.

Despite these bonds, separation from the mother must eventually occur and this separation is a crucial step in child development. With the formation of **ego boundaries** – the sense of separation between "me" and "not me" – infants become aware of themselves and others as separate beings with an ability to influence their surroundings. Along with the formation of ego boundaries is a second developmental task: the formation of gender identity. **Gender identity** refers to people's own sense of themselves as males or females. In psychological terms, it is a "fundamental, existential sense of one's maleness or femaleness, an acceptance of one's gender as a social-psychological construction that parallels one's acceptance of one's biological sex" (Spence 1984: 84).

Not only must infants gain a sense of themselves as a separate entity in the world, they must also develop an awareness of themselves as male or female. For Chodorow and other psychoanalytic theorists, this awareness is helped by – perhaps even dependent upon – another kind of attachment: identification with a same-sex parent or adult. Through this bond children have an opportunity to learn what it means to be male or female. Identification is more than simply modeling an adult, however; it also has emotional significance for the child. Hence, gender identification gives children information about what it means to be male or female, and it motivates and sustains their interest in this aspect of themselves. Psychoanalytic theorists believe that gender identity remains significant to people and is a powerful force in their adult lives.

These processes operate somewhat differently for males and females, however. Because children of both sexes form a primary attachment to their mother, male and female children face different challenges during early stages of development. The formation of males' ego boundaries is helped along by mothers' differences from their sons. Acquiring gender identity, by contrast, is potentially more problematic. Sons are forced to "switch" their identification from their mothers to their fathers, which is emotionally painful and difficult. This is made even harder when – as is typical even in two-parent households – fathers are less involved in caring for their children than mothers.

Girls' development unfolds somewhat differently. Because they are of the same sex as their mother, girls never have to give up their primary identification. Mothers' presence in girls' lives also gives girls a more concrete sense of what it means to be female than boys are likely to receive of what it means to be male from their fathers. What may become problematic for girls, however, is the formation of their ego boundaries – their sense of themselves as separate and independent from others.

These different paths to gender identification are responsible for gender-differentiated female and male personalities and form the backdrop against which males' and females' later development take place. The net result of these differences, according to psychoanalytic theorists, is that males and females acquire distinctly different gender identities, with different forms of "relational potential" (Chodorow 1978: 166). Male gender identity is what Messner refers to as "positional," meaning that the self "is solidified through separation from others" (1992: 32; see also Gilligan 1982). This implies that boys and men, more so than girls and women, will be more comfortable with separation and distance than with connection. In contrast, girls have "a basis for 'empathy' built into their primary definition of self in a way that boys do not. Girls emerge with a stronger basis for experiencing another's needs or feelings as one's own (or of thinking that one is so experiencing another's needs and feelings)" (Chodorow 1978: 167). Hence, women – more so than men – will feel more comfortable when connected to others and prefer relationship to separation.

In addition, psychoanalytic theorists argue that gender identity will have a different significance for women and men. Because women's gender identity develops through their ongoing relations with their mothers, women are likely to acquire a relatively secure sense of themselves as women. Gender identity may be somewhat more amorphous and tenuous for men, who not only are forced to give up their primary attachment to their mother, but also must identify with a more distant father. As a result, while men may feel compelled to "prove" their masculinity to themselves and others, women believe that they are feminine as a result of being female. This difference helps to explain why men seem to have a greater psychic stake in gender than do women.

As we will see in later chapters, this psychoanalytic perspective has been used extensively in gender research. At the same time, it has also been criticized on several counts. Some object to the perspective's Freudian roots, particularly its emphasis on unconscious processes. Critics claim that psychoanalytic arguments like Chodorow's are virtually impossible to systematically test or verify empirically. Another criticism is that this approach falsely universalizes a particular kind of mothering and family organization, thus ignoring how mothering and the creation of gender identity may differ in other social groups and contexts. In particular, some question Chodorow's implicit assumption that gender identity is separate from and develops independently of other identities, such as those involving race, ethnicity, or social class (Spelman 1988). Finally, some suggest that Chodorow's perspective reinforces exaggerated stereotypes about women and men. Her claim that women seek connection and men prefer separation strikes many as oversimplified and contributing to an unrealistic view of differences between women and men.

Chodorow and her followers have responded to many of these criticisms. Although she acknowledges some of the limitations of her early viewpoint, however, Chodorow's major argument remains intact. She believes that gender has an important psychological component that must be taken into account. This component is primarily expressed through people's gender identities. While the specifics of gender identity are unique for each person, the contents of male and female gender identities are not random or arbitrary. As long as women continue to be primary caretakers of infants, and men have limited involvement in the early caretaking of children, women's and men's gender identities will evolve somewhat differently. As Chodorow (1995: 517) explains, "each person's sense of gender – her gender identity or gendered subjectivity – is an inextricable fusion or melding of personally created (emotionally and through unconscious fantasy) and cultural meaning."

Gender theorists like Bem believe that people are capable of reflecting upon their own maleness or femaleness, and assigning meaning to their sex category membership. This perspective has a cognitive emphasis because it regards people's capacities to organize, select, and interpret information as important. Although psychoanalytic views of gender identity also recognize people's abilities to make sense of the world around them, psychoanalytic theorists emphasize unconscious and unreflective processes to a greater degree. Both views, however, share the belief that the meanings people assign to themselves as males or females play important roles in the production and reproduction of gender.

Though they differ in important ways, these theories all aim to explain how women and men acquire gender-appropriate behaviors and beliefs. Because theories of socialization address how people become gendered, these perspectives are of primary significance to those who view gender as an individual characteristic.

CHAPTER SUMMARY

This chapter began with a discussion of the distinction between sex and gender. I also introduced several other related concepts, including sexual dimorphism, sex assignment, and sex category. Sociologists disagree over how best to understand the relations between sex and gender, and these disagreements reflect more fundamental differences about the relations between the biological and the social.

The chapter reviewed several types of "individualist" approaches to gender. Used extensively by gender scholars, these perspectives have a long history of research and development. Individualist approaches treat gender as a characteristic of people. Proponents of these views focus their attention on women and men – their traits, characteristics, and identities – and suggest that gender operates primarily through these aspects of individuals. Examples of individualist approaches discussed in this chapter include sex difference research, biosocial and evolutionary psychology perspectives, and theory and research on gender socialization.

Socialization is the process through which people become gendered. They learn what is expected of them because they are female or male and learn how to display these characteristics. Because most sociologists consider gender distinctions as primarily social in origin, rather than biological, socialization is important to understand. Gender socialization has an especially central role to play in individualist understandings of gender, as these approaches emphasize the ways that gender is embodied in people. The three major theories of socialization – social learning, cognitive, and identification theories – each attempt to explain how people take on characteristics their society sees as appropriate for males and females.

While socialization is important, many sociologists have criticized research that relies exclusively on socialization as an explanation for gender differences. Critics argue that this type of explanation falsely creates a view of women and men as homogeneous groups, possessing internally consistent and unchanging motives, behavioral dispositions, etc. (Gerson 1985, 1993; see also Epstein 1988). Indeed, research by Gerson (1985, 1993) (to be discussed in a later chapter) shows that early childhood experiences and socialization are poor predictors of adult women's and men's work and family decisions. She argues that people's choices are best viewed as "an interaction between socially structured opportunities and constraints and active attempts to make sense of and respond to these structures" (Gerson 1985: 192).

Ultimately, all of the perspectives discussed in this chapter explore how much people's personal characteristics – traits, behaviors, and identities – are shaped by our sex category. They share a belief that people are gendered – that is, that the distinction between masculine and feminine is one that is expressed in individuals. In addition, most agree that sex distinctions are a primary reason for this. Sex, then, is a source of gender and sets limits on the traits, behaviors, and identities of people. Further, because gender is part of the person, it is assumed to be relatively stable. People do not put on and take off gender as they move from place to place, situation to situation, group to group.

In the following chapter we will see how sociologists who adopt an interactionist or gendered institutions perspective account for gender's impact on everyday life. Interactionists believe that situational characteristics interact with, and sometimes offset, internalized personality attributes and behavioral dispositions to create gender distinctions. From a gendered institutions perspective, gender socialization is a less important source of gender distinctions than are features of social structure and social organization.

FURTHER READING

Chodorow, Nancy. 1978. *The Reproduction of Mothering*. Berkeley, CA: University of California Press.

Eagly, Alice H. 1995. "The Science and Politics of Comparing Women and Men." *American Psychologist* 50: 145–58.

Kessler, Suzanne J. 1998. *Lessons from the Intersexed*. New Brunswick, NJ: Rutgers University Press.

Udry, J. Richard. 2000. "Biological Limits of Gender Construction." *American Sociological Review* 65: 443–57.

A CLOSER LOOK

Reading 1: Evolution, Males, and Violence

David P. Barash

Imagine that you were interviewing an intelligent fish, and you asked it to describe its environment. One thing it probably would not volunteer is that

From "Evolution, Males, and Violence," originally published in *The Chronicle of Higher Education*, May 24, 2002.

things are awfully wet down here. Like our hypothetical interlocutor, people are generally insensitive to whatever permeates their lives. So, if you were to ask someone to describe human violence, only rarely would you hear that it is overwhelmingly perpetrated by males. And yet, the truth is that if we could eliminate or even significantly reduce **male violence**, we would pretty much get rid of violence altogether. The maleness of violence is so overwhelming that it is rarely even noticed; it is the ocean in which we swim.

What might be called the "killing establishment" – soldiers, executioners, hunters, even slaughterhouse workers – is overwhelmingly male. Underworld killers such as violent gangs are also people largely by men. Whenever seemingly unprovoked and deadly shootings occur in homes and workplaces, men are typically the mass murderers. Nor is this imbalance limited to the United States: Whether in Kosovo, Rwanda, Cambodia, the Middle East, Guatemala, or Afghanistan, when people kill and maim other people, men are nearly always the culprits. And of course, the lethal operatives of Al Qaeda and its equivalent are reliably male, as are those sent to combat them.

The same gender imbalance applies to the uncountable private episodes of violence that receive little national attention but are the stuff of many a personal tragedy. Admittedly, an occasional Lizzie Borden surfaces, but for every Bonnie, there are about a hundred Clydes. Male brutalizers and killers are so common, they barely make the local news, whereas their female counterparts achieve a kind of fame. A man who kills – even his own children – gets comparatively little notice, whereas when Susan Smith drowned her two sons, in 1994, she received international attention. Violence may or may not be as American as cherry pie, but it is as male as can be.

Violence is also, by and large, something that men direct at other men. As with inner-city crime, in which both the perpetrators and victims are disproportionately members of minority groups, men are disproportionately both the perpetrators and victims of their own violence. This is not intended to romanticize or idealize women, or to deny that they too can sometimes be nasty, brutal, even deadly. Some women are more violent than some men, just as some women are taller, stronger, or have deeper voices or less hair than some men. But the overall pattern is consistent: When it comes to violence, the two sexes simply are not in the same league.

The same pattern is found, by and large, in animals.

Until a decade or two ago, it appeared that other animals – including monkeys – did not kill members of their own species, whereas humans did. But as field studies in animal behavior have become more thorough, the myth of the peaceful primate – or non-murderous animal generally – has largely been dispelled. Orangutans rape, for instance, and chimpanzees murder. Wolves also kill others of their own kind, as do lions, elk, and bison. In fact, nearly every animal species that has been carefully studied sooner or later reveals its penchant for lethal violence. And, to repeat, when such things take place among animals, the perpetrators are almost always males.

Why is this? Evolutionary biology has an answer, and it emanates directly from the very definition of male and female.

Just look at the exterior genitals of a bird. In nearly every species, there aren't any. Males and females simply have a cloaca, the common external opening for excretory and reproductive products. And yet, biologists have no difficulty distinguishing male birds from females; ditto for males and females throughout the natural world. The difference between the sexes has nothing to do with penises or vaginas, beards or breasts. Rather, it is a matter of gametes: the tiny sex cells identifiable as either eggs (if large and produced in small numbers) or sperm (if small and produced in large numbers). This and only this is the meaning of maleness and femaleness: Sperm makers are called males, egg makers females.

The consequences of that distinction are weighty indeed. In brief, since sperm can be made in vast quantities, and with little mandated physiological follow-through, it is possible for males to have large numbers of offspring, the actual output limited by the number of females they succeed in fertilizing. By contrast, females are more likely to maximize their reproduction by producing successful offspring, rather than by outcompeting other females for the sexual attention of males.

To some degree, sexual competition is a replay of fertilization itself, in which numerous males, like hyperactive spermatozoa, compete among themselves for access to females. Just as it is now clear that the egg doesn't merely passively receive suitors, it is increasingly understood that females can be active participants in their own reproduction. Nonetheless, when it comes to sperm makers, success is likely to crown those who outcompete their rivals, and so, in species after species, it is the males who are larger, nastier, more likely to be armed with lethal weaponry and a violent disposition to match. Natural selection has outfitted males with the tools for success in male–male competition, much of it violent.

In the animal world, human no less than nonhuman, competition is often intense. Males typically threaten, bluff, and if necessary fight one another in their efforts to obtain access to females. Among vertebrates in particular, males tend to be relatively large, conspicuous in color and behavior, and endowed with intimidating weapons (tusks, fangs, claws, antlers, etc.) and a willingness to employ them, largely because such traits were rewarded, over evolutionary time, with enhanced reproductive success.

Male–male competition is especially fierce in polygynous, harem-keeping species such as elk, moose, elephant seals, and gorillas. Whereas in such cases each egg maker is likely to be modestly successful (with one pregnancy per year), males play for higher stakes. They end up as harem masters or as evolutionary failures, and not surprisingly, they grow up large, tough, and well-armed: unpleasant bullies, as befits a winner-take-all lifestyle.

Consider elephant seals, behemoths that congregate annually to breed on islands off the coast of California. They are highly polygynous, with successful harem keepers fathering some 40 offspring per year. And not surprisingly, the male elephant seal is truly elephantine, outweighing the female fourfold; he is also strongly disposed to violence, nearly all of it directed at other males. Why? Because among his ancestors, success has been rewarded – 40 times per year.

At the same time, since the sex ratio is one to one, for every harem master, there are 39 disappointed bachelors. As a result, some males will be immensely successful and others will be failures. By contrast, the difference between success and failure is much less extreme among females. Think of it as different degrees of reproductive democracy, or egalitarianism. The payoffs for females are more equitable than for males: one female, one offspring. Males, by contrast, operate in a system that is more inherently unfair and unequal. For them, there is a greater difference between the reproductive "haves" and "have-nots." Hence, males are much more competitive than females.

In species that are monogamous or nearly so – such as most songbirds, geese, eagles, foxes, and gibbons – males and females produce approximately equal numbers of offspring. Not surprisingly, in such cases the two sexes are also nearly equal in size, armament, and aggressiveness. As we come to species that are more polygynous, however, we find a steady progression toward greater inequality in size and aggressiveness, with males getting bigger, and more nasty to each other. Among polygynous primates, for example, we find noticeable size differences between male and female, and also marked differences in behavior, especially when it comes to violence. A similar pattern holds for the deer family, the seals and their relatives, and indeed, pretty much any animal group that is diverse enough to permit comparisons of this sort. In addition, the greater the difference in reproductive payoff (variance in numbers of offspring), the greater the difference in aggressiveness among males. With reproductive success more variable, males are more competitive.

This is not to deny recent findings that animals – even males – often cooperate. My point is simply that because of the basic biology of maleness and femaleness, of sperm and eggs, males are more prone to violence. Incidentally, it has long been thought that the sperm/egg dichotomy also generates profound male/female differences in sexual proclivities. Even though recent DNA studies have revealed that females are more prone to sexual adventuring than had previously been thought, when it comes to violence, the male/female divide is as robust as ever.

[. . .]

This is not to claim that females aren't aggressive in their own way. There are interesting cases of vigorous female–female competition in animals: Among groove-billed anis (large, ravenlike neotropical birds), several females deposit eggs in a communal nest, and the dominant female is especially likely to evict the eggs of subordinates; dominant female African hunting dogs may kill the offspring of lower-ranking females; female red howler monkeys push around other females. In fact, many cases of monogamy among mammals may actually be enforced by subtle aggression by females toward other females. I predict, in fact, that further research will reveal that female–female competition among animals is more widespread than currently recognized. There is no doubt, however, that it is typically less direct, less boisterous, and much less violent than male–male competition.

On the domestic front, violent crime is overwhelmingly male. Studies of prosecution and imprisonment records in Europe, going back several centuries, as well as examinations of modern crime statistics from the United States and around the world show that men consistently outstrip women in criminality by a ratio of at least three or four to one. When it comes to violent crimes, the difference is even greater, with the disparity increasing as the violence intensifies (simple assault versus assault and battery versus manslaughter versus homicide). The only areas, in fact, in which women commit more crimes than men are prostitution (which some would argue is not a crime but an act between consenting adults) and shoplifting.

Another difference is that when women are consistently aggressive, it tends to take a defensive form, as when a woman kills a man who has abused her or her children, or fights to have a murderer condemned to death. The same is true among animals as well. A mother bear with cubs, for example, is notoriously fierce, as are other females who defend their young. Thus, while the aggression of women tends to be reactive, men are more likely to initiate violence, to commit truly "offensive" acts.

When it comes to the most serious violent crime, homicide, men are far and away the most frequent perpetrators. They are also most likely to be the victims, precisely as evolutionary theory predicts. Thus, murder is largely a crime of men against other men, a pattern that, in itself, points an accusing finger at male–male competition. For their book *Homicide*, two Canadian psychology professors, Martin Daly and Margo Wilson, reviewed murder records, specifically looking at cases involving members of the same sex, over a wide historical range and from around the world. They concluded, "The difference between the sexes is immense, and it is universal. There is no known human society in which the level of lethal violence among women even begins to approach that among men."

[. . .]

In 1958, the sociologist Marvin Wolfgang published what has remained the classic study of homicide in America, based on nearly 600 murders in

Philadelphia. Trying to explain why more than 95 percent of the killers were men, Wolfgang – a proponent of social-learning theory and cultural explanations – wrote, "In our culture the average female is . . . less given to or expected to engage in physical violence than the male." We are supposed to infer that things are different in other cultures, but that simply is not so.

There is a powerful bias in the United States, promoted by most contemporary psychologists, anthropologists, and sociologists, that male–female differences have been created solely by differences in upbringing and social expectations. As a result – whether by error or pre-existing bias – social scientists have contributed to the vast myth of the equipotential human being, the idea that every one is equally inclined to behave in any way. Equipotentiality is an appealing sentiment, attractively egalitarian. There is only one problem: It isn't true. Quite simply, it flies in the face of everything known about the biological underpinnings of behavior, and of life itself.

Moreover, if male–female differences derived essentially from arbitrary cultural traditions – the well-known phenomenon in which societies typically imbue young men with the expectation of greater violence – there should be at least some in which the situation is reversed, where young women are socialized to be the more violent sex.

Violence is often seen as primitive or immature. And yet, the reality is that even in this era of gun-toting 12-year-olds, murderous violence is distressingly mature: Overwhelmingly, it is adult behavior. It is also easily triggered. When Marvin Wolfgang conducted extensive interviews with convicted killers in Philadelphia, he was able to identify 12 categories of motive. Far and away the largest, accounting for fully 37 percent of all murders, was what he designated "altercation of relatively trivial origin; insult, curse, jostling, etc." In such cases, people got into an argument at a bar over a sporting event, who paid for a drink, an off-hand remark, or a hastily uttered insult.

To die over something so inconsequential as a casual comment or a dispute about some distant event seems the height of irony and caprice. But in a sense, disputes of that sort are not trivial, for they reflect the evolutionary past, when personal altercations were the stuff upon which prestige and social success – leading ultimately to biological success – were based. It is not surprising, therefore, that young men today will fight and die over who said what to whom, whose prestige has been challenged, and so forth.

Within a group subject to discrimination, the pressures and pains – as well as the tendency to "act out" – will be especially strong. Another way to look at it: The fewer the opportunities for social success, the greater the risks worth taking. From an evolutionary perspective, therefore, it is not surprising that young men, especially those from disadvantaged social and ethnic groups, are overrepresented among drug addicts, violent criminals, prisoners, and death-row inmates. And that angry and alienated men make up the overwhelming majority of violent terrorists.

Others have tried to explain the high rate of **male violence** without regard to biology. For example, advocates of social-learning theory point out that men – whether African-American, Caucasian, Asian, or whatever – are expected to be aggressive; women are supposed to be passive. So people grow up that way, it is claimed, meeting the expectations that society imposes on them. But why should society have such expectations? And why are those expectations virtually the same in every society around the world? And why do both men and women find it so easy to comply?

The British psychologist Anne Campbell, an advocate of social learning and cultural influence, thinks that men are more aggressive than women because men and women interpret aggression differently: Women see it as a loss of self-control and are ashamed of their anger, associating it with being pushy, nasty, and socially isolated. Men, by contrast, see their aggressiveness in a positive light, as a way of gaining control. To men, anger and even rage can mean courage, success, and triumph. Campbell's analysis is probably correct as far as it goes. But why do males associate aggression with success? And why do they view controlling others as more important than controlling themselves? Also, why do women feel so threatened by isolation and anything that smacks of diminished intimacy, while men feel threatened by anything that smacks of diminished prestige and authority? If the "answer" is that women are taught to react as they do, then I must repeat: Why are virtually identical patterns found in every culture on earth? And why are similar patterns even found in the most different "cultures" of all, those of other species?

All of the above is not meant to imply that biology is the sole explanation for the gender gap in human violence. We cannot do a thing about our evolutionary bequeathal; hence, we had better do all we can to ameliorate those conditions that predispose people to violence. And let's face it: Biology does in fact explain a whole lot, such that if we are going to intervene effectively, we would be well advised to understand the nature of our own predispositions. Just like the fictitious fish with which this essay began, it is time for all of us to look around and acknowledge that when it comes to the social construction of sex differences in violence, the traditional view is all wet.

> Barash critiques the idea that male violence is socially constructed. What evidence does he offer to support this critique? Do you agree with this claim?

Reading 2: Ambiguous Genitalia and the Construction of Gender

Suzanne J. Kessler

Physicians conduct careful examinations of intersexed infants' genitals and perform intricate laboratory procedures. They are interpreters of the body, trained and committed to uncovering the "actual" gender obscured by ambiguous genitals. Yet they also have considerable leeway in assigning gender, and their decisions are influenced by cultural as well as medical factors. What is the relationship between the physician as discoverer and the physician as determiner of gender? Where is the relative emphasis placed in discussions with parents and adolescents and in the consciousness of physicians? It is misleading to characterize the doctors whose words are provided here as presenting themselves publicly to the parents as discoverers of the infant's real gender but privately acknowledging that the infant has no real gender other than the one being determined or constructed by the medical professionals. They are not hypocritical. It is also misleading to claim that physicians' focus shifts from discovery to determination over the course of treatment: first the doctors regard the infant's gender as an unknown but discoverable reality; then the doctors relinquish their attempts to find the real gender and treat the infant's gender as something they must construct. They are not medically incompetent or deficient. Instead, I am arguing that the peculiar balance of discovery and determination through-out treatment permits physicians to handle very problematic cases of gender in the most unproblematic of ways.

This balance relies fundamentally on a particular conception of the "natural."[1] Although the deformity of intersexed genitals would be immutable were it not for medical interference, physicians do not consider it natural. Instead they think of, and speak of, the surgical/hormonal alteration of such deformities as natural because such intervention returns the body to what it "ought to have been" if events had taken their typical course. The nonnormative is converted into the normative, and the normative state is considered natural.[2] The genital ambiguity is remedied to conform to a "natural," that is, culturally indisputable, gender dichotomy. Sherry Ortner's claim that the culture/nature distinction is itself a construction – a product of culture – is relevant here. Language and imagery help create and maintain a specific view of what is natural about the two genders and, I would argue, about the very idea of gender – that it consists

From "The Medical Construction of Gender," *Signs* 16 (1990): 3–26.

of two exclusive types: female and male.[3] The belief that gender consists of two exclusive types is maintained and perpetuated by the medical community in the face of incontrovertible physical evidence that this is not mandated by biology.

The lay conception of human anatomy and physiology assumes a concordance among clearly dimorphic gender markers – chromosomes, genitals, gonads, hormones – but physicians understand that concordance and dimorphism do not always exist. Their understanding of biology's complexity, however, does not inform their understanding of gender's complexity. In order for intersexuality to be managed differently than it currently is, physicians would have to take seriously Money's assertion that it is a misrepresentation of epistemology to consider any cell in the body authentically male or female.[4] If authenticity for gender resides not in a discoverable nature but in someone's proclamation, then the power to proclaim something else is available. If physicians recognized that implicit in their management of gender is the notion that finally, and always, people construct gender as well as the social systems that are grounded in gender-based concepts, the possibilities for real societal transformations would be unlimited. Unfortunately, neither in their representations to the families of the intersexed nor among themselves do the physicians interviewed for this study draw such far-reaching implications from their work. Their "understanding" that particular genders are medically (re)constructed in these cases does not lead them to see that gender is always constructed. Accepting genital ambiguity as a natural option would require that physicians also acknowledge that genital ambiguity is "corrected" not because it is threatening to the infant's life but because it is threatening to the infant's culture.

Rather than admit to their role in perpetuating gender, physicians "psychologize" the issue by talking about the parents" anxiety and humiliation in being confronted with an anomalous infant. The physicians talk as though they have no choice but to respond to the parents' pressure for a resolution of psychological discomfort, and as though they have no choice but to use medical technology in the service of a two-gender culture. Neither the psychology nor the technology is doubted, since both shield physicians from responsibility. Indeed, for the most part, neither physicians nor parents emerge from the experience of intersex case management with a greater understanding of the social construction of gender. Society's accountability, like their own, is masked by the assumption that gender is a given. Thus, cases of intersexuality, instead of illustrating nature's failure to ordain gender in these isolated "unfortunate" instances, illustrate physicians' and Western society's failure of imagination – the failure to imagine that each of these management decisions is a moment when a specific instance of biological "sex" is transformed into a culturally constructed gender.

NOTES

1 For an extended discussion of different ways of conceptualizing "natural," see Richard W. Smith, "What Kind of Sex is Natural?" in *The Frontiers of Sex Research*, ed. Vern Bullough (Buffalo: Prometheus, 1979), 103–11.
2 This supports sociologist Harold Garfinkel's argument that we treat routine events as our due as social members and that we treat gender, like all normal forms, as a moral imperative. It is no wonder, then, that physicians conceptualize what they are doing as natural and unquestionably "right" (Harold Garfinkel, *Studies in Ethnomethodology* [Englewood Cliffs, NJ: Prentice Hall, 1967)].
3 Sherry B. Ortner, "Is Female to Male as Nature is to Culture?" in *Woman, Culture, and Society*, ed. Michelle Zimbalish Rosaldo and Louise Lamphere (Stanford, CA: Stanford University Press, 1974), 67–87.
4 John Money, "Psychological Counseling: Hermaphroditism" in *Endocrine and Genetic Diseases of Childhood and Adolescence*, ed. L. I. Gardner (Philadelphia, PA: Saunders, 1975): 609–18.

In rare instances, infants are born with ambiguous genitalia. Normally, intersexed babies are then subjected to extensive medical intervention in an attempt to construct a "normal": male or female. As Kessler argues, however, what's considered a "normal" male or female body in these circumstances is actually one that has been medically constructed. The natural body is the one that existed prior to surgical intervention, and whose genitalia are ambiguous. Is our belief that there are two – and only two – categories of people (male and female) a biological reality or a social construction? What is Kessler's view?

Reading 3: The Science and Politics of Comparing Men and Women

A. H. Eagly

[. . .]

Is psychological research that compares the sexes beneficial or harmful? Does this research foster or hinder the social change that would increase gender equality? These are many-sided questions that are addressed only in preliminary fashion in this article to stimulate debate.

From "The Science and Politics of Comparing Men and Women," *American Psychologist 50* (1995): 155–6.

The fear is often expressed in feminist writing that differences become deficiencies for women because women are an oppressed group (e.g., Unger and Crawford 1992). Anxiety about sex differences is especially strong to the extent that scientists favor biological explanations, because this approach might produce a portrayal of women as innately inferior to men. Yet, contemporary research that has systematically examined whether the traits and behaviors ascribed to women are regarded as inferior to those ascribed to men has not found evidence for this generalized unfavorable perception of women (Eagly and Mladinic 1994; Eagly et al. 1991). This research has shown that the stereotype of women is more positive overall than the stereotype of men, at least in contemporary samples of US and Canadian college students. To the extent that behavioral differences truly do mirror people's stereotypes, scientific research may thus reveal a pattern of differences that shows both sexes to have strengths and deficiencies but that portrays women somewhat more favorably than men, on the whole. Nonetheless, the favorability of the female stereotype may be a mixed blessing because the particular kinds of positive characteristics most often ascribed to women, primarily "niceness–nurturance" qualities, probably contribute to the exclusion of women from certain kinds of high-status roles (e.g., those that are thought to require toughness and aggressiveness). At any rate, the sex differences that scientists have documented do not tell a simple tale of female inferiority.

The possible uses for findings that have demonstrated sex-differentiated behavior will be enhanced to the extent that psychologists understand the causes of the differences. For example, a case has been made for the biological mediation of sex differences in spatial skills (e.g., Gaulin 1993; Thomas and Kail 1991). If this position is correct, women should prefer a different cue system for negotiating spatial tasks, as Kimura (1992) has argued. If so, gender-informed programs to train women in tasks that have an important spatial component could take account of these female preferences. Alternatively, to the extent that sex differences in spatial ability arise from experience (Baenninger and Newcombe 1989), psychologists might help devise ways to give girls and women more equal access to experiences that train high spatial ability. Still, despite these possibilities of positive outcomes, knowledge of sex differences in spatial ability could decrease women's access to jobs and professions for which excellent spatial ability is a prerequisite.

Another example of the potential usefulness of research on sex differences can be found in social psychological investigations of small group behavior. This research documents in exquisite detail how men take charge in task-oriented groups (e.g., Eagly and Karau 1991; Wood and Rhodes 1992). Women who learn about the specific behaviors that mediate male dominance and the causal factors that underlie these behaviors may be pre-

pared to find the points in the sequence of processes where they can intervene to produce a more equal sharing of power. Some women may even
seek out specific training programs designed to increase their dominance
(e.g., assertiveness training). Nonetheless, knowledge of men's more dominant behavior could contribute to exclusion of women from some kinds of
leadership roles. Which type of outcome would predominate would depend
on many factors, including the strength of the women's desire to change
their status, their political power, and their interest in using psychological
research to help them effect change.

In concert with Scarr's (1988) optimistic analysis, social scientific knowledge of sex differences could enhance women's ability to understand the
antecedents of inequality and to improve their status in society. Nonetheless, the aura of danger surrounds research on sex differences. Some critics
urge psychologists to stop this dangerous work or at least censor it in
various ways (e.g., Baumeister 1988; McHugh et al. 1986). Each researcher
must of course weigh the potential costs and potential benefits. If enough
research psychologists conclude that the costs outweigh the benefits,
research comparing the sexes will recede once again because it is too polit-
ically relevant. However, the scientific work now possesses a momentum of
its own, as more investigators become caught up in the sheer excitement of
discovery and theory testing.

Contemporary psychology has produced a large amount of research
revealing that behavior is sex differentiated to varying extents. The knowledge produced in this area of science can be beneficial both in helping
women and men to understand their natures and their society and in suggesting ways to enhance gender equality. Yet there surely are dangers that
the new research will be used in far less beneficial ways by the misogynist
forces of the society. Therefore, the stresses between gender politics and the
science of gender are not going to disappear. Never before in the history of
psychology has such a formidable body of scientific information encountered such a powerful political agenda. The results of this encounter should
be instructive to all psychologists who believe that psychology should serve
human welfare as it advances scientific understanding.

REFERENCES

Baenninger, M. and Newcombe, N. (1989). The Role of Experience in Spatial Test
    Performance: A Meta-analysis. *Sex Roles*, 20: 327–44.
Baumeister, R. F. (1988). Should We Stop Studying Sex Differences Altogether?
    American Psychologist, 43: 1092–95.
Eagly, A. H. and Karau, S. J. (1991). Gender and the Emergence of Leaders: A Meta-
    analysis. *Journal of Personality and Social Psychology*, 60: 685–710.

Eagly, A. H. and Mladinic, A. (1994). Are People Prejudiced Against Women? Some Answers from Research on Attitudes, Gender Stereotypes, and Judgments of Competence. In W. Stroebe and M. Hewstone (eds.), *European Review of Social Psychology* (vol. 5, pp. 1–35). New York: Wiley.

Eagly, A. H., Mladinic, A., and Otto, S. (1991). Are Women Evaluated More Favorably than Men? An Analysis of Attitudes, Beliefs, and Emotions. *Psychology of Women Quarterly*, 15: 203–16.

Gaulin, S. J. C. (1993). How and Why Sex Differences Evolve, with Spatial Ability as a Paradigm Example. In M. Haug, R. E. Whalen, C. Aron, and K. L. Olsen (eds.), *The Development of Sex Differences and Similarities in Behaviour* (pp. 111–30). London, England: Kluwer Academic.

Kimura, D. (1992). Sex Differences in the Brain. *Scientific American*, 267(3): 118–25.

McHugh, M. C., Koeske, R. D., and Frieze, I. H. (1986). Issues to Consider in Conducting Nonsexist Psychological Research: A Guide for Researchers. *American Psychologist*, 41: 879–90.

Scarr, S. (1988). Race and Gender as Psychological Variables: Social and Ethical Issues. *American Psychologist*, 43: 56–9.

Thomas, H. and Kail, R. (1991). Sex Differences in Speed of Mental Rotation and the X-linked Genetic Hypothesis. *Intelligence*, 15: 17–32.

Unger, R. and Crawford, M. (1992). *Women and Gender: A Feminist Psychology*. New York: McGraw-Hill.

Wood, W. and Rhodes, N. (1992). Sex Differences in Interaction Style in Task Groups. In C. L. Ridgeway (ed.), *Gender, Interaction, and Inequality* (pp. 97–121). New York: Springer-Verlag.

What are some of the tensions between the science of gender and the politics of gender, as outlined in Eagly's article? Does gender equality require that women and men be found to be similar?

3

Gender in Interactions and Institutions

CHAPTER OBJECTIVES

- Critically evaluate the main elements of interactionist approaches to gender, including ethnomethodology, status characteristics theory, and homophily research

- Critically evaluate the main elements of institutional approaches to gender

- Discuss the major differences between individual, interactionist and institutional approaches to gender

Have you ever found yourself the only woman (or man) in a group of people, such as a discussion group for a course or perhaps as a member of a work team? Now, think about situations where you were surrounded by others just like you – all women or all men. Did you feel differently in each situation? How did being a member of the majority or the minority (with respect to sex category) affect how you behaved and how others behaved toward you? These are among the issues explored by proponents of the frameworks presented in this chapter.

Recall that gender is a system of social practices that constitutes people as different and that organizes relations of inequality. Thus far, we have looked at gender from the point of view of individuals and have focused on the social practices that produce the gendered person. But the social practices that constitute gender do not operate strictly at the individual level. These social practices also shape social relations and interaction patterns, and they operate as part of larger entities, such as organizations and institutions.

In this chapter, we will explore these alternative frameworks. They include interactional approaches, which attend to social relations; and institutional perspectives, which highlight the structure and practices of organizations and social institutions. In contrast to individualist approaches, which focus on internalized and relatively stable characteristics of individuals, the two frameworks examined here emphasize social forces operating external to the person.

The perspectives examined in Chapter 2 share a belief that people are gendered – that is, that the distinction between masculine and feminine is one that is expressed in individuals. In addition, most agree that sex distinctions are a primary reason for this. Sex, then, is a source of gender and sets limits on the traits, behaviors, and identities of people. Further, because gender is part of the person, it is assumed to be relatively stable – internal and unchangeable. People do not put on and take off gender as they move from place to place, situation to situation, group to group. This claim is disputed by the next set of perspectives we will examine.

INTERACTIONIST VIEWS OF GENDER

Interactionist approaches to gender focus less on individuals and more on the social context within which individuals interact. Although these perspectives acknowledge that women and men may differ in some of the ways noted by individualists, interactionist approaches place greater attention on forces operating outside the individual. In contrast to individualists, who assume people's traits and abilities are relatively stable, interactionists argue that people's reactions and behaviors vary in response to the social context. The social context includes the other participants in a setting and features of the environment where the interaction takes place. These approaches, as Deaux and Major (1990: 91) explain, "presume[s] a repertoire of possibilities from which individual men and women choose different responses on varying occasions with different degrees of self-consciousness." For example, this view would suggest that women might be more nurturant when interacting with others who expect women to behave this way than when interacting with people having fewer gender expectations. Women might also behave in a more nurturant manner in social contexts where women have been traditionally defined as caretakers than when they are in social contexts where women have traditionally held other roles.

In this chapter, we examine three types of interactionist approaches. While they differ in important respects, they all view social categorization as essential to social interaction. **Social categorization** refers to the processes through which individuals classify others and themselves as members of particular groups. Virtually everyone agrees that sex category is an extremely important social category (Aries 1996). For some, as we will see, it is *the* most important social category. There are many other social categories, however, such as those based on racial or ethnic distinctions, age, ability, etc. All of these social categories may be relevant for social interaction in particular situations and settings.

Social categorization is important because it sets into motion the production of gender differences and inequality. The three perspectives examined below differ somewhat in their understanding of how and why that occurs, however. The first interactionist approach – "doing gender" – argues that social interaction is the vehicle through which people present themselves to others as women or men. Status characteristics theory takes a different view, emphasizing the ways in which sex categories become the basis for people's expectations about others' competence. The third interactionist perspective – what I call the homophily approach – emphasizes the consequences of people classifying others as similar or different from themselves. This perspective generally assumes that being different from or similar to others is more important in shaping interaction than *how* one differs or is similar.

Ethnomethodological views: "doing gender"

Sociologists influenced by the ethnomethodological tradition offer an interaction-based view known as "doing gender" (West and Zimmerman 1987). These theorists disagree with those who see gender as a stable set of personality traits or behavioral capacities. Instead, from a "**doing gender**" perspective, gender – or, rather, the belief that the world is divided into two, mutually exclusive categories – is understood as an "accomplishment" – a product of human effort.

Like the previous interactionist accounts, ethnomethodologists believe that sex categorization is a habitual, virtually automatic, and rarely questioned aspect of social interaction. Sex categorization both reflects and contributes to "the natural attitude" regarding gender (Garfinkel 1967; see also Chapter 1). Ethnomethodologists believe that sex categorization and the "natural attitude" are social constructions rather than biological or physical realities. Understanding how social interaction produces a gender-differentiated world is the central goal of these approaches.

West and Fenstermaker (1995) recently extended this view: "Doing difference" is their attempt to describe the exercise of power and production of inequality more generally, not just in relation to gender. West and

Fenstermaker argue that the same dynamics that "accomplish" gender in interaction also produce other forms of inequality and power differentials, such as those stemming from social class and race. This implies that not only gender, but race and social class as well, are products of social interaction, not essential characteristics of people. "Doing difference" is West and Fenstermaker's way of explaining multiple types of inequality with a single analytic framework.

From an ethnomethodological perspective, gender is "done" in virtually all social situations. Ethnomethodologists claim that because sex categories are always present, they are always available as a basis for interpreting others' behavior. "In short," as West and Fenstermaker explain, "persons engaged in virtually *any* activity can hold themselves accountable and be held accountable for their performance of that activity *as women* or *as men*" (1993: 157; emphasis in original). This claim – that gender is being "done" always and everywhere – distinguishes ethnomethodological approaches from other interactionist accounts.

Ethnomethodologists, in general, are somewhat skeptical of broad theoretical accounts, preferring instead to show how gender (and other forms of difference) is produced and maintained in particular social encounters. In some people's eyes, this unwillingness to generalize makes their approach more descriptive than explanatory. Further, some believe that ethnomethodologists go too far in emphasizing the fluidity and variability of gender. For example, Thorne (1995) argues that ethnomethodologists' preoccupation with gender as a "performance" or as something that is "done" in social interaction underemphasizes the factors that shape or constrain people's ability to produce gender displays. Extending the metaphor of the performance, we could say that ethnomethodologists focus on each performance's unique details to the exclusion of how performances differ systematically and how these differences may be shaped by the theatre, the stage, and the props that form its backdrop. To fully understand these influences, we turn to other interactionist accounts.

Status characteristics theory: the importance of expectations

How does social interaction help produce gender distinctions and inequalities? Status characteristics theory (also referred to as the theory of "expectation states") offers a straightforward answer to this question: Because interaction requires that people orient themselves to one another, it is necessary to have some basis for categorizing others *vis-[ag]-vis* oneself (Ridgeway 1997). In Risman's words: "Gender is something we do in order to make social life more manageable" (1998: 33).

Sex categorization serves this purpose better than any other categorization system, according to Ridgeway and other status characteristics theorists. Continuing reliance on sex categorization as a way to organize interaction, however, tends to create gender expectations and stereotypes. People learn to expect certain kinds of behaviors and responses from others, based on their sex category. These expectations serve as cognitive reminders of how we are supposed to behave in any given situation. Risman refers to them "as accurate folklore that must be considered in every interaction" (1998: 32). People thus respond to others based on what they believe is expected of them and assume that others will do likewise.

To explain why and how categorizing others by sex produces gender expectations and stereotypes, these theorists introduce the idea of a **status characteristic**. A status characteristic is "an attribute on which individuals vary that is associated in a society with widely held beliefs according greater esteem and worthiness to some states of the attribute (e.g., being male) than others (being female)" (Ridgeway 1993: 179). Gender in American society – and in most contemporary societies – is clearly a status characteristic. Men are generally regarded more positively than women. Once a characteristic like sex category has status value, it begins to shape expectations and form the basis for stereotypes.

Gender is not the only basis on which people differentially assign power and status, however. For example, age is also a status characteristic; adults are generally ascribed more status and power than children. Similarly, racial distinctions may also operate in this way. Gender thus is not unique or distinctive as a status characteristic. Further, expectation states theory recognizes that multiple status characteristics may be activated in any given situation.

Status characteristics theory was developed to explain goal-oriented interaction, such as occurs in workplaces, classrooms, or in any group oriented toward a collective end. In these kinds of settings the important expectations are those relating to performance. That is, group members assess how competent each is and how much value to attach to each other's contributions. People form their expectations about others' competence by weighing each status characteristic in terms of its relevance to the task at hand. This weighting process is not assumed to be conscious or precise; rather, expectation states theorists believe that people seek cues as to how others will perform in a particular situation and use status characteristics to assess this. These performance expectations tend to disadvantage those with lower status value (in the case of gender, women). Women are expected to be less competent than men and their contributions are expected to be less valuable.

Status characteristics theory recognizes that the effects of gender on social interaction may vary from situation to situation. This is why this theory provides a contextual account of gender: It assumes that status characteristics such as gender are more likely to be "activated" (i.e., central to people's awareness) in some situations than others. Ridgeway expects gender to be most influential when two conditions hold: when the interactants are members of different sex categories, and when gender is relevant to the task or purpose of the interaction.

Many kinds of social interactions meet these conditions. For example, consider a meeting of a student group attended by both women and men. According to the status characteristics approach, how women and men interact in this setting context will depend in part on the nature of their task. If the group works on a task that the larger culture strongly identifies with men (e.g., organizing a softball tournament), we would expect men to display interactional styles associated with power and competence (e.g., more talking, speaking longer, etc.). If the task is more closely associated with women, however, then women would be more likely than men to behave in these ways.

Contrast this interactionist approach with one focusing on gender socialization. A socialization account would emphasize how women and men learn to behave in dominant or assertive ways. The interaction styles associated with dominance thus would be treated as personality characteristics, and these styles would undoubtedly be viewed as more typical among men than among women. Status characteristics theory instead treats interaction styles as less a matter of individual personality and more a function of the setting, including the group's sex composition and task orientation. In this view, the fact that men may interact in dominant ways more often than women has less to do with men's personalities or socialization and more to do with the types of settings where women and men typically encounter each other.

Like the ethnomethodological approach, status characteristics theory suggests that gender differences emerge out of more general processes that shape interaction. Their methods for studying social interaction differ considerably, however. Ethnomethodologists prefer fine-grained, qualitative studies of particular settings and tend to resist abstract theorizing. By contrast, status characteristics theorists have developed their ideas primarily through laboratory experiments. Further, these theorists aim to create a formal theory of status processes. Through these efforts, status characteristics theory is constantly being refined and expanded. Researchers work to better understand the kinds of situations that activate gender and other status characteristics (Ridgeway 1993; Ridgeway and Diekema 1992).

For status characteristics theorists, a group's sex composition helps to determine how gender will shape the group's interactions. The third interactionist approach focuses explicitly on the role of sex composition. From this perspective, the meaning and impact of one's own sex category depends on the sex composition of the group. A person's own sex category is less relevant to any particular interaction than the sex category memberships of those with whom she is interacting.

Opposites attract – or don't they? Homophily and gender

We are probably all familiar with the adage "opposites attract." Like many forms of conventional wisdom, however, this one is not accurate. In fact, a better description of social relations is "birds of a feather flock together." Similarity tends to be a much stronger source of interpersonal attraction than difference. Indeed, much research suggests that social ties of all types tend to be organized according to the homophily principle: Social ties tend to be between people who are similar on salient sociodemographic dimensions (Popielarz 1999).

There are at least two reasons why this occurs. Partly, it reflects people's preferences. **Homophily**, then, is a term used to describe people's preference for sameness, a preference that is expressed in their interpersonal relations. In addition, however, the homophilous social ties experienced in everyday life are reinforced – and developed – in the groups to which people belong. Groups include such things as the neighborhoods where people live, the clubs and organizations they belong to, or their church membership. As McPherson et al. (1992) explain, "We argue that most homophily occurs because ties are shaped by the opportunities presented to people in groups. We do not encounter people who are seriously different enough from us frequently enough for them to become social network contacts" (1992: 168).

What does it mean to say that people's interpersonal relations are governed by homophily? What kinds of similarity matter? Do some forms of similarity matter more than others? When sociologists say that similarity attracts, they mean that people are drawn to those whose attitudes, values, and beliefs are similar to their own. People who share our views affirm us, thus positively reinforcing who we are and how we live. We may also feel that people like us in these ways are easier to communicate with than those who do not share our views. We may trust them more and feel a greater sense of kinship with them. Conversely, when people are different from us, we may feel threatened and find communication difficult. Trust may be lacking or simply be harder to achieve.

These ideas about the importance of similarity in social life have tremendous implications for understanding gender and the relations between women and men. To understand why, we must consider how it is that people decide who shares their views of the world and who does not. The best way to make this determination would be to get to know on a personal level each individual with whom we interacted. It takes time and effort to really learn about a person, though. Hence, it is unrealistic to assume that we would ever be able to acquire this type of knowledge about all of the people in our daily lives. Moreover, would we even want to devote time and energy to this task, given other life priorities? Under these circumstances, most of us are much more selective. We may get to know some people in our lives very well, but will not expend so much energy on everyone. Instead, in the absence of information about people's attitudes and beliefs, we rely on a sort of "social shorthand": We infer information about them – and their degree of similarity to us – from characteristics that are easily visible and accessible. We use these visible and accessible characteristics as "proxies" for qualities that would be time-consuming to determine, such as values, attitudes, and beliefs.

Ascribed characteristics, such as sex, race, and age, are the kinds of proxies most often used to infer similarity (or dissimilarity) with another. Recall that ascribed characteristics are relatively immutable and not voluntarily chosen. Sex, race, and age are important ascribed characteristics in social life because they are so easily observed and difficult to hide. The power of these characteristics also derives from the fact that sex, race, and age are highly institutionalized statuses and, hence, each is laden with layers of social meaning. This increases their value as "proxies" for similarity and dissimilarity since they are believed to be reliably associated with particular characteristics.

The similarity-attraction hypothesis implies that being a member of a group containing all women (if you are a woman) or all men (if a man) would be preferable to being in a more sex-integrated group (other factors being equal). In other words, people should prefer to interact with others like themselves and feel uncomfortable, threatened, and less committed when they are in more heterogeneous groups. These issues have received significant attention from researchers and have been especially important in understanding women's and men's work experiences (see Part II). For example, studies have focused on people's experiences in groups of varying sex composition. They are interested in whether people have different experiences in mixed-sex groups than in groups that contain all men or all women. In general, the similarity-attraction hypothesis assumes that both women and men would prefer settings where they were in the majority to those where they were less well represented. Researchers are also interested in the performance of those groups. Is conflict higher in some types of groups than in others?

These dynamics were captured in a provocative study by Tsui et al. (1992). These researchers examined the consequences of "being different" for workers' attachment to their firms. They hypothesized that people who were more different from other members of their work groups would be less attached (e.g., less psychologically committed, more likely to be absent from work, and more likely to quit) than those who were more similar. Several forms of difference were examined, including sex, age, race, education, and tenure with the employer.

Consistent with the arguments presented above, Tsui et al. found that being different from one's co-workers on ascribed characteristics (i.e., age, race, and sex) had negative consequences on attachment, while being different with respect to education or tenure with the employer did not have these consequences. Moreover, these authors found that whites and men – that is, those who were members of the historically dominant categories – reacted more negatively to being different than non-whites and women. This research thus suggests that being different is difficult for people, especially when it involves difference on an ascribed characteristic, like sex.

While Tsui et al. (1992) focused on the reactions of those who are different from others in the group, others have examined the majority's reactions or looked at the interactions between the majority and the minority. Rosabeth Moss Kanter explored these issues in her 1977 classic, *Men and Women of the Corporation*. Kanter argued that the relative proportions of different "social types" in a group shape members' social relations. "As proportions shift," she suggests, "so do social experiences" (Kanter 1977: 207). Proportions have this effect because they influence how people perceive one another.

Kanter (1977: 208) was particularly interested in what she called, "skewed groups." In these groups, one social type is numerically dominant and the other is a very small numerical minority (e.g., 15 percent or less). Kanter's focus on this type of group stemmed from the fact that this is likely to be the situation experienced by "newcomers" to a social setting. Women who enter jobs or workplaces historically dominated by men, for example, are apt to enter as a minority of this type, as are people of color who enter jobs historically dominated by whites. Because it is unlikely that an employer would hire large numbers of women or people of color at one time, sex (and race) integration happens slowly, one or two people at a time. Members of the numerical minority in skewed groups are called **tokens**. For Kanter, this term is not pejorative, nor does it refer to people who are assumed to have been hired *because of* their sex or race. Instead, the term "token" is a neutral label, referring to those whose "social type" constitutes 15 percent or less of a group.

Kanter argues that relations between tokens and dominants in skewed groups are shaped by three perceptual tendencies: **visibility, contrast,** and **assimilation**. First, tokens – because they are different from the majority – are easily noticed. In the organization she studied Kanter found that token women in high-level positions were "the subject of conversation, questioning, gossip, and careful scrutiny" (1977: 212). Moreover, tokens' behavior was often attributed more to their social category membership than to their own individual characteristics. Thus, tokens carry an extra burden: they represent their entire social category (Kanter 1977). Tokens responded to these "performance pressures" in numerous ways. Some overachieved, while trying hard not to stick out too much, thus avoiding the resentment of dominants. Others enjoyed being the only woman and thus emphasized their uniqueness, while still others kept low profiles and tried to become socially invisible. In all cases, however, tokens were performing under very different conditions than dominants.

Contrast is the second perceptual tendency associated with tokenism. As Kanter notes, "The presence of a token or two makes dominants more aware of what they have in common at the same time that it threatens that commonality" (1977: 221–2). Tokens are threatening to dominants because their presence creates uncertainty: Norms, beliefs, and styles of communication that dominants take for granted may be challenged or misunderstood. At its most extreme, dominants' uncertainty and discomfort can be expressed in hostility toward tokens and result in efforts to isolate or exclude them from social interaction. More typical perhaps are dominants' attempts to exaggerate and affirm their differences from tokens, a set of behaviors Kanter refers to as "boundary heightening" (1977: 229).

The third perceptual tendency associated with tokenism is assimilation. Dominants see tokens less as individuals and more as representative members of their social category. Moreover, because the characteristics dominants associate with a token's social category are often overly simplified or inaccurate stereotypes, assimilation contributes to the dominants' misperceptions of the token. Kanter contends that these processes ultimately force tokens into highly restricted and caricatured roles. This "role encapsulation" may make dominants more comfortable in tokens' presence, but it can be detrimental to tokens. Because the roles that tokens are constrained to perform may inhibit rather than enhance job success, Kanter refers to these as "role traps."

As this discussion suggests, being a token can be a highly stressful experience. Even if successful in terms of their overall job performance, the conditions under which tokens work are different than those of the dominant group and may be psychologically burdensome. Of course, some tokens will not experience these stresses and some may even derive self-esteem from successfully overcoming the challenges associated with token status. Nevertheless, Kanter's point is that how people experience work is shaped in part by how many of their social type are present.

Can men be tokens? Although Kanter's research focused on female tokens, she believed that the processes associated with tokenism were genderless and thus would operate regardless of whether tokens were male or female. In the years since Kanter made these arguments, many researchers have explored this question. For example, in a 1986 study, Floge and Merrill examined male nurses and female physicians in a hospital. Because maleness is generally associated with more positive expectations about competence, knowledge, and leadership capability than femaleness, male tokens often benefit from their status, while female tokens do not. To better understand this point, recall the theory of "expectation states" discussed above. Floge and Merrill are drawing on this perspective when they suggest that maleness is a status characteristic associated with more positive expectations than femaleness.

Other approaches to this issue draw more heavily on the "doing gender" perspective. For example, in their study of male clerical temporaries, Henson and Rogers (2001) pose the question: How do men "do masculinity" in a predominantly female job? The vast majority of clerical workers are women, and this is also true among those in temporary jobs. Henson and Rogers (2001) note that prior to the 1960s, most temporary employers of clerical workers (e.g., Kelly Girl – later Kelly Services) did not even accept male applicants. Not surprisingly, then, men who become clerical temporaries are likely to face questions, surprise, and disapproval from their peers and co-workers. One man interviewed by Henson and Rogers (2001: 223) commented:

> People are looking at me like, "What are you doing here?" Like they're thinking, "Gee, what's the deal? Shouldn't you be, I don't know, doing something else?" I mean it's sort of fine if you're just out of school. They kind of expect well, you're just doing this until you get a regular job.

In response, male clerical temporaries reasserted their masculinity using several strategies designed to set them apart from and superior to women. For example, they reframed the work, replacing the term "secretary" with more masculine or gender-neutral descriptions, such as bookkeeper or word processor (Henson and Rogers 2001). They used "cover stories" to create an alternative occupational identity, such as actor or writer, and minimized the significance of their temporary job. The male clerical temporaries in Henson and Rogers's (2001) study also asserted their masculinity by refusing to perform the deference (see Chapter 6) typically required of subordinates – especially women (Pierce 1995).

While these researchers focus on tokens, others are interested in how people's experiences differ across the full range of group types. Allmendinger and Hackman's (1995) study of symphony orchestras provides an example of this line of research. These researchers were interested in how the sex composition of a symphony orchestra affected its members' attitudes. This study relies on cross-national data; the researchers examined 78 orchestras in four geographical locations (the USA, United Kingdom, the former East Germany, and the former West Germany). Historically, women have been only a small percentage of players in professional orchestras, and this is true worldwide. In this study, the percentage of women ranged from 2 to 59 percent.

Allmendinger and Hackman's (1995) findings are generally consistent with the similarity-attraction hypothesis, though they show that it is more complicated than one might assume. For example, they found that while women were less satisfied when they were in orchestras dominated by men (i.e., 90 percent or more male) than those that were more balanced (i.e., between 40 and 60 percent women), they were especially dissatisfied in orchestras that contained between 10 percent and 40 percent women. Male orchestra members also were less satisfied when women were greater than 10 percent but less than 40 percent of members. These findings held true in all four countries, underscoring the power of group composition. Allmendinger and Hackman suggest that once women become a significant minority (i.e., greater than 10 percent), they gain power and cannot be as easily overlooked by their male counterparts. In their words: "Together, these processes result in tightened identity group boundaries for both genders, increased cross-group stereotyping and conflict, less social support across gender boundaries, and heightened personal tension for everyone" (Allmendinger and Hackman 1995: 453).

Summary of interactionist views

The three interactionist perspectives agree that social categorization – particularly sex categorization – is an important social process. In addition, all three approaches emphasize the ways that gender emerges and is reproduced in social interaction. In this way, they diverge from individualist approaches, which see gender as residing primarily within individuals. Interactionist approaches are a useful counterpoint to individualist understandings of gender. While individualists see gender as a relatively stable property of people, interactionist approaches emphasize the ways that social context and social interaction influence the expression and significance of gender.

GENDERED ORGANIZATIONS/GENDERED INSTITUTIONS

Much of social life is organized and routine. People are employed by organizations, such as business firms or the government. They attend school from kindergarten – or even preschool – through high school, or college and perhaps graduate or professional school. They are members of churches or voluntary associations, such as neighborhood groups. In fact, many of the interactions people have take place within organizations. An **organization** is a social unit established to pursue a particular goal. Organizations have boundaries, rules, procedures, and means of communication (Hall 2002). The social practices that are associated with organizations play an especially important role in the production and reproduction of gender and gender inequality.

Institution is a somewhat more abstract and more all-encompassing concept. In simplest terms, sociologists define an **institution** as "an organized, established pattern" or even more simply, "the rules of the game" (Jepperson 1991: 143). Institutions, then, are those features of social life that seem so regular, so ongoing, and so permanent that they are often accepted as just "the way things are." Each major social institution is organized according to what Friedland and Alford call "a central logic – a set of material practices and symbolic constructions" (1991: 248). These logics thus include structures, patterns, and routines, and they include the belief systems that supply these with meaning.

As this discussion reveals, institutions incorporate more of the social landscape than organizations. In fact, many institutions contain several different types of organizations. For example, education is a social institution made up of schools of all kinds, school boards, administrative offices, teachers' groups, as well as organizations of students and parents. Given this, I will refer to this framework as the gendered institutions approach, recognizing that it includes aspects of organizations as well.

Gendered institutions

Acker (1992b) observes that many of the institutions that constitute the "rules of the game" in American society – and, indeed, most societies – embody aspects of gender. As she defines it, to say that an institution is gendered means that

> gender is present in the processes, practices, images and ideologies, and distributions of power in the various sectors of social life. Taken as more or less functioning wholes, the institutional structures of the United States and other societies are organized along the lines of gender . . . [These institutions] have been historically developed by men, currently dominated by men, and symbolically interpreted from the standpoint of men in leading positions, both in the present and historically. (1992: 567)

Further, from this perspective, aspects of social life that are conventionally treated as "genderless" or gender-neutral are, in fact, expressions of gender. This way of thinking about gender directs attention to the organization, structure, and practices of social institutions, and it emphasizes the ways that these entrenched, powerful, and relatively taken-for-granted aspects of the social order produce and reproduce gender distinctions and inequality.

Gendered institutions in everyday life: sport and higher education

Two examples may help you better understand these ideas. Sport and education are two institutions familiar to most students. Both institutions are gendered in important ways. Sport in American society is comprised of many different types of organization – schools, governing bodies such as the NCAA (National Collegiate Athletic Association), professional organizations, media, and large corporations, such as Nike. It is almost impossible to describe sport in American society without taking these organizations into account. Millions of boys and girls are introduced to sports in schools. Media, such as newspapers, magazines, and television, influence people's exposure to sports, teams, and particular athletes. Governing bodies and professional organizations also play a powerful role shaping sports practices, policies, and procedures.

Gender permeates virtually all of these aspects of sport. For example, research shows that by almost all criteria – from access to funding to media coverage to fan support – organized sports has favored men over women (Birrell and Cole 1994; Messner and Sabo 1990). Research on sports media shows that women's sports are reported very differently than sports involving men; daily newspapers devote roughly 80 percent of their space to men's sports (Messner et al. 1992). Sport helps to create ideas about male and female bodies and their physical capabilities or limitations – the muscular male football player and the petite female figure skater. Sports journalist Joan Ryan argues that the popularity of sports such as gymnastics and figure-skating stems in part from their highly feminized presentation, "free of the sticky issues of power, sexual orientation and aggression that encumber most other female athletes" (1995: 68). Coakley suggests that American sport reflects a "gender logic," such that "when people participated in sports, they often learned that 'common sense' led to the conclusion that women were 'naturally' inferior to men in any activity requiring physical skills and cognitive strategies" (1998: 9–10).

Now we turn to higher education – another important (gendered) institution. We begin by considering the sex composition of teaching. Unlike elementary school, junior high, and high school, where students are likely to encounter teachers of both genders (and, in the early years, have more female than male teachers), roughly half of full-time, college professors were white men in 1999. White women made up slightly more than one-quarter (i.e., 27.9 percent) of this population, with the remaining 14 percent consisting of women and men of color (United States Department of Education 2001). Male and female students attending the most elite colleges and universities are least likely to be taught by female faculty members, while students attending public community colleges are most likely to be taught by a woman. Hence, the sex composition of the faculty and the type of institution a student attends are related.

In addition, unlike the earlier years of schooling when all students more or less take the same kinds of classes, the curriculum at the college level is highly specialized. Because women and men tend to major in different fields, this means that classrooms in higher education – unlike the early years of schooling – are likely to vary widely in their sex composition. This variation sets into motion some of the interactional processes described earlier in this chapter. Students of both genders are more likely to be taught by female professors in those fields where women students predominate. Roughly half of all full-time faculty members in education, for example, were women in 1992, as compared to less than 5 percent in engineering. African-American women faculty are more likely to be found in education than in any other area (United States Department of Education 1999).

Observe your own classes to gain a better sense of these patterns. In what kinds of courses have you had a female professor? A male professor? A male or female professor of color? Are the students in your classes mostly male or mostly female? Does the sex composition of your classes vary depending upon the subject matter of the course? These observations are likely to reveal patterns consistent with other material presented in this chapter. Variation in the sex composition of faculty and students across fields and types of higher education curriculum is a persistent feature of this institution and is one reason why education is a gendered institution.

Although women and men continue to major (and become faculty members) in different fields, this pattern has declined over time. This can be seen in three respects. First, higher education itself has become more gender-integrated. While women represented 43 percent of all bachelor's degree recipients in 1970–1, by 1997–8, women were earning over half (56 percent) of all bachelor's degrees. Women earned a higher percentage of bachelor's degrees than men in all racial-ethnic groups (i.e., American Indian, Hispanic, Asian, African-American, and White). In addition, a majority of master's degree recipients were women and women received 40 percent of all PhD's (United States Department of Education 2001).

The tendency for women and men to major in different fields has also declined over time. During the 1997–8 school year, women earned over half of all the bachelor's degrees in the biological and life sciences and just under half of all business degrees. By contrast, in 1970–1 women received approximately one-quarter of all biology degrees and less than 10 percent of all degrees in business (National Center for Education Statistics 2001). While men received over 80 percent of all undergraduate engineering degrees in 1997–8, less than 1 percent of engineering degrees went to women in 1968. About three-quarters of all degrees in education went to women in 1995–6, approximately the same percentage as in 1970–1 (National Center for Education Statistics 2001). Overall, then, gender segregation has declined in higher education since the 1960s, but women and men in college continue to enter somewhat different fields.

In conclusion, these examples reveal several important aspects of institutions. First, institutions are an important source of cultural beliefs about the social world, including beliefs about gender. Institutions provide scripts that become guides for action. For example, as we will see in Part II, gender has been a tremendously important element of the institutional logics governing work and family in the United States. These institutions are the source of many of people's beliefs about how women and men are and should be. Beliefs about gender also feed back into these institutions, shaping their organization and practices. No one can really escape these institutional forces. Even those who may not share the logics that govern institutions must nevertheless respond to them as they organize their lives.

A second important feature of institutions, revealed in the examples of sport and education, is that they tend to be self-perpetuating, almost taking on a life of their own. This implies that there need not be – and often is not – any conscious intent to create or reproduce gender differences and inequalities. Instead, beliefs are taken for granted and past practices continue unless and until a conscious and large-scale effort is made to change them. It was not until 1972 and the passage of Title IX that sex discrimination in education became illegal and girls and women had equal access to organized sports in high school and college. The struggle for gender equity in sport and education continues to this day, emphasizing the tremendous inertia that is built into the largest and most powerful social institutions.

A related feature of institutions is that, because they are taken for granted, they produce a socially shared "account" of their existence and purpose. The availability of these accounts helps explain why institutions are so rarely challenged or scrutinized: People believe that their purpose and functioning are self-evident. When I ask my students why Olympic gymnastics is a sport for petite, prepubescent young girls and strong, muscular men (and thus why there are few gymnastics opportunities for adult women and prepubescent boys), they offer a quick and ready answer. In my students' eyes, it is unremarkable and completely obvious that people would rather watch young girls and adult men than the alternative. The question of why this should be true is not something many have ever considered, thus underscoring the power of institutions to avoid scrutiny.

The gendered institutions approach directs researchers' attention away from individuals and interaction patterns to the study of social structure and culture. Gender thus is not viewed as something individuals possess, but rather is conceived as an aspect of social organization. But are all organizational structures and practices "gendered"? Or is the "gendering" of institutions a matter of degree and form?

These are difficult questions that gender scholars are only beginning to explore (Britton 2000). In the meantime, however, England (1998) provides one useful way to address these issues. She draws on legal doctrines to propose two ways to identify whether and how an organization (or practices and policies within an organization) are gendered. She suggests that practices, policies, or procedures that treat women and men differently represent a form of "disparate treatment," while practices, policies, or procedures that do not specify differential treatment, yet have a "disparate impact" on women and men, represent a second form of gendering. In England's view, either or both practices may be sufficient to identify an organization as gendered. As we will see in later chapters, proponents of a gendered institutions perspective have uncovered both forms of gendering in the key social institutions of American life.

TOWARD A MULTILAYERED CONCEPTION OF GENDER

Interactionist approaches argue that students of gender should focus less on individuals and more on social interaction and social relations. For these theorists, gender emerges and is sustained within social interaction; hence, social context – the groups and settings where people gather – plays a much greater role in these views than in individualist approaches. Institutional perspectives capture the ways that gender is embedded within social structure and is a part of the taken-for-granted reality in contemporary society. Both approaches can be contrasted with an individualist perspective, which treats gender as an attribute of people. None of these approaches alone is sufficient, however. Instead, gender is a multilayered system of practices and relations that operates at all levels of the social world (Ridgeway and Smith-Lovin 1999; Risman 1998).

As a multilevel system affecting individuals' identities and characteristics, patterns of social interaction, and social institutions, the gender system shapes social life in crucial ways. In Part II, we will examine this system's operation in two key arenas: work and family. Each of the three frameworks introduced in this and the previous chapter will us in this investigation.

No discussion of gender would be complete without attending to work and family. Both spheres directly affect the daily lives of adult women and men, and their children. Work, family, and gender have been intertwined historically. As the organization of work and family life have changed, so too, have women's and men's lives. In addition, beliefs about gender – about what men and women are and should be – are conditioned by these institutions.

CHAPTER SUMMARY

This chapter examined interactionist and institutional approaches to gender. Interactionists focus on the social relations that produce gender distinctions and inequalities. The key perspectives within this tradition include ethnomethodology (i.e., "doing gender"), status characteristics theory, and theory and research on homophily. Though they differ in important respects, the process of social categorization is central to all three perspectives.

Institutional perspectives focus on gender as aspects of social structure and culture. Institutional perspectives thus direct attention to the practices and policies of organizations, and to the material and symbolic dimensions of large-scale social institutions, such as education, work, or family. Institutions are an important source of beliefs about gender. In addition, because they tend to be self-perpetuating, institutions play a central role in the perpetuation of gender distinctions and inequalities. The chapter concluded with a discussion of gender as a multilayered system, operating at the individual, interactional, and institutional levels.

FURTHER READING

Acker, Joan. 1990. "Hierarchies, Jobs, and Bodies: a Theory of Gendered Organizations." *Gender & Society* 4: 139–58.

Acker, Joan. 1992. "Gendered Institutions." *Contemporary Sociology* 21: 565–9.

Ridgeway, Cecilia L. 1997. "Interaction and the Conservation of Gender Inequality." *American Sociological Review* 62: 218–35.

West, Candace and Fenstermaker, Sarah. 1995. "Doing Difference." *Gender & Society* 9: 8–37.

West, Candace and Zimmerman, Don H. 1991. "Doing Gender." In Judith Lorber and Susan A. Farrell (eds.), *The Social Construction of Gender*. Newbury Park, CA: Sage.

Reading 1: "If you let me play": Nike Ads and Gender

Robert Goldman and Stephen Papson

[. . .]
When play is transformed into sport, the physical body is made social.[1]

One of Nike's most talked about TV ads debuted in August 1995. Titled "If you let me play," this ad gave voice to the consequences of denying girls the same opportunities for sports that boys routinely receive. This ad combines quick camera takes and slow-motion shots of preteen and teenage girls on a park playground signified by swing sets, monkey bars, and a simple merry-go-round. The spot features a turn-taking of girls' voices as they recite the long-term advantages in their lives if they play sports. Shown in tight facial close-ups, the young girls solemnly speak in soundbites that sound as if they have been scripted by social scientists and women's health advocates. The encounter with children speaking adult thoughts is initially startling, as they stare into the camera and flatly intone:

> If you let me play
> If you let me play sports
> I will like myself more.
> I will have more self-confidence.
> If you let me play sports.
> If you let me play
> If you let me play
> I will be 60% less likely to get breast cancer
> I will suffer less depression.
> If you let me play sports
> I will be more likely to leave a man who beats me.
> If you let me play
> I will be less likely to get pregnant before I want to.
> I will learn
> I will learn what it means to be strong

From "Transcending Difference? Representing Women in Nike's World," in *Nike Culture*, (Thousand Oaks, CA: Sage Publications, 1998).

To be strong
If you let me play
Play sports
If you let me play sports.

Just do it
[*Swoosh* symbol]

Nike represents a new breed of advertisers who try to make ads serve their own narrow commodity agendas by trying to give the ad a place in the field of **public culture** – a space where public debate is raised. The creators of "If you let me play" – Janet Champ, Rachel Nelson, Jennifer Smieja, and Angelina Vieira – have been explicit about their intentions.

> What we hoped to create with this advertisement was twofold. One, we wanted to help end the discrimination every little girl – and woman – is faced with when it comes to organized sports. And two, to alert fathers, mothers, teachers, friends, family members and girls themselves to the profound, and unsettling, benefits that sports and fitness can give them if they start young enough. (T)he benefits (of sports for women) are astounding.[2]

In another interview, Janet Champ stressed her concern that without realizing it, parents and teachers buy into the ideology that little girls need to be protected. This, Champ observed, results in lower self-esteem and confidence, and precipitates a self-fulfilling gender prophecy.[3]

Indeed, the ad brings together elements that otherwise rarely co-exist in the entertainment world of advertising. Advertising normally tries to avoid serious issues, because such issues are apt to generate controversy on the part of some audiences. But generating controversy is precisely the agenda here. Obviously, Nike is not alone in challenging these boundary norms – witness the advertising of Benetton in recent years, or the pro-environmental spots put forward by Esprit, or the Liz Claiborne billboards which focus on violence against women.

"If you let me play" exemplifies Wieden & Kennedy's effort at breaking through the clutter of television advertising. Remember that every other marker of women's athletic shoes and apparel was also fashioning some blend of feminism and consumption. The Nike ad broke through the clutter not just because of its message about women's health and well-being, but also because it violated conventions about how ads address or hail us.

This ad startled viewers as an adventurous effort at changing what is acceptable within the field of advertising discourse. It is immediately obvious that the young girls are reading lines given them by others. They have been instructed not to "act" but to recite their lines as if reading them. This rhetorical trope allows them to speak about their future in such a way that the children become both the subjects and objects of their own discourse. Newspaper reviews of the ad called it "chilling" or "eerie." We are not used to little girls looking straight into the camera and reciting "facts" about "adult" subjects in the low-affect tones of social scientists.

Though Nike and Wieden & Kennedy may have had a specific message they wanted to get across, this ad invites multiple interpretations. It should be quickly noted, however, that multiple interpretations are of no concern to Nike because the goal of "If you let me play [sports]" was to "stir the pot." And that is what the ad did: it generated talk.

> The first time I saw the commercial, it stopped me cold in my living room, and I had to sit down for a moment, just to absorb what had been said. Part of me was thrilled by what I was seeing. Part of me was profoundly disturbed. More than 20 viewings later, I am still pulled in two directions.[4]

This ad worked like a Rorschach test, eliciting a range of interpretations and emotional intensities based on what the viewer brought to its interpretation. A survey by sociology-anthropology students at Lewis & Clark College found that wealthier and more educated young women were more likely to negotiate the ad's meaning in a cynical and skeptical way. They tended to question Nike's agenda for running the ad, whether Nike's commitment was to the lives of adolescent girls or to garnering more sales. Typical of this response was a student who wrote on the survey, "Does Nike really have a social conscience, or are they just trying to sell shoes?" Of course, these are not necessarily mutually exclusive goals; but in the minds of many young people who have been exposed to thousands and thousands of ads, there does seem to be a distrust of pecuniary motives even when they are accompanied by rhetorics of concern for others. Alternatively, young women from working class families, or whose families do not have a history of college education, or who are from small towns, seemed to embrace the ad more enthusiastically and with fewer qualifications. Young women who self-identified as athletes were most likely to see the ad favorably.

But girls were only one audience for this ad. Liz Dolan, Nike's Vice President of Marketing, stated bluntly that the ad was aimed at parents. "We felt we needed to talk to adults about the benefits if girls get to play." "Our intention was to be provocative; we wanted adults to think" about barriers to girls' participation in sports. Nike's women's sports marketing manager, Sue Levin, added that "Dads with daughters – my greatest allies are dads with daughters. They want their kid to have every opportunity in sports that they did."[5] Indeed, if it has become "socially acceptable for girls to play – and excel – at sports," one major reason is that the current generation of fathers want to share the experience of sports with their daughters. "We finally have the first generation of men who lived through the women's movement," Billie Jean King said. "They may not want to admit it, but they're making a difference with their daughters. These dads want their daughters to have opportunities."[6]

NOTES

1 John Wilson, *Playing by the Rules: Sport, Society, and the State* (Wayne State University Press, Detroit, 1994), p. 37.
2 pubweb.acns.nwu.edu/~ksa878/wchb/astound.htm.
3 Karen Anderegg, "Women Who Shape Our Ideas of Fitness: Janet Champ," *Mirabella*, March 1996, p. 33.
4 Jennifer Frey, "Nike Puts Shoe on Other Foot: It Fits, Though Perhaps Not Comfortably," *The Washington Post*, October 15, 1995, p. D7.
5 Jeff Manning, "Corporate America is Finally Embracing Women's Athletics," *The Oregonian*, July 2, 1995, p. A15.
6 Tom Zucco, "Giving Girls a Crack at the Bat," *St Petersburg Times*, May 21, 1996, p. 1D.

> Goldman and Papson suggest that this ad elicited different reactions from different segments of the population. What is your reaction to this advertisement? One purpose of the ad was to be provocative and generate controversy. Does this ad challenge the "gender logic" of sport?

Reading 2: Resources for Doing Gender

Candace West and Don Zimmerman

[. . .]

Doing gender means creating differences between girls and boys and women and men, differences that are not natural, essential, or biological. Once the differences have been constructed, they are used to reinforce the "essentialness" of gender. In a delightful account of the "arrangement between the sexes," Goffman (1977) observes the creation of a variety of institutionalized frameworks through which our "natural, normal sexedness" can be enacted. The physical features of social setting provide one

From "Doing Gender," in *Gender & Society* 1: 125–51.

obvious resource for the expression of our "essential" differences. For example, the sex segregation of North American public bathrooms distinguishes "ladies" from "gentlemen" in matters held to be fundamentally biological, even though both "are somewhat similar in the question of waste products and their elimination" (Goffman 1977: 315). These settings are furnished with dimorphic equipment (such as urinals for men or elaborate grooming facilities for women), even though both sexes may achieve the same ends through the same means (and apparently do so in the privacy of their own homes). To be stressed here is the fact that:

> The *functioning* of sex-differentiated organs is involved, but there is nothing in this functioning that biologically recommends segregation; that arrangement is a totally cultural matter . . . toilet segregation is presented as a natural consequence of the difference between the sex-classes when in fact it is a means of honoring, if not producing, this difference. (Goffman 1977: 316)

Standardized social occasions also provide stages for evocations of the "essential female and male natures." Goffman cites organized sports as one such institutionalized framework for the expression of manliness. There, those qualities that ought "properly" to be associated with masculinity, such as endurance, strength, and competitive spirit, are celebrated by all parties concerned – participants, who may be seen to demonstrate such traits, and spectators, who applaud their demonstrations from the safety of the sidelines (1977: 322).

Assortative mating practices among heterosexual couples afford still further means to create and maintain differences between women and men. For example, even though size, strength, and age tend to be normally distributed among females and males (with considerable overlap between them), selective pairing ensures couples in which boys and men are visibly bigger, stronger, and older (if not "wiser") than the girls and women with whom they are paired. So, should situations emerge in which greater size, strength, or experience is called for, boys and men will be ever ready to display it and girls and women, to appreciate its display.

Gender may be routinely fashioned in a variety of situations that seem conventionally expressive to begin with, such as those that present "helpless" women next to heavy objects or flat tires. But, as Goffman notes, heavy, messy, and precarious concerns can be constructed from *any* social situation, "even though by standards set in other settings, this may involve something that is light, clean, and safe" (Goffman 1977: 324). Given these resources, it is clear that any interactional situation sets the stage for depictions of "essential" sexual natures. In sum, these situations "do not so much allow for the expression of natural differences as for the production of that difference itself" (Goffman 1977: 324).

Many situations are not clearly sex categorized to begin with, nor is what transpires within them obviously gender relevant. Yet any social encounter can be pressed into service in the interests of doing gender. Thus, Fishman's (1978) research on casual conversations found an asymmetrical "division of labor" in talk between hetero-sexual intimates. Women had to ask more questions, fill more silences, and use more attention-getting beginnings in order to be heard. Her conclusions are particularly pertinent here:

> Since interactional work is related to what constitutes being a woman, with what a woman is, the idea that it is work is obscured. The work is not seen as what women do, but as part of what they are. (Fishman 1978: 405)

We would argue that it is precisely such labor that helps to constitute the essential nature of women as women in interactional contexts.

Individuals have many social identities that may be donned or shed, muted or made more salient, depending on the situation. One may be a friend, spouse, professional, citizen, and many other things to many different people – or, to the same person at different times. But we are always women or men – unless we shift into another sex category. What this means is that our identificatory displays will provide an ever-available resource for doing gender under an infinitely diverse set of circumstances.

Some occasions are organized to routinely display and celebrate behaviors that are conventionally linked to one or the other sex category. On such occasions, everyone knows his or her place in the interactional scheme of things. If an individual identified as a member of one sex category engages in behavior usually associated with the other category, this routinization is challenged. Hughes (1945: 356) provides an illustration of such a dilemma:

> [A] young woman ... became part of that virile profession, engineering. The designer of an airplane is expected to go up on the maiden flight of the first plane built according to the design. He [sic] then gives a dinner to the engineers and workmen who worked on the new plane. The dinner is naturally a stag party. The young woman in question designed a plane. Her co-workers urged her not to take the risk – for which, presumably, men only are fit – of the maiden voyage. They were, in effect, asking her to be a lady instead of an engineer. She chose to be an engineer. She then gave the party and paid for it like a man. After food and the first round of toasts, she left like a lady.

On this occasion, parties reached an accommodation that allowed a woman to engage in presumptively masculine behaviors. However, we note that in the end, this compromise permitted demonstration of her "essential" femininity, through accountably "ladylike" behavior.

Hughes (1945: 357) suggests that such contradictions may be countered by managing interactions on a very narrow basis, for example, "keeping the relationship formal and specific." But the heart of the matter is that even – perhaps, especially – if the relationship is a formal one, gender is still something one is accountable for. Thus a woman physician (notice the special qualifier in her case) may be accorded respect for her skill and even addressed by an appropriate title. Nonetheless, she is subject to evaluation in terms of normative conceptions of appropriate attitudes and activities for her sex category and under pressure to prove that she is an "essentially" feminine being, despite appearances to the contrary. Her sex category is used to discredit her participation in important clinical activities, while her involvement in medicine is used to discredit her commitment to her responsibilities as a wife and mother. Simultaneously, her exclusion from the physician colleague community is maintained and her accountability *as a woman* is ensured.

In this context, "role conflict" can be viewed as a dynamic aspect of our current "arrangement between the sexes" (Goffman 1977), an arrangement that provides for occasions on which persons of a particular sex category can "see" quite clearly that they are out of place and that if they were not there, their current troubles would not exist. What is at stake is, from the standpoint of interaction, the management of our "essential" natures, and from the standpoint of the individual, the continuing accomplishment of gender. If, as we have argued, sex category is omnirelevant, then any occasion, conflicted or not, offers the resources for doing gender.

We have sought to show that sex category and gender are managed properties of conduct that are contrived with respect to the fact that others will judge and respond to us in particular ways. We have claimed that a person's gender is no simply an aspect of what one is, but, more fundamentally, it is something that one does, and *does* recurrently, in interaction with others.

What are the consequences of this theoretical formulation? If, for example, individuals strive to achieve gender in encounters with other, how does a culture instill the need to achieve it? What is the relationship between the production of gender at the level of interaction and such institutional arrangements as the division of labor in society? And, perhaps most important, how does doing gender contribute to the subordination of women by men?

REFERENCES

Fishman, Pamela. 1978. "Interaction: The Work Women Do." *Social Problems* 25: 397–406.

Goffman, Erving. 1977. "The Arrangement Between the Sexes." *Theory and Society* 4: 301–31.

Hughes, Everett C. 1945. "Dilemmas and Contradictions of Status." *American Journal of Sociology* 50: 353–9.

What are some of the "resources" for doing gender mentioned in this extract? Can you think of any other resources besides those mentioned?

Part II

Gender in Context

4

Work and Family as Gendered Institutions

CHAPTER OBJECTIVES

- Define and discuss the sexual division of labor

- Explore the changing relations between gender, work, and family as these have developed historically

- Discuss the factors that "pushed" and "pulled" women into the paid labor force after the Second World War

- Present a portrait of the contemporary labor force

- Define sex segregation, explain how it is measured, and discuss variations in sex segregation across time and place

- Explore the meaning of family and family diversity

- Examine the changing relations between work and family

Gender, work, and family are inextricably intertwined; changes in work and family give rise to changes in gender relations and changes in gender relations give rise to changes in family and work. As women's and men's lives have changed, so too have work and family. Work and family are gendered institutions. Understanding these relationships – where they come from and their consequences – is one goal of this chapter. We will also look closely at the structure and organization of work and family, paying particular attention to the ways these have evolved historically and their contempo-

LIVERPOOL JOHN MOORES UNIVERSITY
LEARNING SERVICES

rary expression. This chapter sets the stage for a more in-depth look at family and work from individual and interactional perspectives (Chapters 5 and 6).

THE DIVISION OF LABOR

Throughout history and the world, divisions of labor have developed along the lines of sex. Hence, while work is an activity performed historically by both women and men, sex in virtually all societies has been an important basis of societal organization. The **sexual division of labor** thus refers to the process through which tasks are assigned on the basis of sex. This division of labor is one of the most fundamental ways that sex distinctions are expressed in social institutions. Many argue that sex and age represent the oldest forms of the division of labor. Even at the dawn of the twenty-first century, however, sex continues to be a key basis on which tasks are divided.

There are many different views as to why societies differentiate labor on the basis of sex. Some locate the origins of the sexual division of labor in the fact that women historically have had primary responsibilities for the care of children. Children's dependence on their mothers' care shapes the type of labor women can perform (Collins et al. 1993). Conversely, men's greater average physical strength makes other activities more likely to be their responsibility. In hunting and gathering societies, for example, women were more likely to be gatherers and men to be hunters. While each set of tasks contributed to the group's survival by providing food that supplied necessary calories, women's labor provided most of the food supply (Lenski et al. 1995; Tanner and Zihlman 1976).

Over time, societies in many parts of the world adopted systems of agriculture based on the plow. Plow-based agriculture required greater physical strength than less intensive forms of food production, such as gathering or early horticulture, and thus was an activity performed most often by men (Boserup 1970; Lenksi et al. 1995). Hence, in these societies, men provided more of the necessary calories than women. More generally, evidence suggests that when women's labor is less vital to family survival than men's, their relative social status also declines (Guttentag and Secord 1983). Historical and geographical variations in female infanticide and resulting sex ratios thus can be correlated with the relative value of female labor.

These arguments suggest that the sexual division of labor whereby women and men specialize in different activities is also linked to the relative status of each sex. In particular, the relative contributions of women's and men's labor to survival influence the degree to which each sex is socially valued – and hence the degree of sex inequality. Women and men are more equal in societies where the value of their labor is more similar.

Not everyone accepts this argument, however, and its relevance for understanding the sexual division of labor in today's society is quite limited. An alternative explanation for the sexual division of labor views it less as a response to women's and men's differing childcare responsibilities than as a cultural practice that justifies the devaluation of women. In this view, the sexual division of labor is rooted in gender, not sex. Moreover, these analysts question the relevance of attempts to explain the "origins" of the sexual division of labor, preferring instead to focus on how the sexual division of labor is reproduced in contemporary societies.

The first hunting and gathering societies emerged thousands of years ago. Yet, even at the beginning of the twenty-first century, women and men continue to do different kinds of work. Within families, the sexual division of labor is reflected most directly in women's and men's differential responsibilities for child-rearing. Women (and not men) give birth – a biological fact – but women in most societies have primary responsibility for children's care and rearing. Gender differences in the responsibility for children are an important component of family as a gendered institution, and shape many aspects of women's and men's work and family lives. In the paid labor force, the sexual division of labor is expressed in the sex segregation of employment at all levels. Though women represent close to half of those participating in the paid labor force (roughly 48 percent), women and men are employed in different occupations, firms, and jobs (Reskin and Padavic 1994). Below, I discuss the historical evolution of these patterns.

GENDER, WORK, AND FAMILY IN HISTORICAL PERSPECTIVE

The US economy during the latter part of the nineteenth century was primarily based on agriculture. Work and family were closely intertwined and the distinction between home and workplace was nonexistent. As Hodson and Sullivan (1990) note, the word "housework" was not introduced into the written English language until 1841, suggesting that the distinction between work performed at home and work performed elsewhere did not exist in previous eras. The situations of native-born families in pre-industrial United States have received much attention from historians and historical sociologists (Cowan 1983; Hareven 1990). These accounts describe the functioning of family economies within which wives, husbands, and children contributed their labor to the household and produced goods for sale in the market. Although tasks were divided on the basis of gender and age, neither women nor men experienced a separation between the worlds of family and work.

Industrialization profoundly altered these arrangements. According to Hareven (1990), families not only responded to changes brought about by industrialization, they also helped make these changes possible. The most important changes taking place during this time were the nature of work itself and the geographical separation of work and family life. This latter shift severed the interdependence of work and family that characterized pre-industrial America. It did not eliminate the connections between these realms, however, but instead altered the nature of work–family linkages.

With the creation of factories, goods production moved out of the home, and families began sending one or more of their members to work in these industrial settings. In some New England villages, for example, entire families went to work in local textile mills. This "family employment system," which often involved fathers paying wives, children, and other relatives out of their own wages, represented one way that work organizations in the industrial era began to reflect familial influences. The New England "mill girls" offer another example of the early industrial workplace. The "mill girls" were young women from rural backgrounds sent by their families to work in factories for a few years before their marriage (Hareven 1990). These women, whose labor was viewed as less necessary to the family farm than the labor of sons, contributed to their family's economic well-being by sending their wages home (Tilly and Scott 1978). Gradually, the "mill girls" were replaced by newly arriving European immigrants. Immigrant workers, who could be employed more cheaply than the "mill girls," were often recruited as families in a manner similar to the "family employment system" described above.

The experiences of African-Americans under slavery diverged from this pattern. As Jones (1987) shows, the institution of American slavery undermined slaves' ability to maintain family life. In Jones's words, "If work is any activity that leads either directly or indirectly to the production of marketable goods, then slave women did nothing *but* work" (1987: 85; emphasis in original). Within the confines of a brutal slave system, however, African-Americans did attempt to carve out a private life where familial obligations and sentiments could be expressed. Slavery represents perhaps the clearest example of a system of work organized so as to eliminate family life altogether.

As industrialization unfolded, it was associated with other important changes in American society, such as urbanization. These developments, in turn, shaped and were shaped by employment relations. Not all groups within the population were affected the same way, however. For the growing middle class of managers and professionals, work and family continued to grow apart, both geographically and symbolically. As Kanter explains, "Those who could afford to remove their residences to 'pastoral' surroundings far from places of employment often did so, also removing, in the process, points of contact between the rest of the family and the organization" (1977: 13). This separation was facilitated by zoning laws and various architectural arrangements that created clearly defined boundaries between industrial and residential areas. These physical boundaries between work and family were further reinforced by a gender division of labor. Among the middle class, the workplace became men's domain, while families were seen as populated by women and children. Because middle-class wives cooked, cleaned, raised children, provided emotional support, entertained, and sacrificed their own ambitions for their husbands' careers, it was as if married, middle-class men brought two people to work, rather than one. Accordingly, despite the geographical separation of work and family, middle-class marriages and family lives during the industrial era were shaped by the demands of middle-class work.

Industrialization had a different effect on the working class. These workers, employed in blue-collar, clerical, and service jobs, could not afford to relocate to the suburbs and hence lived much closer to the workplace than their middle-class counterparts. The cities thus became home to workers, who lived in densely populated areas not far from their workplaces. Unlike the middle class, where most women worked exclusively at home caring for their families, many working-class women combined their family responsibilities with a wage-earning job. Working-class men were employed in factories, while their wives worked in clerical or service positions. These gender-segregated work environments spilled over into the social lives and activities of the working class, which some have characterized as more gender-segregated than those of the middle class.

Many members of the working class are racial minorities. Because racial minorities of both genders have historically received lower earnings than whites, two wage earners rather than one has been a typical pattern among minority families. Although the work and family configurations of these families are themselves diverse, minority men have generally been employed in factories or in agriculture. Minority women have found employment in these settings as well. During the early stages of industrialization, many minority women were also employed as domestic servants in middle-class homes. This freed white middle-class women for other pursuits, such as leisure, volunteer work, or even careers (Glenn 1992).

These descriptions of the industrial workplace illustrate the complex evolution of work and family arrangements over time, and they reveal the ways these relations were shaped by social class and race (as well as gender). The physical separation of work and family that accompanied industrialization had important impacts in the middle class, where work and family came to be seen as distinct domains inhabited by different genders. Middle-class men's roles were organized around the statuses of "worker" and "breadwinner," while the roles of "mother" and "homemaker" were assigned to middle-class women. Industrialization had different consequences for working-class families, who could often not afford a full-time homemaker and thus sent both women and men out to seek waged work. Ironically, minority women often found such work as domestic servants in middle-class homes.

Industrialization's impact on work and households was intrinsically connected to its role in reshaping gender roles. Despite the fact that many working-class and minority women were employed for pay, the experiences of the middle class became the basis for cultural norms and employer practices that defined the workplace and workers as "male." As Reskin and Padavic observe:

> the sexual division of labor that assigned men to the labor force and women to the home encouraged employers to structure jobs on the assumptions that all permanent workers were men and that all men had stay-at-home wives. These assumptions freed workers (that is, male workers) from domestic responsibilities so they could work 12- to 14-hour days. These assumptions also bolstered the belief that domestic work was women's responsibility, even for women who were employed outside the home. (1994: 23)

One implication of these changes involved the emergence of what historians and sociologists have called "**the doctrine of separate spheres**" (Cancian 1987). This doctrine drew an association between the separation of home and work and the qualities deemed desirable in women and men. The paid workplace came to seen as an arena of competition, rationality, and achievement – qualities that then became attached to men as the primary inhabitants of this sphere. Conversely, the home was portrayed as a "haven" from work and a realm characterized by domesticity, purity, and submissiveness. These characteristics, in turn, were ascribed to those who were seen to be primarily responsible for this domain – namely, women. As Cancian explains: "In sum, the ideology of separate spheres reinforced the new division of labor, and portrayed a world of independent, self-made men and dependent, loving women. The ideal family was portrayed as a har-monious, stable, nuclear household with an economically successful father and an angelic mother" (1989: 17).

The doctrine of separate spheres was aimed as much at *prescription* as description, however. In other words, this doctrine supplied a cultural jus-tification for men working for pay and women staying home to care for their family. The normative nature of this view is revealed in the treatment and views of those who deviated from its prescriptions. Men who were pre-vented from working altogether or whose work was too minimal to support their families were *denigrated not merely in their roles as workers, but as men*. Workers were men and, conversely, men were workers. Not working hence signaled being less than a man. The late sociologist Jessie Bernard referred to this association between manhood and paid work as "**the good-provider role**": "To be a man one had to be not only a provider but a good provider. Success in the good-provider role came in time to define masculinity itself. The good provider had to achieve, to win, to succeed, to dominate. He was a bread*winner*" (Bernard 1992: 207; emphasis in original). This view implied that men fulfill their obligations to their family through their paid work; men who could not accomplish this were deemed unfit husbands and fathers (Gerson 1993).

Women had different obligations to fulfill: "An ideal woman centered her life on love of husband and children, a love expressed mainly through emotions and piety, not through practical action" (Cancian 1989: 16). These qualities made women unsuited for paid work, however, just as the qualities required of the paid worker make them unsuited for family caretaking. Moreover, just as the doctrine of separate spheres penalized men unable or unwilling to be good providers, it stigmatized women unable or unwilling to be full-time family caretakers. As women, they are unsuited to be workers, while, as workers, they are unsuited to be women.

The separation between home and workplace thus corresponded to changes in women's and men's lives. Men – including the native-born, immigrant, and eventually former slaves – gradually came to dominate factory work. In fact, the paid labor force in the United States became gradually more male during the nineteenth century and into the early twentieth century; less than 5 percent of married women were employed in 1890 (Reskin and Padavic 1994). Those women who did work for pay tended to be young and unmarried, African-American or Asian-American, or poor. Native-born, married, white women were likely to find themselves at home caring for family and children. The social category of full-time homemaker thus emerged during this time period and became a way of life for some women.

As this history reveals, the fact of women's steadily increasing rates of labor-force participation in the twentieth century, though important, obscures a much more complicated picture. Two points are especially worth repeating. First, men were not "naturally" or "automatically" the labor force of choice for early employers. Popular cultural conceptions of men as "workers" and "breadwinners" thus took time to emerge. Second, while rates of female participation in the twentieth century have varied over time and increased dramatically in the last three decades, women have been a part of the paid labor force in the USA for centuries. What has changed over time, then, is not so much the fact of female labor-force participation, but the composition and size of that labor force. By far, the biggest change in the female labor force since the 1960s has been the entrance of married women with children (Goldscheider and Waite 1991; Johnston and Packer 1987; Reskin and Padavic 1994).

The industrial era was extremely important in shaping our views of women, men, and work. We began to judge men by their work and judge workers according to whether they possessed characteristics attributed to men. Because men were expected to achieve through work, their interest in and opportunities for participating in family life were constrained. Because workers were assumed to be men, women employed for pay were often forced to decide whether to be a woman or a worker. Success in one role, however, implied failing at the other. In addition, men who worked for pay were assumed to be fulfilling their family obligations through this act, while employed women were assumed to be abandoning their family responsibilities. How did these cultural views change as more and more women entered the paid labor force?

THE POST-INDUSTRIAL ERA: MARRIED WOMEN'S RISING LABOR-FORCE PARTICIPATION

During the past half-century, women's rates of labor force participation have been rising across the industrialized world. Women's movement into paid work is "the single most influential change in the labor markets of industrialized countries in the postwar period" (Gornick et al. 1998: 35). Especially striking have been the increased rates of mothers' employment. As we will see below, these increases can be traced to several, interrelated economic, political, and social changes.

Manufacturing industries, such as auto, electronics, and steel, were the economic backbone of industrial society. These goods-producing industries expanded their share of employment until the 1950s, but have declined steadily since that time. The percentage of the population employed in agriculture has also been declining steadily; this sector now employs only about 2 percent of the labor force. By contrast, service-producing industries, such as finance, insurance, and real estate, have been increasing their share of employment over time. These employment trends document that the United States has become a "service" economy, or, in Daniel Bell's words, a "post-industrial society" (Bell 1973).

In contrast to the kinds of products generated by a goods-producing economy, such as cars or machinery, the products of a post-industrial economy are services. Services, such as depositing money in one's bank account or consuming a meal in a restaurant, are intangible products, because they are produced and consumed simultaneously (Hochschild 1983). Social interaction between the customer and the service provider is also a key aspect of service work .

American society's shift to a service economy is associated with a sharp increase in women's labor-force participation. Many of the women who entered the labor market in the decades following the Second World War filled predominantly female jobs in service industries. This increase in women's labor-force participation was not confined to single or childless women, but included substantial numbers of married women with children.

Explaining post-Second World War changes in women's labor-force participation

What other social forces lay behind the changing rates of female labor-force participation? One way to answer this question is to consider the influences on women's decision to enter the labor force as a series of "pushes" and "pulls" (Gerson 1985). "Pushes" refer to those factors that make *not* working for pay increasingly difficult; hence, they reflect the costs of staying out of the labor market. "Pull" factors are those that attract people to the work force; they represent the rewards of working for pay.

In the last three decades, women – especially married women – have been pushed and pulled into the paid labor force. Both the costs of staying at home and the rewards of working for pay have increased. The forces pushing women out of the home were both economic and social. The major economic force was the declining wages of men. As Figure 4.1 shows, wages for workers other than managers and professionals increased steadily from the 1950s to the early 1970s, fluctuated over the next few years, and, around 1977, began to decline (Mishel et al. 2001). Wages for these workers did not begin to rise until the mid-1990s. Disaggregating these trends by gender shows that, from the late 1970s to the early 1990s, male workers' earnings generally fell more than women's earnings (Gordon 1996). As men's wages fell, it became more and more difficult for them to support their wives and children. This economic reality helped to push many married women into the paid labor force. While women's paychecks were not equal to those of men's, women's salaries helped considerably to ease the economic burdens on families. Indeed, households with two wage-earners continue to earn considerably more than households with only one employed adult.

While economic forces were important, rising divorce rates and the consequent decline of stable marriage were another set of forces helping to push women into the labor force. Divorce rates in the USA rose steadily from the 1960s, reaching their highest levels around 1980, after which they stabilized and declined somewhat (Casper and Bianchi 2002).

There are at least two reasons why rising divorce rates might propel women into the labor force. First, a woman's own divorce might necessitate a move into the paid labor force. Second, regardless of an individual's own circumstances, as divorce becomes more common, it may begin to

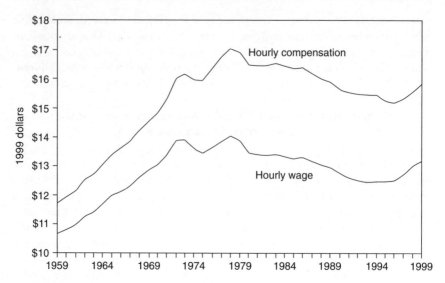

Figure 4.1 Hourly wage and compensation growth for production/non-supervisory workers, 1959–99
Source: Lawrence Mishel, Jared Bernstein, John Schmitt, and Economic Policy Institute (2001), *The State of Working America, 2000–2001* (Ithaca, NY: Cornell University Press). Reprinted by permission of the publisher.

influence the ways that young people – even those yet to marry – assess their options. In particular, women may be less willing to become economically dependent on men and instead make a greater commitment to work and career (Gerson 1985).

Relations between divorce rates and women's employment are complex, however. Not only may higher divorce rates lead people to plan their futures differently, but paid employment itself may contribute to divorce. A 1984 study by Booth et al. found a positive relationship between wives' employment and marital instability (including, but not limited to, divorce). This pattern was especially strong if wives worked more than 40 hours per week. These authors suggested that wives' employment required a reorganization of family life for which neither sex's upbringing fully prepared them. These results underscore the tremendous forces of social change that both produced and were produced by women's rising labor-force participation.

The relations between women's employment and marital instability have continued to generate research and debate. Tzeng and Mare (1995) found that marital instability was higher in marriages where wives had higher levels of work experience than in marriages where wives' levels of work experience were lower than that of their husbands. In a review of research addressing these issues and the more general claim that women's economic independence has contributed to marital instability, Oppenheimer (1994) suggests that trends are not as clear as they may seem. She suggests that families with working wives are better positioned to survive in the post-industrial era than those without working wives.

Not only have the costs of staying home risen for women, but so have the rewards of going to work for pay. Prior to the 1970s most employed women worked in a narrow range of low-paying, predominantly female occupations. Several factors contributed to this pattern. Women were excluded from certain jobs by law. For example, "protective legislation," ostensibly designed to prevent women from harm at work, prevented them from applying for some predominantly male (typically blue-collar) jobs. Many professional schools also routinely denied women admission, thus limiting women them from entering fields such as medicine or law. Restricted opportunities in the workplace reduced the rewards women could obtain from the labor market. Women worked for pay only when they were compelled by circumstances such as poverty or divorce, or when they were young and unmarried.

Women's opportunities for paid employment expanded greatly during the 1960s and 1970s, however. Legislation such as the 1963 Equal Pay Act, Title VII of the 1964 Civil Rights Act, and the 1972 Education Amendments, as well as various Supreme Court decisions, began to break down some of the legal barriers to paid employment for women. Opportunities expanded accordingly, as women found jobs in fields previously closed to them. Though sex segregation remained high, it began to edge downward as some groups of women started to move out of traditionally female fields.

In addition to legal changes, two other social forces were reshaping work opportunities for women. The first is one that has already been mentioned: the transformation of the economy from one centered on goods production to an economy based on services. This shift can be seen as both cause and consequence of women's rising labor-force participation. For example, many service jobs involve tasks that have been performed historically by women in the home. As jobs such as food preparation, child care, and care for the elderly have been transformed from unpaid to paid work, women have also moved from the status of homemaker to worker. The increasing availability of services, in turn, makes families less dependent upon women's unpaid work in the home, thus making it possible for women with families to seek paid employment.

In addition to services, the expanding service economy created many opportunities for employed women in clerical occupations. Services and clerical jobs rapidly feminized in the latter half of the twentieth century. In 2001, roughly half of all women working for pay were employed in these two occupational sectors. Opportunities in the professional ranks also expanded, however. The loosening of legal barriers to education enabled women to enter professions, like law and medicine, that had previously been much harder for them to pursue. Hence, the expansion of work opportunities for women was not confined to lower-paying jobs, but included some professional positions as well.

The final factor contributing to women's expanded job opportunities involved education. As noted, women's entrance into the professions was made possible in part by legal challenges to sex discrimination in education. The percentage of women with college degrees has risen substantially since the early 1970s, while the percentage of men with college degrees has stayed about the same. In 1971 18 percent of women between the ages of 25 and 29 had a college degree, whereas 29 percent of women in this age group had a college degree in 1998. With expanded educational opportunities came more options in the paid labor market.

Thus far, I have considered two "pushes" and one "pull" as factors responsible for the increased numbers of married women in the labor market. A final "pull" factor concerns the changing cultural milieu and its growing support for women's education and employment. The 1960s and early 1970s marked the height of the second wave of the women's movement. Middle-class women, in particular, began to encounter gender egalitarian ideologies in college. Some gravitated to feminism as a direct result of their participation in the civil rights or anti-war movement, while others were attracted to the ideals of women's liberation itself. While many young white and middle-class women participated in the women's movement directly, other women (and men) were exposed indirectly to the movement's goals and philosophies. Economic independence and equal opportunity in the workplace were among the most important of these.

Current research on women who attended college during the late 1960s and early 1970s offers powerful evidence of the personal and cultural transformations brought about by the women's movement. As Blair-Loy observes in her study of female finance executives: "Yet virtually all women who finished college between 1969 and 1973 discussed exposure to feminism as either a reinforcing or primary reason they pursued [finance careers]" (1999: 17). One of Blair-Loy's respondents, an owner of a consulting firm who was interviewed when she was in her late 40s, describes the impact of feminism in this way:

> Most of the people in my age group were formed in college in the late 1960s. It shaped how we viewed life. Friedan, Steinem, Viet Nam, all of it. Most of us [women] defined ourselves outside the home for the first time. Very few people I went to college with don't work. A lot of them didn't have kids. Many that did are now single moms . . . The late 60s was a tough time . . . There was lots of social upheaval. It was the defining period of a whole gen-

eration of us . . . I started college in 1965. I was a good little sorority girl. I
had to wear nylons and skirts. Then from 1965 to 1969, the whole world
changed. It went to hell in a hand basket. (Blair-Loy 1999: 16–17)

The women's movement was not the only source of cultural change
during the 1960s and early 1970s. Each of the previous factors – including
the declining wages of men, rising rates of divorce, equal opportunity legislation, increased numbers of women in college, and women's employment
itself – all contributed to a new cultural landscape. While majorities of
women and men in the 1950s and 1960s agreed that "It is much better for
everyone involved if the man is the achiever outside the home and the
woman takes care of the home and family," these percentages have been
declining almost continuously since (Farley 1996; Goldscheider and Waite
1991). Employment outside the home is now normative for women, even
those who are not desperately poor and who are married and have children.
   In sum, the lives of women and men changed dramatically during the
decades after the Second World War. Changes in women's lives have been
more pronounced than those in men's lives, however. As Goldscheider and
Waite note, "The entry of women into the paid labor force represented a
major shift from earlier periods, since for most of the nineteenth century
and early twentieth century, it was *men* who were moving into the paid
labor force from joint production with their wives and from continuous
involvement in the lives of their families" (1991: 9). Like all forms of uneven
social change, this disjuncture between the pace of change in women's and
men's lives has produced areas of tension and conflict between genders, both
at work and at home (Hochschild 1989).

PORTRAITS OF FAMILY AND WORK

Thus far, we have been focusing on women's and men's work and family
lives as these have evolved historically. Now, we turn to the contemporary
era for a snapshot of work and family today.

The contemporary labor force

The sex composition of the paid labor force in the United States has varied
dramatically over time. At the beginning of the twenty-first century, women
made up approximately 47 percent of employed workers (Jacobs 1999).
Women have formed the bulk of new labor force entrants for the past 30
years, though the feminization of the labor force appears to be slowing
somewhat (Johnston and Packer 1987). Men's labor-force participation

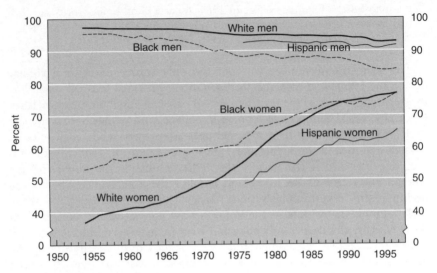

Figure 4.2 Labor-force participation rates of persons aged 25 to 54
Note: Prior to 1972, data for blacks include all non-whites.
Source: Council of Economic Advisors for the President's Initiative on Race (1999),
Changing America: Indicators of Social and Economic Well-Being by Race and Hispanic Origin (Washington, DC: US Government Printing Office).

rates have declined slightly during this time, fluctuating in response to business cycles and the relative attractiveness of alternatives to employment for adult men, such as school or retirement.

As Figure 4.2 shows, the vast majority of women and men today work for pay. Moreover, majorities of both sexes are employed full time. Men and women work for pay even when they are parents. Rates of labor-force participation for both sexes during the primary child-bearing years (i.e., 25–45) are over 70 percent. In 1995, 55 percent of all women who had a child in the previous year were employed (Statistical Abstracts 1997). Paid employment is typical for women and men of all racial groups. Slightly over 60 percent of African-American women, 53.4 percent of Latinas, 60 percent of Asian-American women, and 59.1 percent of white women worked for pay in 1996, as did majorities of men in each group (Statistical Abstracts 1997; Shinagawa and Jang 1998). These figures underscore that demographic diversity by sex and race is an important characteristic of the contemporary US labor force, and it is one that is expected to increase during the first half of the twenty-first century.

Further insight into the contemporary labor force can be gained by looking at each race and sex group's distributions across occupational categories. These data are shown in Figure 4.3. In 1997, white and Asian men

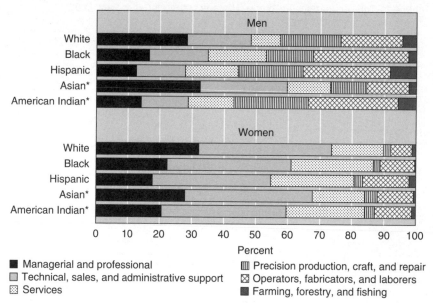

Figure 4.3 Occupations of employed persons, 1997
Note: *Data for Asians and American Indians are for 1990.
Source: Council of Economic Advisors for the President's Initiative on Race (1999). *Changing America: Indicators of Social and Economic Well-Being by Race and Hispanic Origin* (Washington, DC: US Government Printing Office).

were mostly likely to be employed in managerial and professional occupations. By contrast, "precision production, craft, and repair" occupations employed the largest percentages of African-American, Hispanic, and Native American men. Figure 4.3 shows that women, regardless of race or ethnicity, are most likely to be found in "technical, sales, and administrative support" occupations.

Women and men thus are not randomly distributed across occupations. Table 4.1 sheds more light on this pattern by listing the ten largest occupations for six categories of workers in 2000. Women are more likely than men to be nurse's aides, cashiers, or secretaries; men are more likely than women to be truck drivers or managers.

Sex segregation and the division of labor in paid work

Sex segregation – the concentration of women and men into different occupations, firms, and jobs – is a pervasive feature of the American workplace,

Table 4.1 Top occupations for blacks, Hispanics, and whites, by sex, 2000

Black women	Number (in thousands)	Black men	Number (in thousands)
Total labor force	8,247	Total labor force	6,990
Nurse's aide, orderly	606	Truck driver	448
Cashier	422	Janitor, cleaner	307
Secretary	234	Salaried manager, administrator, n.e.c	196
Teacher, elementary school	214	Cook	181
Registered nurse	188	Salaried sales supervisor, proprietor	165
Cook	183	Laborer, except construction	162
Janitor, cleaner	166	Guard	151
Salaried manager, administrator, n.e.c.*	159	Misc. machine operator, n.e.c.	136

Hispanic women		Hispanic men	
Total labor force	5,912	Total labor force	8,446
Cashier	299	Truck driver	369
Secretary	214	Cook	345
Nurse's aide, orderly	193	Janitor, cleaner	301
Private household cleaner, servant	193	Farm worker	293
Janitor, cleaner	182	Gardener, groundskeeper	271
Cook	160	Salaried manager, administrator, n.e.c.	253
Maids, "housemen"	157	Construction laborer	237
Salaried manager, administrator, n.e.c.	136	Salaried sales supervisor, proprietor	216

White women		White men	
Total labor force	48,872	Total labor force	55,827
Secretary	2,441	Salaried manager, administrator, n.e.c.	4,848
Salaried manager, administrator, n.e.c.	2,139	Salaried sales supervisor, proprietor	2,517
Salaried sales supervisor, proprietor	1,691	Truck driver	2,070
Cashier	1,635	Carpenter	1,120
Registered nurse	1,612	Sales rep., mining, mfg., and wholesale	1,043
Teacher, elementary school	1,493	Janitor, cleaner	955
Bookkeeper	1,451	Computer systems analyst	887
Nurse's aide, orderly	967	Supervisor, production occupations	763

Note: Figures for 2000 are averages of 1998, 1999, and 2000 Current Population Survey data. Blacks and whites include people of Hispanic origin.

* The US Census Bureau uses the abbreviation *n.e.c.* to denote miscellaneous occupations that are "not elsewhere classified."

Source: Irene Padavic and Barbara Reskin (2002), *Women and Men at Work* (Thousand Oaks, CA: Pine Forge Press). Reprinted by permission of the publisher.

yet it is one that is often overlooked by the casual observer. One reason sex segregation is often overlooked is because it is such a taken-for-granted aspect of the workplace. A trip to the doctor's office, for example, is unlikely to prompt reflection on why all of the nurses happen to be women. This reflection might only be prompted by the presence of male nurse – an exception to the dominant pattern. What we expect and are used to, however, rarely attracts our attention. A second reason why sex segregation may be invisible to the casual observer stems from the forms segregation often assumes. For example, you might walk into an office and see both women and men at work. Only by looking more closely at their job assignments and titles, however, would it become clear that women and men are, in fact, performing different jobs.

On a broader level, however, sex segregation in the workplace is easily spotted. Many people know, for example, that nursing is a predominantly female occupation, while engineering is dominated by men. Many would be surprised to encounter a child-care worker, a receptionist, or an elementary school teacher who was not female, just as they would be to meet an auto mechanic, a surgeon, or a plumber who was not male. In this respect, sex segregation is a part of people's understanding of work.

Types and amounts of sex segregation

Sex segregation can occur at the job, occupation, or firm levels. Occupational sex segregation refers to the concentration of women and men into different occupations. Due to the large amount of contemporary and historical data on occupations, most studies focus on this form of segregation. In recent years, however, more data have become available on the sex composition of jobs and firms (Tomaskovic-Devey 1993; Tomaskovic-Devey et al. 1996). This has enabled researchers to examine the degree to which women and men are segregated into different jobs both within and across firms.

Two general conclusions have emerged from this research. First, sex segregation at the job level is more extensive than sex segregation at the level of occupation. By focusing only on occupational sex segregation, researchers underestimate the degree to which women and men work in different jobs and firms. A second conclusion is that women and men hardly ever truly work together. Women and men are not distributed evenly across occupations and even when they are members of the same occupation, they are likely to work in different jobs and firms.

Measuring sex segregation

The most widely used measure of sex segregation is the **index of dissimilarity** (also referred to as the index of segregation). The index of segregation ranges from 0 to 100. A score of 100 indicates that there is complete segregation in the entity being measured: This means that the units (e.g., occupations, jobs, etc.) comprising that entity (e.g., labor force, firm, etc.) are all either 100 percent female or 100 percent male. A score of 0 indicates complete integration of the entity being measured: This means that every unit (e.g., occupations, jobs, etc.) comprising the entity has the same proportion of women and men in it as the entity as a whole.

An example may help further illustrate these ideas. As mentioned earlier, the US labor force is approximately 47 female and 53 percent male. If there were no occupational sex segregation in the labor force we would find every occupation to be 47 percent female and 53 percent male. On the other hand, if the labor force were completely sex-segregated by occupation, we would find that all occupations were either 100 percent female or 100 percent male. According to recent studies, the level of occupational sex segregation in the US labor force was approximately 51.5 in 1990 (Cotter et al. 1995). In other words, the level of occupational sex segregation in the labor force is moderately high.

A more graphic way to illustrate what this means is to consider the exact interpretation of the index of dissimilarity: The value of this index can be interpreted as the percentage of either sex who would have to change occupations in order for the sex composition of every occupation to be the same as the sex composition of the labor force as a whole. Hence, 51.5 percent of either women or men – more than half of either category – would have to move to another occupation in order to bring about an occupationally sex-integrated labor force.

Sex segregation and race segregation

Sex is not the only form of ascriptively-based segregation in the US labor force. Occupations and jobs are also segregated by race and ethnicity (Padavic and Reskin 2002; Tomaskovic-Devey 1993). Due to limitations in the availability of data, most studies of racial segregation in employment focus on segregation between African-Americans and whites. These studies reveal one important pattern, which can be easily spotted by examining Figure 4.4. Levels of occupational segregation by race are lower than levels of occupational sex segregation. Women and men thus are more likely to work in different occupations than are blacks and whites. Moreover, sex segregation among both blacks and whites is greater than racial segregation among women and among men. Black men and black women are as likely to be segregated from one another as white women are to be segregated from white men. As Figure 4.4 shows, the indices of racial segregation among both women and men were around 30 at the end of the 1980s, while the indices of sex segregation among whites and among African-

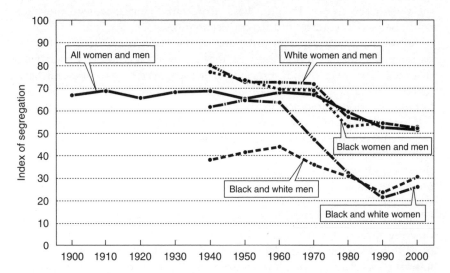

Figure 4.4 Indexes of occupational sex and race segregation, 1900–2000
Note: Figures for 2000 are averages of 1998, 1999, and 2000 Current Population Survey data.
Source: Irene Padavic and Barbara Reskin (2002), *Women and Men at Work* (Thousand Oaks, CA: Pine Forge Press). Reprinted by permission of the publisher.

Americans each were around 60. Jobs are also more likely to be segregated by sex than by race (Tomaskovic-Devey 1993).

The US labor market is not comprised only of African-Americans and whites, but rather contains many members of other racial and ethnic groups, and is increasingly diverse with respect to other characteristics of workers, such as age, nationality, and sexual orientation. Research suggests that, while all of these characteristics shape the kinds of occupations and jobs people obtain, some characteristics are more important than others. Sex is clearly the most important of these characteristics, though race is also relevant.

Trends in occupational sex segregation

Although problems with the comparability of occupational categories over time do complicate matters, researchers have examined trends in occupational sex segregation from the beginning of the twentieth century to the present (see Figure 4.4). These studies show that occupational sex segregation was relatively stable during most of the twentieth century, then began to decline in the 1970s. This relative stability is a stunning finding given all of the other social, economic, and cultural changes that occurred during the twentieth century. Despite these profound changes, women and men continue to concentrate in different occupations.

From an historical perspective, one of the fascinating aspects of occupational sex segregation is the way that many occupations have changed their sex label over time. Librarians, clerical workers, teachers, and bank tellers are examples of occupations that used to be mostly filled by men, but are now dominated heavily by women. The feminization of occupations – the movement of women into fields dominated by men – is primarily responsible for the decline in aggregate levels of occupational sex segregation that occurred during the 1970s (Reskin and Roos 1990). During this time period, women's representation increased markedly in fields such as public relations, systems analysis, bartending, advertising, and insurance adjusting. The feminization of occupations continues. For example, while women students were rare in schools of veterinary medicine in the 1960s, they are now in the majority (Gose 1998). The number of female veterinarians has doubled since 1991, while the number of male veterinarians has fallen by 15 percent. Women are expected to become the majority in the field by 2005 (Zhao 2002).

There are far fewer examples of occupations that have shifted in the other direction – from mostly female to mostly male. Hence, while Reskin and Roos (1990) identified 33 occupations that feminized in the 1970s, they could find only three (cooks, food-preparation kitchen workers, and maids and housemen) where the percentage of men significantly increased. Despite these changes, however, it is important to note that the sex composition of the vast majority of occupations remained fairly stable during the time period studied by Reskin and Roos. The processes that create and maintain a sex-segregated occupational structure are ongoing and the sexual division of labor is maintained even as particular occupations experience changes in their sex composition.

Researchers have also used the index of dissimilarity to compare levels of occupational sex segregation across societies. This is a difficult task, given the tremendous variability across countries in the quality and availability of occupational data (Charles 1998; Jacobs 1999). Nevertheless, these studies have yielded some useful information. For example, they show that occupational sex segregation is a feature of all industrial societies, though the form it takes varies widely. In general, a country's level of occupational sex segregation depends upon a variety of economic, social, and cultural factors. Women generally have greater access to predominantly male occupations in countries with low birth rates and strong egalitarian belief systems, while sex segregation is increased when countries have large service sectors (Charles 1992). Governmental policies relating to gender also play a role in shaping a country's level and pattern of occupational sex segregation.

Chang (2000) distinguishes between "interventionist" and "non-interventionist" governments; interventionist governments actively attempt to influence women's labor force participation by passing legislation guaranteeing equal opportunity in the workplace, or by providing direct benefits to families, such as state-subsidized child care or paid family leave. Depending upon the level and type of intervention they engage in, governments help to define their country's "sex segregation regime" (Chang 2000).

Job-level sex segregation

The index of dissimilarity can also be used to measure the sex segregation of jobs within or across firms. For example, a researcher studying a single organization may want to know how women and men are distributed across job titles within the company. On a larger scale, researchers have estimated levels of job-level sex segregation among a random sample of workers employed in many kinds of firms. These studies have shown that the sex segregation of jobs is significantly higher, on average, than levels of occupational sex segregation. For example, Baron and Bielby (1985) measured levels of sex segregation by job among over 60,000 workers employed by roughly 400 California firms (see also Bielby and Baron 1984). They found that only about 10 percent of workers were employed in job titles that contained members of both sexes. These authors note that "men and women shared job assignments in organizations so rarely that we could usually be certain that an apparent exception reflected coding or key-punch error . . . We were amazed at the pervasiveness of women's concentration in organizational ghettos" (Baron and Bielby 1985: 235).

Family and family diversity

The family is perhaps the most taken-for-granted of all social institutions. In part, this is because the family is sometimes assumed to be natural, biological, or somehow "functional" for society, rather than being seen as a social construction whose configurations vary historically and culturally (Thorne 1982). People's uncritical faith in these assumptions, which reinforce the taken-for-grantedness of the family as an institution, are what provokes anxieties and concerns at a time when family life is changing.

The word **family** means different things to different people. The US Census (1990) defines a family as "two or more persons who are related by birth, marriage, or adoption who live together as one household" (cited in Coltrane 1998: 3). This definition might be too narrow for some people, however; it does not view adults who share a household but are not related legally through marriage as families. Gay and lesbian couples, for example, are excluded from the Census definition, as are heterosexual cohabitors. When asked to identify members of their families, many middle-class Americans are likely to name members of their immediate family – parents, siblings, grandparents, children, and partner. Members of other social groups, both within the United States and outside it, may conceive of their families more broadly, including more distant relatives or even what Stack (1974) calls "fictive kin." Fictive kin are not related by blood, but rather assume the roles of a family member.

Although people's definitions of family are somewhat subjective, it is possible to identify at least one common element: Families cooperate in daily living. They pool resources and provide for one another. Although family members' willingness, need, and ability to assume these obligations for others' well-being varies, for course, the existence of these obligations indicates a family bond. Blood ties or ties formed by marriage or adoption are relevant as well; however, these ties do not exhaust the definition of family. This broad definition of family thus includes people legally prevented from marrying, such as gay and lesbian couples, and it includes various kinds of **fictive kin** – people who recognize obligations towards each other and contribute to each other's survival.

Unfortunately, it is impossible to completely map my definition of family onto existing Census data. It is possible, however, to use these data to draw some conclusions about the role of families in people's living arrangements. Figure 4.5 shows the composition of US households from 1960 to 1998. No single type of household dominated in 1998. Married couples with children made up only about one-quarter of all households, a proportion that has declined substantially since 1960, when over 40 percent of all households were married couples with children. Roughly a third of all households contain married couples without children, a figure that has remained fairly stable over time. Remarkably, however, Figure 4.5 indicates that slightly more than a third of all households fall into other categories – that is, they include a single parent and children, people living alone, or other kinds of arrangements, such as cohabitation or group living. While the number of childless couples and never married people has grown in the last few decades, most couples do have children, as do many unmarried women. Coltrane (1998) cites US Census predictions that less than 15 percent of women born in the 1950s will remain childless and that the average woman will have two children. There are other ways to become a parent than through bearing a biological child and these methods – such as adoption – are also being used at least as frequently as in past decades.

The relatively stable birth rate in the US overall masks some important changes in parenthood over time, as well as variations across social groups. For example, while most couples eventually have children, many women are delaying childbirth until after age 30 – births to mothers over 30 have

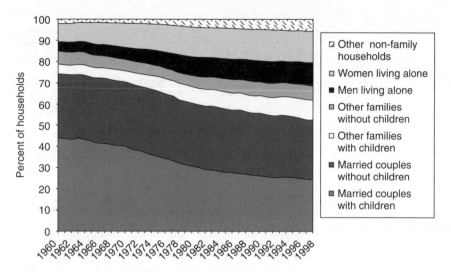

Figure 4.5 Households by type, 1960–98
Source: Lynne M. Casper and Suzanne M. Bianchi (2002), *Continuity and Change in the American Family* (Thousand Oaks, CA: Sage Publications). Reprinted by permission of the publisher.

increased faster than among any other group, now accounting for roughly one-third of all births (Coltrane 1998). Delaying parenting in this fashion is most common among middle-class, employed women (McMahon 1995). Another change involves the rate of births to unmarried women. This includes women involved in cohabiting relationships and single women living alone, a population whose birth rates have increased in recent years – especially among whites (Coltrane 1998). This increase, coupled with an increase in divorce rates, means that a much higher percentage of children live in single-parent households now than in 1970. Single-parent households comprised roughly 18 percent of all households in the US in 1994 (Shinagawa and Jang 1998). The vast majority of single-parent households (86 percent) are, in fact, female-headed households, though the percentage of households headed by single men is growing.

Based on this portrait, we can conclude that American households and the families they contain are diverse and have grown more so over time. Family diversity also appears when we consider racial and ethnic differences in family composition. These data are shown in Figure 4.6. Even if we restrict attention to married couples and single parents, we can see significant variations in family composition. Married couples are more common among Non-Hispanic Whites and Asian-Pacific Americans than

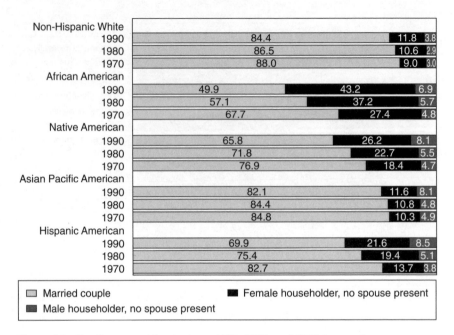

Figure 4.6 Family composition by race, 1970, 1980, and 1990 (percent)
Source: Larry Hajime Shinagawa and Michael Jang (1998), *Atlas of American Diversity* (Walnut Greek, CA: Alta Miera Press, a division of Rowman & Littlefield Publishers, Inc.). Reprinted by permission of the publisher.

among African-Americans, Hispanics, or Native Americans. Conversely, single parents of both sexes are least common among Non-Hispanic Whites and Asian-Pacific Americans and more common among other racial and ethnic groups. The percentage of families containing single parents has risen since 1970 for all racial and ethnic categories, however.

While these data are helpful, we know much less about other kinds of family arrangements. For example, although the numbers of people cohabiting have risen from about 500,000 in 1970 to around 4 million in the late 1990s (Waite and Gallagher 2000; see also Coltrane 1998), there is still more to learn about how cohabiting relationships differ from or are similar to heterosexual marriage. Similarly, the numbers of gay men and lesbians living as couples and/or raising children are also hard to precisely discern, although some estimate that there are anywhere from 1 to 5 million lesbian mothers and 1 to 3 million gay fathers (Patterson 1995). In addition, it is important to note that gay and lesbian families are themselves quite diverse in terms of their racial and ethnic make-up (Demo and Allen 1996).

Family diversity is a social fact. But this reality is often obscured by a set of taken-for-granted beliefs about the family as a social institution. Together, these beliefs represent a set of cultural assumptions about how families are and should be. When people refer to "the family," they often have a modern, nuclear family in mind, consisting of wife, husband, and children (Thorne 1982). Implicitly, then, the family is assumed to be a heterosexual unit, containing one woman and one man, who reproduce biologically. Within the family, the roles of women and men are carefully divided. Women are mothers and family caretakers, and men are fathers and breadwinners.

These assumptions are reinforced by the practices and beliefs of other institutions, such as religion, work, and law. More important, these assumptions about families and family roles form the context in which people make choices about their lives. As we have seen, institutions provide people with scripts that may guide their behavior and beliefs. No one can really escape these institutional forces. Even families that do not conform to the dominant cultural views must nevertheless respond to them as they organize their lives.

A Broader View: Gender and Social Organization

These portraits reveal some of the ways that gender is bound up with the organization of family and work. We have also seen how these gendered institutions have developed historically. In this section, I examine some of the ways that men's and women's daily lives are shaped by their participation in gendered institutions. In the process, I will provide examples of how a gendered institutions perspective can be combined with other frameworks. These include individualist research on gendered personalities and roles, and interactionist concerns with social networks and social relations. In the concluding part, I examine women's and men's involvement in work and family life more broadly, focusing on the changing relations between these realms.

Institutions, roles, and social networks

Both in paid work and in families, women and men tend to engage in different activities, with different responsibilities. Sociologists have long been interested in the meaning and significance of these different kinds of involvements. Talcott Parsons was among the first sociologists in the postwar era to explore the consequences of the sexual division of labor in work and family. Although his views have been highly criticized, they are important for their attempt to link gendered institutions with gendered personalities.

Several decades ago, Parsons (1964; Parsons and Bales 1955) used the sexual division of labor in the family as the basis for his conceptions of male and female "sex roles." For Parsons, a division of labor whereby men have responsibility for the instrumental tasks associated with being a wage-earner and women are responsible for the expressive tasks of caring for children and providing emotional support was functional for both family solidarity and the larger society. Parsons thus seemed to believe that bio-logical distinctions between women and men laid the foundation for them to occupy different social roles. These roles were transmitted to each gen-eration through processes of socialization. By internalizing societal expec-tations for their sex, differences between women and men were produced and expressed through personality and behavior.

Parsons's views on sex roles went further, as he also commented on the content of these roles and their contributions to the larger social system. In this way, he was attempting to link personalities to the organization of work, family, and society. Parsons's basic argument was that the mainte-nance of gendered institutions required that people develop gendered per-sonalities (Chodorow 1978). The male sex role, according to Parsons, was oriented toward instrumental action, while the female sex role was expres-sively oriented. Defined in very general terms, **instrumental action** involves action focused on the external environment, while **expressive action** is geared to internal integration. More concretely, this distinction came to be associated with occupational roles and family roles. Men were expected to work for pay and be the family breadwinner, while women were expected to care for children and maintain the home. Because both roles are essen-tial to the functioning of the system, Parsons saw the instrumental/expres-sive distinction as reflecting role complementarity.

Parsons's views have been criticized on many levels. Most take issue with his overarching framework, which suggests that institutions and societies have "needs" that are almost automatically satisfied. More specifically, gender scholars believe that the instrumental/expressive distinction reifies gender stereotypes and provides a highly inaccurate account of women's work in the home. Others suggest that Parsons's views ignore power rela-tions in families, particularly husbands' power over wives (Stockard and Johnson 1992). By focusing on the complementarity between the sexes, Parsons ignored the ways that women and men are unequal (Lorber 1994; Stacey and Thorne 1985). For example, Parsons did not acknowledge that the instrumental and expressive roles were associated with distinctly different levels of power and status in families and the larger society. As Stacey and Thorne (1985) note, sociologists never use the term "class roles" or "race roles" because it is implicitly understood that class and race differences imply inequality. But the inequality implicit in "sex roles" went unnoticed.

Eagly's (1987) social role theory extends Parsons's ideas. Eagly defines gender roles as "those shared expectations (about appropriate qualities and behaviors) that apply to individuals on the basis of their socially identified gender" (1987: 12). These expectations derive from the positions women and men typically occupy in the social structure. For example, because women have primary responsibility for childcare and domestic work, they are expected to behave in **communal** ways – emotionally expressive and generally concerned with others' welfare. Men's occupational roles are the basis for gender role expectations involving **agentic** behaviors (i.e., stressing competence and independence). From this perspective, men and women behave differently because they are each attempting to comply with distinct gender role expectations.

Unlike Parsons, proponents of social role theory do not claim that gender differentiation is "functional" for society, nor do they assume that the instrumental/expressive distinction adequately captures differences in women's and men's social roles. Eagly (1987) thus agrees with Parsons's critics on this latter point. Instead, social role theorists are concerned with understanding specifically how people form expectations about women and men, and the consequences of those expectations for behavior. Despite these departures from Parsons, social role theorists share his concern with linking differences in women's and men's behavior with the roles each assumes in the wider society. In this respect, social role theorists are more concerned with gender differentiation and gender distinctions than with gender inequality.

Role theorists focus on the ways that gendered institutions supply women and men with gendered role expectations and personalities. This is one way that a gendered institutions framework can be linked to more individualist concerns. Others link gendered institutions with social relations and social interaction. Here, the focus is on the ways that women's and men's participation in gendered institutions provides them with different experiences and brings them into contact with different people.

Research suggests that men's and women's **social networks** – the people with whom they interact with on a regular basis – are quite distinct (Munch et al. 1998). Women's personal networks are more diverse than men's and contain a higher percentage of kin and a lower percentage of co-workers (Marsden 1987; Moore 1990). More important, child-rearing – independent of employment status – decreases the size of women's social networks, while men's networks are not influenced by the presence of children (Munch et al. 1998). Becoming a parent thus seems to affect women's social ties to a greater degree than men's.

These differences are also revealed in the types of voluntary associations to which women and men belong. Voluntary associations include groups such as the PTA (Parent–Teacher Association), veterans' groups, recreational clubs, and the like. Voluntary associations are highly segregated by sex; in fact, most voluntary associations are completely gender exclusive, having only male *or* only female members (McPherson and Smith-Lovin 1986; Popielarz 1999; Smith-Lovin and McPherson 1993). In addition, women and men belong to different kinds of voluntary associations; men are more likely to belong to work-related groups, while women are more likely to participate in groups focusing on social or religious activities (McPherson and Smith-Lovin 1986). Voluntary associations tend to be segregated in other dimensions as well, most notably age, marital status, employment, and education. Women's voluntary associations, in particular, tend to be highly segregated by age and education, as well as gender (Popielarz 1999). This means that women's voluntary associations are likely to be more homogeneous than men's on these dimensions.

These differences in social networks and group memberships have important consequences. The ties we form to others, through our networks or in our group memberships, represent social resources that can be used to achieve particular goals, such as finding a job or obtaining useful information or support (i.e., Lin 1999; Portes 1998). Segregation means that women and men have access to different kinds of resources. Moreover, separate is not equal (McPherson and Smith-Lovin 1986). Access to financial and political resources, in particular, is more likely to be provided by the kinds of groups to which men belong than those of which women are most likely to be members. The sex segregation of voluntary associations also limits women's and men's opportunities for contact, informal ties, and the exchange of useful information with each other.

These differences are not total, of course, nor are they static and unchanging. Women and men do encounter each other in many settings. Most important, heterosexual women and men form intimate ties and share households. As a result, women and men are less spatially and geographically isolated than are members of different racial or ethnic groups, or social classes (Jackman 1994; see also Chapter 7). In addition, there is some evidence that the level of sex segregation in voluntary associations is changing somewhat. For example, as women have entered the paid labor force, they have been less likely to be members of exclusively female voluntary associations. Full-time homemakers are more likely than employed women to be members of voluntary associations containing high percentages of women (Rotolo and Wharton 2003).

While change is ongoing, it would be a mistake to downplay the ways in which gender permeates the organization of the social world. Women and men are not randomly distributed across the various activities that comprise social life. And these differences shape their experiences, as well as their opportunities and rewards. In particular, the care of children remains largely women's responsibility. This social arrangement is reflected in and has helped to shape the organization of work and family life.

WORK AND FAMILY REVISITED

Work–family relations have been intertwined historically with conceptions of gender. A belief that work and family were "separate worlds" corresponded with a belief that women and men had distinct, non-overlapping responsibilities and roles. Accordingly, women's move into the paid labor force has been accompanied by a recognition that work and family are not separate, but rather they intersect in complex ways. As relations between women and men continue to change, relations between work and family are likely to be redefined as well. Work and family are not static, unchanging institutions, but reflect and adapt to developments in the wider society.

The time bind

To illustrate the changing nature of work and family life in the United States, we turn to *The Time Bind* (1997), Arlie Hochschild's study of the work and family lives of women and men employed by a large, US corporation. Hochschild argues that work–family conflict caused by a shortage of time is a serious problem for working parents – mothers *and* fathers. Because of increased demands and rewards available to people in the paid workplace, families face a time deficit. As people spend more and more time at work, they are forced to be more efficient and time-conscious at home. In the process, work and family are experienced as "reversed worlds": work becomes a "haven" where people can relax and feel in control, while home becomes a workplace where people feel pressure and frustration. As she explains: "As the first shift (the workplace) takes more time, the second shift (at home) becomes more hurried and rationalized. The longer the workday at the office or plant, the more we feel pressed at home to hurry, to delegate, to delay, to forgo, to segment, to hyperorganize the precious remains of family time" (Hochschild 1997: 214–15). These pressures culminate in what she calls a "**third shift** – noticing, understanding, and coping with the emotional consequences of the compressed second shift" (215).

Both genders in Hochshild's study experienced the time bind and the difficulties of coping with "the third shift," although women's and men's experiences were by no means identical. Because women have primary responsibility for housework and childcare, the time bind was particularly problematic for women as they returned home to face the "second shift." By contrast, the men in Hochschild's study experienced somewhat different pressures. Because of the lingering expectations of the "good provider," it was hard for men to cut back on their work hours and take more time for family life. Many men she interviewed were reluctant to display this type of concern for their family because they feared it would be costly at work, signaling to their employer that they were not committed workers. As Hochschild explains: "Traditionally, 'family man' meant a good provider, one who demonstrated his love of wife and children by toiling hard at the office or factory. In the modern workplace, however, 'family man' has taken on negative overtones, designating a worker who isn't a serious player. The term now tacitly but powerfully calls into question a worker's masculinity" (1997: 132).

Hochschild's research on these issues is consistent with Larson et al.'s (1994) study of employed parents (see also Larson and Richards 1994). These researchers asked a sample of employed mothers and fathers to carry pagers for a week and report their emotional states at random intervals when signaled by the pager. Some of their results are shown in Figure 4.7. As this figure shows, these researchers found that women with children – particularly married women with children – experience a positive shift in mood as they moved form home to work, while men's emotional states improve as they moved from work to home.

Larson and his research team suggest that women are in better moods at work than at home because paid employment offers opportunities for social interaction and the ability to work more deliberately and in a less hurried way than at home. The employed mothers in their study did not enjoy housework, especially when it was not shared with a spouse. By contrast, employed fathers reported more positive emotional states at home than at work, a pattern Larson et al. (1994) attribute to fathers' tendency to feel constrained by their work obligations and to experience more freedom at home.

Whether all workers face the kind of time bind Hochschild described is still under debate, as some suggest that excessively long work hours are most likely to be found among college-educated professional and managerial workers (Jacobs 1999). Nevertheless, because most two-parent households with children now contain two wage earners and single-parent households typically contain one employed adult, the time bind is a reality for many families. The problems it poses are compounded by the fact that "the rules of the road for working mothers and fathers are still being

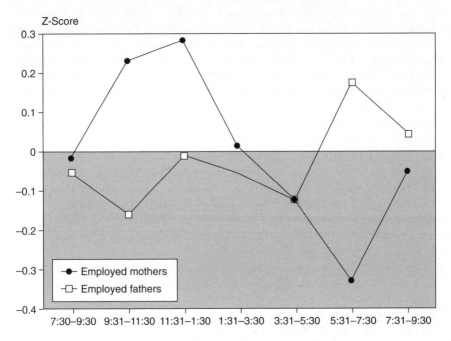

Figure 4.7   Employed mothers' and fathers' emotion across the day
Note: Based on weekdays only. Shows only mothers and fathers who were employed full-time.
Source: Reed Larson and Maryse H. Richards (1994), *Divergent Realities: The Emotional Lives of Mothers, Fathers, and Adolescents* (New York: Basic Books), p. 66. Reprinted by permission of the publisher.

worked out" (Jacobs 1999: 1504). While mothers, fathers, and children have sought ways to cope with the time bind and the resulting "third shift," American workplaces are only beginning to address their workers' needs for a balanced life. As an institution, the workplace has been particularly slow to change, forcing individuals to adapt in ways that may not always be their choice.

CHAPTER SUMMARY

Women and men have always worked, but the work they do has changed over time. Prior to industrialization, women and men both worked at home. In this agriculture-based economy, women and men each contributed to the tasks essential for survival, such as raising food. Industrialization changed the ways that people lived and worked. Women – young women from farm families – entered the factories first as wage laborers, but were soon replaced by male and female immigrants. Eventually, most people in the USA survived by working for wages for someone else. Women and men both worked for pay, with the exception of middle-class women whose lives revolved around the care of children and family. During the years since the end of the Second World War, married women and women with children have entered the labor force in large numbers. Women currently comprise close to half of all paid workers.

Women and men rarely work together, however; it is unusual for women and men to hold the same job title in the same firm. Women and men enter different occupations and even when in the same occupation find themselves working in different jobs and firms. Occupational- and job-level gender segregation thus are pervasive and highly resilient features of the workplace in the United States and elsewhere. This aspect of the sexual division of labor is a key feature of a gendered institution.

The family is also a gendered institution. American families, like the USA as a whole, are increasingly diverse. They differ according to members' racial and ethnic composition, marital status, sexual orientation, and living arrangements. The "Leave it to Beaver" family – comprised of a breadwinning father, stay-at-home-mother, and children – is a minority of all families today.

Work and family are increasingly intertwined. Balancing these two spheres is not always easy, however. The "time bind" refers to the difficulties people face as they try to meet their employer's expectations and their obligations to their partner and children. Hochschild argues that some people have begun to prefer their work lives over their home lives; they feel a sense of accomplishment on the job and increasingly rushed and frustrated at home. Women with families may be especially likely to feel this way, since women have primary responsibility for household work and childcare.

FURTHER READING

Hochschild, Arlie. 1997. *The Time Bind*. New York: Metropolitan Books.
Jones, Jacqueline. 1987. *Labor of Love, Labor of Sorrow: Black Women, Work, and the Family from Slavery to the Present*. New York: Vintage Books.
Milkman, Ruth. 1987. *Gender at Work: The Dynamics of Job Segregation by Sex During World War II*. Urbana, IL: University of Illinois Press.
Oppenheimer, Valerie Kincade. 1994. "Women's Rising Employment and the Future of the Family in Industrialized Societies." *Population and Development Review* 20: 293–342.

A CLOSER LOOK

Reading 1: Constructing Jobs as Women's Work in World War II

Ruth Milkman

The economic mobilization for World War II dramatically transformed women's relationship to the labor market. They poured by the millions into jobs previously done only by men. As military conscription reduced the ranks of available workers and war production generated rapid economic expansion, the labor surplus of the 1930s was quickly replaced by a labor shortage – especially a shortage of male labor. Suddenly there was deep uncertainty about where the boundaries between "men's" and "women's" work should be drawn. Not only were women integrated into "men's jobs" on an unprecedented scale, but also, with conversion to war production, many entirely new occupations emerged – with no clear sex labels.

The war is often viewed as a period when job segregation by sex was broken down, albeit temporarily. Yet what is most striking about the wartime transformation is the way *new* patterns of occupational segregation developed in the industries opened to women. The boundaries between "women's" and "men's" work changed location, rather than being eliminated. If the most remarkable aspect of the sexual division of labor in the depression was its stability in the face of dramatic economic and political change, the wartime experience highlights something even more fundamental: the reproduction of job segregation in the context of a huge influx of women into the work force and a massive upheaval in the division of labor.[1]

Rather than hiring women workers to fill openings as vacancies occurred, managers explicitly defined some war jobs as "suitable" for women, and others as "unsuitable," guided by a hastily revised idiom of sex-typing that adapted prewar traditions to the special demands of the war emergency. As married women and mothers joined the labor force in growing numbers during the war, occupational segregation and the sex-typing of war jobs helped to reconcile women's new economic position with their traditional family role. Wartime propaganda imagery of "woman's place" on the nation's production lines consistently portrayed women's war work as a

From *Gender at Work: The Dynamics of Job Segregation by Sex During World War II* (Urbana, IL: University of Illinois Press, 1987), pp. 49–50, 61.

temporary extension of domesticity. And jobs that had previously been viewed as quintessentially masculine were suddenly endowed with femininity and glamour for the duration. The war mobilization era not only illustrates the resilience of job segregation by sex, but also graphically demonstrates how idioms of sex-typing can be flexibly applied to whatever jobs women and men happen to be doing.

[. . .]

"Note the similarity between squeezing orange juice and the operation of a small drill press," the Sperry Gyroscope Company urged in a recruitment pamphlet. "Anyone can peel potatoes," it went on. "Burring and filing are almost as easy." An automotive industry publication praised women workers at the Ford Motor Company's Willow Run bomber plant in similar terms. "The ladies have shown they can operate drill presses as well as egg beaters," it proclaimed. "Why should men, who from childhood on never so much as sewed on buttons," inquired one manager, "be expected to handle delicate instruments better than women who have plied embroidery needles, knitting needles and darning needles all their lives?"[2] The newsreel *Glamour Girls of '43* pursued the same theme:

> Instead of cutting the lines of a dress, this woman cuts the pattern of aircraft parts. Instead of baking cake, this woman is cooking gears to reduce the tension in the gears after use. . . .
> They are taking to welding as if the rod were a needle and the metal a length of cloth to be sewn. After a short apprenticeship, this woman can operate a drill press just as easily as a juice extractor in her own kitchen. And a lathe will hold no more terrors for her than an electric washing machine.[3]

In this manner, virtually any job could be labeled "women's work."

Glamour was a related theme in the idiom through which women's war work was demarcated as female. As if calculated to assure women – and men – that war work need not involve a loss of femininity, depictions of women's new work roles were overlaid with allusions to their stylish dress and attractive appearance. "A pretty young inspector in blue slacks pushes a gauge – a cylindrical plug with a diamond-pointed push-button on its side – through the shaft's hollow chamber," was a typical rendition.[4] Such statements, like the housework analogies, effectively reconciled woman's position in what were previously "men's jobs" with traditional images of femininity.

NOTES

1   Karen Skold has documented the persistence of job segregation by sex in the wartime shipbuilding industry in "The Job He Left Behind: Women Shipyard

Workers in Portland, Oregon during World War II," in *Women, War and Revolution: A Comparative Perspective*, eds. Carol Berkin and Carol Lovett (New York: Holmes and Meier, 1980), 55–75. See also Karen Anderson, *Wartime Women: Sex Roles, Family Relations and the Status of Women in World War II* (Westport, Conn.: Greenwood Press, 1981), 35f.

2 "There's a Job for You at Sperry . . . Today" (pamphlet), Records of UE District 4, UE Archives, folder 877; "Hiring and Training Women for War Work," *Factory Management and Maintenance* 100 (Aug. 1942): 73; "Engineers of Womanpower," 4.

3 The transcript of this newsreel was made available to me by Rosie at the Riveter Film Project, Emeryville, California.

4 "Engineers of Womanpower," *Automotive War Production* 2 (Oct. 1943): 4–5 (emphasis added). This was the organ of the Automotive Council for War Production, an industry association that included all the major auto firms except Ford.

As Milkman shows, during wartime many jobs traditionally done by men were redefined as appropriate for women. How was this accomplished? Milkman argues that "the idiom of sex-typing" is extremely flexible. Do you agree?

Reading 2: Work–Family Arrangements in Four Countries

Laura Den Dulk

[. . .]

SWEDEN: EXTENSIVE GOVERNMENT INVOLVEMENT

The Swedish government offers people who combine work and family life a broad range of facilities. As early as 1974, working parents could take paid parental leave with the right to return to the same job or a similar position in the organization. In this period, parents who took parental leave

From "Work–Family Arrangements in Organizations: An International Comparison," in Tanya van der Lippe and Liset van Dijk (eds.), *Women's Employment in a Comparative Perspective* (New York: Aldine de Gruyter, 2001), pp. 59–84.

received 90 percent of their normal salary. In the 1990s this percentage was lowered from 85 to 80 percent, and finally to 75 percent. In 1998, however, the percentage was raised again to 80 percent. At present, parental leave is allowed for 450 days per child; 360 days are paid at 80 percent of one's normal earnings and the remaining 90 days at a flat rate (90 Swedish crowns a day). Every parent has the right to his or her own month of leave ("the daddy or mommy month"); the remaining period can be divided between partners (Haas and Hwang 1999). Leave is granted until the child reaches the age of eight, and can be taken on a full-time, half-time, or quarter-time basis. Maternity leave after a child is born is included in the parental leave. But working mothers have the right to pregnancy cash benefit (80 percent of their normal earnings) for a maximum of 50 days during the last two months of pregnancy. Fathers are entitled to 10 days of paid leave when a child is born (80 percent of normal earnings). Leave for family reasons (or temporary parental leave) is 60 days per child per year until the child reaches the age of twelve (National Social Insurance Board 1996). In most cases, this leave is used to look after sick children or to mind children when the regular caretaker is ill. Each year, two days can be taken off to visit children at day care centers or schools. In addition, all parents with a child under the age of eight are entitled to reduce their working week to thirty hours (75 percent of a normal working week). They have the right to return to full-time hours after two months' notice to the employer (Sundström 1991).

Besides various types of leave and the right to reduce working hours, Sweden has a substantial system of public childcare. Legislation in 1995 gave all working or studying parents the right to a place in publicly funded childcare services for children from one to twelve years. Most local authorities are able to meet current demand.

Due to economic problems at the beginning of the 1990s, the Swedish government cut public expenditures (Sainsbury 1996; Stephens 1996). Among other things, replacement rates for leave benefits were lowered. However, equal access to a wide range of public work–family policies remains intact.

The combination of a large number of working women and a long tradition of work–family arrangements can create a climate in which people are expected to have caring responsibilities besides their job. This can stimulate employers to enhance statutory provisions. However, given the various public benefits and services, there is not much scope left for employers to develop work–family arrangements. Since childcare is considered the responsibility of the community, it is not very likely that organizations will offer duplicate services. Regarding leave, employers do have the possibility to supplement statutory provisions and add flexible working arrangements.

THE NETHERLANDS: SHARED RESPONSIBILITY

The breadwinner model has strongly influenced social policy in the Netherlands. For a long time government policy was based on the traditional division of paid and unpaid work between men and women. During the 1980s the Dutch government began to individualize social policy. However, it was not until the 1990s that measures to facilitate the combination of work and family life were actually implemented.

Part-time work is a widely adopted strategy for Dutch women to combine paid work and caring tasks. Almost 60 percent of all working women have a part-time job. Compared to other European countries, the Netherlands has the largest share of (male and female) part-time workers in the labor force (Plantenga 1995). This development was supported by government policy, which tried to improve the position of part-timers. For instance, since the end of 1996, employers have to treat part-timers and full-timers equally with regard to employment conditions (TK 1996–7).

The Maternity Leave Act entitles Dutch working mothers to take sixteen weeks fully paid maternity leave. The Parental Leave Act (1991) gives both parents the right to a period of six months unpaid, part-time leave, which can be taken until children reach the age of eight. The Parental Leave Act is considered a minimum policy, which can be supplemented by collective agreements or individual firms. Presently, there is no statutory paternity leave for fathers in the Netherlands. Most collective agreements (91 percent), however, provide for two days paternity leave (SZW 1997). Also, working parents do not have a legal entitlement to leave for family reasons. The government considers further development of these forms of leave to be the responsibility of the social partners, although currently a proposal to introduce ten days unpaid leave for family reasons is being discussed (SZW 1999). From the perspective of the government, trade unions and employers organizations are the right actors for developing facilities that fit the needs of both employers and employees. The role of the government is to remove existing barriers and stimulate the further development of work–family arrangements in collective agreements and in organizations (TK 1994–5). For instance, in order to stimulate the use of the right to leave, the Act on Career Breaks (1998) came into force. This act gives employees who take a career break for education or caring responsibilities financial compensation if they are temporarily replaced by unemployed workers. The act does not entitle employees to take such a break. This will be a matter of collective agreement.

Public childcare is available on a limited scale in the Netherlands. During 1990–5, the Dutch government stimulated the increase of the number of childcare facilities by providing subsidies. The Stimulation Measure on

Childcare was intended primarily to expand the number of childcare places for working parents, and employers were expected to contribute to this by buying places in subsidized childcare centers. The Stimulation Measure has increased the number of childcare places considerably. However, supply still does not meet demand. In 1998, 17 percent of all children under four had a place in public childcare, of children aged four to twelve years this was 3 percent. In 1989, figures for the two age groups were 5 and 1 percent, respectively (SGBO 1999).

To summarize, in the Netherlands most work–family policies are relatively new. There is not a long tradition of public work–family arrangements as there is in Sweden. The Dutch government provides a minimum standard of facilities, which have to be further developed by social partners and organizations. Employers are encouraged to develop work–family arrangements but are relatively free in their decision to actually do so.

ITALY: FAMILY MODEL

In Italy, work–family arrangements are not as hotly discussed as in the other three countries. The idea of family-friendly organizations does not seem to be taking off (Trifiletti 1999; Network on Childcare 1996). Trifiletti (1999) argues that the unwillingness to put work–family issues high on the public and political agenda has something to do with Italy's totalitarian past and the role of the family in the Italian welfare state. Family policies are historically linked to the old totalitarian regime, which created this reluctance to put the issue of the family on the political agenda. Furthermore, in the Italian welfare state, family problems are expected to be solved privately; the state only intervenes when the family is unable to cope. Nevertheless, work–family issues are presently becoming a matter of public debate.

Public policies in Italy, such as parental leave, suggest that the reconciliation of work and family is primarily seen as a women's issue. Working women have the right to five months maternity leave (two months before and three months after the childbirth), paid at a rate of 80 percent of average earnings. In the case of a child being sick, parents are entitled to take unpaid leave if a child is younger than three years old. There exists no legal right of fathers to paternity leave. Likewise, parental leave was until recently targeted at the mother. In the first instance, it was only the mother who was entitled to parental leave, but she could transfer all or part of it to the father on the condition that she gave up her own entitlement. Recently, however, this situation has changed. The Italian parliament accepted a new Act on Parental Leave that focuses also on fathers. This new act entitles parents to ten months parental leave, but is extended to eleven months if the father takes at least three months leave (Moss and Deven 1999).

With respect to the use of leave, the division between well-protected workers in the official labor market and those in the deregulated gray economy is important. In most cases, only workers in "secure" jobs are able to make use of existing regulations. The same applies to the workplace arrangements.

Childcare for children under three is not widely available in Italy, and there are great differences within the country. For instance, far more facilities are available in the north than the south. Public day care for children under three is mainly provided by day care centers, managed by local authorities. In 1991, 6 percent of all children under the age of three had a place in a public day care center. Preprimary schooling is provided for children between three and the compulsory school age (of six). About 91 percent of this age group are in preprimary schooling. However, opening hours vary and care is only provided in term time. In 1991/1992, 72 percent of all eligible children attended for five to eight hours a day; 17 percent attended for more than eight hours. Private childcare facilities hardly exist in Italy. On the other hand, the role of grandparents is very important when it comes to the minding young children (Network on Childcare 1996).

Because the concept of work–family arrangements only recently entered the public debate and the traditional family still plays an important role in Italy, as yet not much pressure is being exerted on employers to take action. The development of work–family arrangements will depend first and foremost on the circumstances of individual organizations.

THE UNITED KINGDOM: LIMITED GOVERNMENT INVOLVEMENT

In the United Kingdom, there is almost no national legislation concerning work–family arrangements. Since 1994, all working women have the right to fourteen weeks maternity leave regardless of the duration of service. Women who have been working for their employer for two years or longer have the right to twenty-nine weeks of maternity leave. During the first six weeks women receive 90 percent of their normal earnings; after that they get a flat rate payment for a further twelve weeks. The remainder of the period is unpaid. These legal provisions are a minimum standard and organizations can extend maternity rights (*Equal Opportunities Review* 1995). Public childcare is minimal. The publicly funded childcare services that do exist are targeted on children "in need."[1] However, the government is pressured to develop a national childcare policy. There are various pressure groups, such as Parents at Work and Employers for Childcare, who campaign for a national childcare strategy.

The Conservative government, which was in power from 1979 to 1997, pursued a neoliberal policy of minimal regulations for employers. The current Labor government pays more attention to work–family issues. Maternity leave regulations are being updated, mainly to remove anomalies and complexities. After the previous government's exemption from the European Union's Social Chapter had been reversed, parental leave rights were introduced by the end of 1999 to comply with the EU Parental Leave Directive. However, at the time this study was conducted, the Conservative government was still in power.

In the absence of public provisions, there is a lot of scope for UK employers to develop work–family arrangements. Suzan Lewis (1999) argues that, in this context, a business case for work–family arrangements has been the most persuasive. The business case focuses on benefits to employers, especially cost benefits, which means that employers will only implement work–family arrangements if these benefit the organization. Consequently, differences between organizations can occur.

[. . .]

NOTE

1   "In need" is defined "in terms of actual or potential problems of health, development or disability; it does not include children needing care by reason of their parents' employment, education or training" (*Network on Childcare* 1996, pp. 117–18).

REFERENCES

Equal Opportunities Review (1995). No. 63, September/October.

Haas, L. and Hwang, P. (1999). Parental Leave in Sweden. In P. Moss and F. Deven (eds.), *Parental Leave: Progress or Pitfall? Research and Policy Issues in Europe.* Brussels: NIDI CBGS.

Lewis, S. (1999). Work–Family Arrangements in the UK. In L. den Dulk, J. van Doorne-Huiskes, and J. Schippers (eds.), *Work–Family Arrangements in Europe.* Amsterdam: Thela-Thesis.

Moss, P. and Deven, F. (eds.) (1999). *Parental Leave: Progress or Pitfall? Research and Policy Issue in Europe.* Brussels: NIDI CBGS.

National Social Insurance Board (1996). *Social Insurance Facts 1996: Statistics up until 1995.* Stockholm: Author.

Network on Childcare (1994). *Leave Arrangements for Workers with Children: A Review of Leave Arrangements in the Member States of the European Union and Austria, Finland, Norway and Sweden.* Brussels: European Commission

Network on Childcare and other Measures to Reconcile Employment and Family Responsibilities.

Network on Childcare (1996). *A Review of Services for Young Children in the European Union, 1990–1995.* Brussels: European Commission Network on Childcare and Other Measures to Reconcile Employment and Family Responsibilities.

Plantenga, J. (1995). Labor-Market Participation of Women in the European Union. In J. van Doorne-Huiskes, J. van Hoof, and E. Roelofs (eds.), *Women and the European Labor Markets.* London: Paul Chapman.

Sainsbury, D. (1996). *Gender, Equality, and Welfare States.* Cambridge: Cambridge University Press.

SGBO (1999). *Kinderopvang in gemeenten. De monitor over 1998* [Public Childcare in Municipalities. The 1998 Monitor]. The Hague: Vereniging van Nederlandse Gemeenten [Association of Dutch Municipalities].

Stephens, J. D. (1996). The Scandinavian Welfare States: Achievements, Crisis, and Prospects. In G. Esping-Andersen (ed.), *Welfare States in Transition: National Adaptations in Global Economies.* London: Sage.

Sundström, M. (1991). Sweden: Supporting Work, Family, and Gender Equality. In S. B. Kamerman and A. J. Kahn (eds.), *Child Care, Parental Leave, and the Under 3s: Policy Innovation in Europe.* New York: Auburn House.

SZW (1997). *Emancipatie in arbeidsorganisaties* [Emancipation in Work Organizations].The Hague: Arbeidsinspectie, Ministerie van Sociale Zaken en Werkgelegenheid [Labor Inspection, Ministery of Social Affairs and Employment].

SZW (1999). *Op weg naar een nieuw evenwicht tussen arbeid en zorg* [The Road to a New Equilibrium between Labor and Care]. The Hague: Ministerie van Sociale Zaken en Werkgelegenheid [Ministry of Social Affairs and Employment].

TK (1994–5). *Combineerbaarheid van betaalde arbeid met andere verantwoordelijkheden. Nota om de kwaliteit van arbeid en zorg: investeren in verlof* [Possibilities of Combining Paid Work and Other Responsibilities. Note on the Quality of Labor and Care. Investments in Leave]. *Tweede Kamer*, 24: 332.

TK (1996–7). *Gelijke behandeling deeltijd-/voltijdwerkers* [Equal Treatment of Full-time and Part-time Workers]. *Tweede Kamer*, 24: 498.

Trifiletti, R. (1999). Work–Family Arrangements in Italy. In L. den Dulk, J. van Doorne-Huiskes, and J. Schippers (eds.), *Work–Family Arrangements in Europe.* Amsterdam: Thela-Thesis.

What are the major differences in work–family arrangements between these four countries? What do you think best explains these differences? Do you see one type of arrangement as better than others? Which one? Why?

5

Gender, Childhood, and Family Life

CHAPTER OBJECTIVES

- Discuss the research on parental treatment of girls and boys
- Explain how children learn to apply gender stereotypes to themselves and others
- Discuss the research on the household division of labor
- Explore the differences between "his and her" marriage and the ways that gay and lesbian relationships differ from heterosexual marriages

The multilayered conception of gender developed in previous chapters will help us as we make sense of the vast amount of research on children, family, and households. For example, researchers often focus on gender differences in the experiences associated with family life – such as childhood socialization practices, marriage or cohabitation, parenting, and household work. Some of this research embraces a strictly individualist perspective, but much examines how gender emerges through social interaction – between children and their peers or partners in a relationship, for example. The gendered institutions approach will also make an appearance, although this perspective as it applies to both work and family was highlighted in the previous chapter.

"IS IT A BOY OR A GIRL?" GENDER CONSTRUCTION
IN CHILDREN

This is probably the first – and most often – question asked when a baby is born. The simplest explanation for why this is true is that a child's gender gives us important clues about him or her. Specifically, a child's gender conveys to us information, expectations for behavior and personality, and offers some guidelines for interaction. The fact that people rely on gender – even in a newborn – to provide these clues reaffirms once more the power of gender as an important social category. Of course, simply because people rely on gender as a source of information does not mean that it is a *reliable* source. What matters is that we take for granted gender's ability to provide information about people and thus rely on it almost unconsciously. What is important, then, is that people *act as if* gender is a reliable source of information and behave accordingly. The Thomas Theorem, associated with W. I. Thomas (1966: 301 [1931]), is relevant here: "Situations defined as real become real in their consequences."

Once a person is categorized as female or male, gender is used to organize and interpret additional information about that person and to shape expectations for behavior. This starts at birth or even earlier. Recall that in Chapter 2 I discussed how gender is assigned to a child at birth. Normally, this is done by inspecting the child's genitals. In those rare cases where genitals are ambiguous, doctors and parents almost always attempt to assign the child to a sex category and construct appropriate genitalia (Kessler 1990). Most cultures adhere strongly to the belief that a child must be *either* male or female. Consequently, infants who cannot be easily categorized are normally subjected to complicated and extensive medical procedures to "correct" their ambiguous genitalia.

Assigning a child to a gender category, however, is just the beginning. Assignment sets into motion many other processes that all help to produce a gendered individual. As Coltrane (1998: 124) observes: "Male and female infants are similar to one another, but most adults go to great lengths to make them appear dissimilar." For example, when expecting parents learn they are going to have a girl, they may decorate the nursery in pink or yellow rather than blue, or in pastel colors rather than colors that are more bold. Girls' rooms tend to be painted in a wider variety of colors than the rooms of boys, which are mostly blue (Pomerleau et al. 1990). Parents' knowledge of their child's gender will also shape the kinds of clothes and toys they purchase: Clothes for infant girls tend to be soft, pink, and decorated with lace or bows, while clothes for male infants may be made of more rugged fabrics, such as denim, and decorated with sports imagery. Parents buy girls more dolls than boys, while they buy more sports equipment, tools, and vehicles for boys (ibid.). Not all toys are so strongly gender-differentiated, however: Toys such as animals, balls and balloons, books, musical and talking toys, and even kitchen appliances and utensils for children are as likely to be purchased for girls as for boys (ibid.).

Do parents treat girls and boys differently?

From an individualist perspective, parental socialization is the primary source of most gender differences in traits and personality dispositions. To gain support for this view, these researchers design studies to examine whether and in what areas parents relate differently to their daughters and sons. Demonstrating that parents treat their male and female infants and very young children differently, however, is more difficult than it seems.

A 1974 study aimed to uncover these differences by asking mothers and fathers of newborns to describe their infants (Rubin et al. 1974). Parents were given a list of adjectives, presented as pairs on an eleven-point scale, and were asked to choose how closely each described their baby. Eighteen pairs were provided, such as firm/soft, large featured/fine featured, strong/weak, hardy/delicate, etc. While infants as a group were generally described in positive terms (e.g., strong, friendly, alert, cheerful, easy-going), daughters were rated as softer, finer-featured, littler, and more inattentive than sons. Although the infants had been selected to be similar in weight, length, and muscle tone, parents of daughters described their children very differently than parents of sons did.

Because the infants were physically very similar, the researchers concluded that parents were not reacting to real differences between children as much as they were applying gender stereotypes that could possibly result in differential treatment of their male and female children. For example, those who saw their child as delicate may be less likely to engage in physical play than those who saw their child as strong and coordinated. While their child's gender is not the only thing that new parents attend to, of course, it is very important – a "distinctive," "definitive," and "normative" characteristic (Rubin et al. 1974: 517). This is because parents and newborns are just getting acquainted and parents at this stage have very little additional knowledge about their child. In general, people seem to rely on gender to "fill in the gaps" in their assessments of others, and this is especially true when little else is known about a person (Stern and Karraker 1989).

Although studies such as the one described above are useful in showing that parents have different expectations for males and females, this research does not directly address the question of whether (and under what conditions) these expectations shape how parents behave toward their young daughters and sons. Studies exploring this latter issue have yielded some fairly consistent findings. Researchers from Maccoby and Jacklin (1974) to Lytton and Romney (1991) have concluded that in many areas of behavior parents *do not* differentiate between their infant daughters and sons. The results of Lytton and Romney's (1991) meta-analysis of 172 published studies of parental treatment of boys and girls showed few significant differences in treatment for most areas of socialization. Lytton and Romney (1991) also found little evidence that parental treatment of boys and girls has become significantly less sex-differentiated since the 1950s, nor did they find any strong effects of social class and education on parental behavior. This research thus suggests that boys and girls, on average, receive the same amount of nurturance, warmth, responsiveness, encouragement, and attention from parents.

Along with these similarities, however, are some differences in the ways parents relate to children. One important area of difference concerns toys, games, and childhood activities. Research by Maccoby and colleagues (Maccoby 1998; Maccoby et al. 1984; see also Lytton and Romney 1991) showed that when given a choice, parents offered girls and boys different types of toys, such as dolls for girls and toy footballs for boys. Moreover, the kind of toys chosen for children shaped the way that parents and children interacted during play. Because boys were more likely than girls to be offered activity-oriented toys, such as balls, parents' play with boys tended to be rougher and more physical than play with girls. Maccoby notes that: "The father–son dyad displayed the highest levels of roughhousing: three times as much rough play occurred between fathers and sons as between mothers and daughters" (1998: 125).

Punishment and parental responses to misbehavior are another widely researched topic in the area of gender socialization. In general, research conducted in Western countries suggests that boys are more likely than girls to receive physical punishment, though this varies somewhat across samples (Lytton and Romney 1991). Some believe that these differences in exposure to physical punishment contribute to sex differences in aggression by indirectly encouraging physicality in boys. In general, however, there is little direct evidence that parents *encourage* aggressive behavior in their children – regardless of sex. Rather, it appears that parents attempt to discourage aggression in their children, though they may be somewhat more likely to tolerate it in their sons than in their daughters (Lytton and Romney 1991; Maccoby 1998). Focusing only on punishment, however, may obscure a more complicated pattern of parental involvement in children's lives. Maccoby (1998) argues that mothers may be more assertive with their daughters than with their sons and give girls less autonomy in their behavior.

Even as infants, children live in a gendered social world and these experiences shape their development as females and males. Though infants and very young children have not yet developed a gender identity, the foundations of their gender schemas are being established. As Coltrane observes:

> Infants enter the world much more prepared to extract information from their environments than social scientists once thought . . . By the age of seven months, infants can discriminate between men's and women's voices and generalize this to strangers. Infants less than a year old can also discriminate individual male and female faces. Even before they are verbal, young children are developing gender categories and making generalizations about people and objects in their environments . . . (Coltrane 1998: 125)

This ability to categorize others on the basis of gender is not just a human trait, but also extends to other species (Maccoby 1998).

Mothers and father

Until now, I have referred mainly to *parents'* role in the socialization process rather than to the roles of *mothers* and *fathers*. However, if boys and girls are treated differently from birth, we might expect that upon becoming parents, fathers and mothers might relate differently to their male and female children. In fact, studies suggest that fathers' and mothers' interactions with their children do differ, but only in limited respects and these differences vary depending upon the age of the child.

Summarizing 39 studies that compared fathers' and mothers' treatment of daughters and sons, Siegal (1987) concluded that fathers did socialize with their sons and daughters somewhat differently than mothers. Fathers were most likely to differentiate between sons and daughters in the areas of physical punishment and discipline. Specifically, numerous researchers have found that fathers react more negatively than mothers to sons engaging in cross-gender-typed play (i.e., playing games or with toys considered more appropriate for the other gender) (Lytton and Romney 1991). Young boys appear to understand their fathers' preferences. In a study of preschoolers, Raag and Rackliff (1998) found that many more boys than girls believed their fathers would react negatively to them engaging in cross-gender play. In fact, in this study, boys believed that fathers more than any other familiar person (e.g., mother, daycare worker or babysitter, sibling, best friend) would have a negative reaction to their cross-gender play.

Fagot and Hagan (1991) report other differences in mothers' and fathers' interactions with children. Fathers of children 18 months of age reacted less positively to sons playing with female-typed toys, while mothers' reactions to sons were not influenced by their toy choice. In addition, these authors found that fathers had more positive interactions (as compared to instructional or negative interactions) with children than mothers. In general, studies suggest that fathers spend more time with their sons than their daughters, and they engage in more physical play with their sons (Ross and Taylor 1989). Fathers also seem to expect their sons to be both physically and emotionally tougher than their daughters, an expectation that can be expressed in the form of emotional distance between father and son and in fathers' rejection of sons' dependence. In areas such as affection and every-day speech with infants and toddlers, however, research has revealed few differences in mothers' and fathers' interactions with their children (Siegal 1987).

Several factors may explain these differences between fathers and mothers, particularly fathers' more negative reactions to sons' cross-gender play. First, they may occur because mothers generally spend more time with their children (especially during infancy) than fathers and typically are more involved in children's daily care. Because these day-to-day caregiving responsibilities are not particularly gender-specific (all children need to be fed, clothed, bathed and so on), the roles of *parent* and *child* may be more significant than the roles of mother and daughter or son.

Bem's gender schema perspective (discussed in Chapter 2) offers another explanation for these differences between mothers and fathers. Because gender schemas tend to be highly androcentric, Bem's approach predicts that males have stronger motives to avoid all that is associated with females and femininity than females have to avoid all that is associated with males and masculinity. Fathers would be expected to encourage this orientation in their sons and be more concerned than mothers that their sons display masculine characteristics. Psychoanalytic theory (discussed in Chapter 2) offers a somewhat similar explanation. Recall that this perspective views male gender identity as less firmly established than female gender identity. Because males experience a painful psychological separation from their mothers in the course of establishing their gender identity as males, they learn to reject femininity and all that they associate with females. Psycho-analytic theorists suggest that fathers (and men in general) would have a stronger psychic motive than mothers (and women in general) to reinforce gender distinctions in their children. Can you think of any other factors that may account for these differences between mothers and fathers?

Turning the focus on children: learning gender

Although parents play a critical role in shaping their children's experience of gender, children themselves become increasingly skilled at decoding gender messages in the world around them. This "self-socialization" starts in infancy, and once they acquire gender identity, children become even more active participants in the socialization process. By the time they are three, most children can correctly identify themselves as female or male and can identify others as same or different with respect to gender (Maccoby 1998). As we saw in Chapter 2, this ability to self-identify as female or male signifies the formation of a **gender identity**. Children's ability to self-identify as female or male influences their preferences for playmates – children who are aware of their gender being more likely than those whose gender identity is not developed to prefer same-sex playmates and gender-typed toys.

Children also learn to apply the labels "male" and "female" to others, using characteristics such as clothing and hairstyle (Coltrane 1998), and they learn **gender stereotypes**. Gender stereotypes can refer to characteristics associated with each gender, such as the belief that girls are soft, and they include beliefs about gender-appropriate activities, such as the belief that trucks are for boys. Beginning as early as age three, for example, "children will sort pictures of such items as a hammer, baseball, shirt and tie, razor and shaving cream, into a box for men and pictures of a dress, vacuum cleaner, cooking pot, cosmetics, handbag, into a box for women" (Maccoby 1998: 165). Once children assign gender labels to objects and activities, they use these labels to guide their preferences and their expectations of others. Martin et al. (1995: 1454) explain this process: "a girl will reason that a doll is something girls usually like, I am a girl, therefore I will probably like to play with the doll. In some situations, this kind of reasoning may become so well learned that it is done virtually automatically."

Young children do not associate every object, activity, or characteristic with a particular gender, of course. However, once these associations have been made, what Martin et al. (1995: 1468) call **gender-centric reasoning** (i.e., what one gender likes the other does not; what a person of one gender likes, others of the same gender will also like) is likely to be employed, especially by younger children. Children from similar backgrounds who are exposed to similar cultural messages tend to agree on the content of those gender associations that do exist and use that information to organize their social worlds. Children are aware of the expectations their society attaches to gender and can associate these expectations with a wide variety of cultural objects and activities.

Gender stereotypes seem to be most entrenched among children aged five to eight – a period Maccoby refers to as "the most 'sexist' period of life" and a time when "deviations from [gender stereotypes are seen as] positively *wrong*, not just misguided" (1998: 169; emphasis in original). Of course, children in this age group are not really sexist in any intentional way. Rather, they are actively applying the gender stereotypes they have absorbed from their cultural surroundings and using gender to organize information about people and things. Children's ability to do these things is rather remarkable, since many of the gender associations they acquire are learned not through direct observation, but rather through inference and reasoning. As Fagot et al. (1992: 229) observe, how else could we explain why it is that children will associate a "fierce-looking bear" with boys and a "fluffy cat" with girls? Children's ability and willingness to make these associations signifies that they have in fact learned some of their culture's messages about gender; that is, they have been gender socialized. Over time, as children continue to mature, their ideas about gender-appropriate activities and behavior grow more sophisticated and they are less inclined to believe that gender stereotypes must always be adhered to.

One final point about gender labeling and stereotyping among children is worth noting: There is some evidence that children's ability to assign gender labels and the degree to which they embrace gender stereotypes are influenced by their parents' behaviors. In particular, Fagot et al. (1992: 229) found that children they call "early labelers" were more likely than others to come from households where mothers encouraged more gender-typed play and embraced more gender-traditional attitudes. This finding suggests that children's ability and inclination to use gender as a basis for making choices and organizing information varies to some extent, based on parents' characteristics. Not surprisingly, children who grow up in homes where gender assumes an important role in daily life may rely on it more in their own lives than children for whom gender is less salient to everyday life. This may explain why at least some studies have found that white children – especially those from higher socioeconomic backgrounds – express more gender-stereotyped views than African-American children and those from lower socioeconomic backgrounds (Bardwell et al. 1986). Members of the dominant social group may be more likely to embrace traditional societal values and norms than members of other social categories.

The importance of same-sex peers

Another important aspect of children's experience of gender is the involvement of peers. As children move out of infancy and into their preschool and school-age years, a greater proportion of their play and interactions involve other children, such as siblings or peers. Parents are still important, of course, as they influence their children's choice of playmates, but their direct roles in the socialization process become somewhat less important.

One of the most widely studied aspects of children's relations with peers is their sex-segregated nature. Studies of sex segregation sometimes rely on an individualist framework, as they attempt to understand why girls and boys prefer same-sex playmates. More often, however, this research embraces a more interactionist approach; the focus is on the social relations of childhood groups and the nature of interaction within those groups.

By about age three, both girls and boys prefer same-sex playmates, though girls' preferences are the first to emerge (Fagot and Leinbach 1993). This preference for same-sex peers continues when children enter school, generally lasting until adolescence: "In fact, in nearly every study of school situations where kids from age three through junior high are given the opportunity to choose companions of the same age, girls have shown a strong preference to be with girls, and boys with boys" (Thorne 1993: 46). Sex segregation in childhood intrigues researchers, in part because it is spontaneous and reflects the preferences of both girls and boys (Thorne 1993). Sex segregation among children is more likely to be found in settings where few adults are present than ones where adults are in charge (e.g., on the playground rather than in the classroom). A preference for same-sex peers has been found among children in many societies, including nonindustrial societies (Maccoby 1998).

The segregation of children's peer groups adds another layer of complexity to our understanding of the socialization process, and it challenges us to consider the broader set of social relations within which children are embedded. Because of sex segregation, much of what children learn from peers is acquired in a same-sex context. Boys are socialized by and with other boys, while girls' socialization is by and with other girls. This implies that the *content* of what is learned also varies by gender. One consequence of this is that girls and boys relate to one another as "familiar strangers," people "who are in repeated physical proximity and recognize one another, but have little real knowledge of what one another are like" (Thorne 1993: 47). Although sex segregation in childhood is by no means total, and boys and girls do have opportunities to interact with each other, their friendships and closest bonds are with same-sex peers.

Why children prefer same-sex peers has been explained in several ways. Perhaps these choices reflect gender differences in play styles, with children choosing to interact with those whose styles of play are more similar to their own. Research does suggest that groups of boys play differently than groups of girls (Maccoby 1998) and these differences in play style may partly explain children's preferences for same-sex peers. Cognitive theories of gender socialization provide an alternative explanation, as they suggest that children's preference for same-sex peers is related to a more general tendency to prefer and more highly value those labeled as having a similar gender to oneself, regardless of play style.

Alexander and Hines (1994) conclude that both explanations of children's same-sex playmate preferences have some validity. These researchers interviewed children ranging in age from four to eight about their preferences for imaginary playmates. They found that play style was more strongly related to boys' preferences for playmates than the preferences of girls: boys of all ages were more likely to choose to play with girls who displayed a masculine play style than boys displaying a feminine play style. By contrast, the factors shaping girls' preferences changed with age. Consistent with cognitive theoretical accounts, younger girls chose imaginary playmates based on gender rather than play style, while play style had a stronger influence on the preferences of older girls. This study suggests that no single theory can account for children's preferences for same-sex playmates.

Are these differences universal?

Most of the research discussed in the preceding sections was conducted in North America among samples that were predominantly (though not exclusively) white. Given this, can the findings and patterns reported here be generalized to other cultures? The answer to this question is more than a simple "yes" or "no." In fact, a comprehensive, in-depth study of children in six cultures (India, Okinawa, Philippines, Mexico, Kenya, and the USA) found some similarities in patterns of gendered behavior across societies, but concluded that "the differences are not consistent nor so great as the studies of American and Western European children would suggest" (Whiting and Edwards 1988: 296).

In general, these researchers found that girls displayed more nurturing behaviors than boys, while boys' play was more aggressive (e.g., "rough and tumble") and dominance-seeking than girls'. Whiting and Edwards conclude that these universal gender differences reflect some similarities in *socialization contexts* – that is, in learning environments – across cultures. In general, girls tend to interact much more than boys with infants and younger children, while boys spend more time than girls interacting with older children. Because each type of interaction tends to require different kinds of skills and abilities, boys and girls are socialized somewhat differently and acquire somewhat different preferences and styles of interaction. Consistent with this argument, Whiting and Edwards (1988) found that in societies where boys are expected to participate in domestic tasks, including caring for infants, there are fewer differences between girls and boys. Although there are some broad similarities in gender socialization across cultures, societies vary in the size of gender differences in behavior. These differences tend to be *smaller*, on average, than studies focusing solely on North America have suggested.

Childhood socialization reconsidered

Think back once more to your own early childhood. Do you fit the patterns described here? If you are female, were your close friends mostly girls? Did you play with dolls more than with trucks? If you are male, do your memories of early childhood friendships mostly contain boys, with whom you played games such as baseball or other sports? Some of you will answer "yes" to these questions and will have seen your childhood experiences reflected in the previous pages. For others, however, the general patterns uncovered by sociologists will be at odds with your childhood memories. Moreover, regardless of our own experiences, we probably all remember some childhood peers who preferred to play with the other gender and who had little interest in what were considered gender "appropriate" activities. In fact, it is likely that all of us at one time or another did not conform to what was expected of us as boys or girls. How can we account for these atypical socialization experiences? What explains why some children behave in what parents and peers consider "gender appropriate" ways, while others reject at least some of this socialization? Addressing these questions helps remove one of the most common misconceptions about the socialization process.

Socialization is never completely consistent, nor is it total or all-encompassing. These inconsistencies and disruptions in the socialization process stem from many factors. For example, children may receive different kinds of messages from different agents of socialization in their lives. Saturday morning cartoons may present children with different images of how girls or boys are supposed to behave than those received from a parent. In addition, children are not blank slates; temperament – which many believe is partially shaped by genetic factors – may shape what children learn and how they interpret gender messages. More important, as we have seen, how children are socialized as well as the content of the gender messages they receive vary by a number of factors such as race and ethnicity, social class, religion, etc., so it is doubtful than any two people have been socialized in exactly the same way. For all of these reasons, we should not expect that the kinds of patterns uncovered in sociological research would ever fully capture all of the variation and complexity in males' and females' experience of childhood.

Crossing gender boundaries: tomboys and sissies

One set of childhood experiences that differ from the typical pattern has been of special interest to researchers – the experiences of those who cross gender boundaries. Here, I am referring to those girls and boys commonly (and, in the case of boys, pejoratively) referred to as "tomboys" and "sissies." A sissy is a boy who "has ventured too far into the contaminating 'feminine,' while 'tomboys' are girls who claim some of the positive qualities associated with the 'masculine'" (Thorne 1993: 111). When Thorne conducted her research on elementary-school children in the early

1990s, she found that few children used the term "tomboy" (t.
meaning was understood). Nevertheless, several girls in her study
gender boundaries on the playground and in other school setting\
regularly played games with boys and sat with them in the cafe,
although they moved just as easily among the girls. Moreover, Thorne found
that girls were more likely than boys to want to join the other gender's
activities. By contrast, the term "sissy" was an unambiguously negative
label and the boys in Thorne's study mostly avoided joining girls' games.
Moreover, when they did attempt to participate in girls' activities, boys
often did so disruptively, rather than as serious participants.

Sex differences in crossing gender boundaries are consistent with other
material presented in this chapter. Girls seem to face less pressure than boys
to conform to gender stereotypes, are more likely than boys to cross gender
boundaries, and girls receive less negative attention than boys when they
do participate in activities or games with the other gender. The gender
socialization that occurs during childhood thus appears to be more restric-
tive for boys than for girls. Boys' behavior and activities are more closely
monitored for their gender appropriateness by parents (especially fathers)
and peers than the behavior and activities of girls. Hence, although both
genders experience socialization, girls seem to have a wider range of options
for behavior than boys.

THE HOUSEHOLD DIVISION OF LABOR AND THE FAMILY

Childrearing is just one of many activities that take place in families. Maintaining a household also requires that adults perform many other tasks. The
division of labor in the family (or, as it is also called, the **household division of labor**) is among the topics most often studied by sociologists interested in gender and family life. Much effort has been devoted to describing
the kinds of activities women and men perform in the family. Ferree (1990)
divides studies into those focusing on the physical labor of housework and
childcare, and those concerned with the symbolic meaning of these activities. Researchers who conceive of household work as physical labor are
typically concerned with identifying gender differences in the amount and
type of work performed, and hence tend toward an individualist view of
gender. By contrast, researchers interested in the symbolic meanings associated with household work are more likely to view gender as an emergent
feature of social interaction.

Doing housework and childcare

In order to study the division of household work, researchers must decide what activities count as housework. Should we count only activities involving physical labor, such as cooking or cleaning, or should the "emotion work" of providing support and showing care for others also count? Is childcare a form of housework or should it be considered something else? While what counts as housework varies somewhat across studies, most researchers define it as "unpaid work done to maintain family members and/or a home" (Shelton and John 1996: 299). Some researchers include childcare in this definition and some do not.

According to Blair and Johnson, "Virtually every study investigating the division of household labor has come to two basic conclusions: women perform approximately twice as much labor as men; and women perform qualitatively different types of chores than men" (1992: 570). More recent data show little change. According to Bianchi et al. (2000), women in 1995 spent about 17.5 hours a week doing housework (excluding childcare), while men averaged 10 hours a week. Men's reported hours of housework have not declined since 1985.

There is some evidence that the division of household work is more egalitarian in African-American families than in white households, though African-American women still perform more housework than men. As Figure 5.1 shows, African-American husbands perform slightly more housework than white husbands in virtually every category, except those tasks where men have typically dominated (i.e., outdoor, auto, and bills). These patterns may reflect differences in white and African-American husbands' commitment to gender equality in the family. In particular, Landry (2000) argues that, compared to white men, African-American men have long been stronger supporters of wives and mothers working for pay and contributing to the family income.

If we broaden our time frame, however, it is clear that there have been some significant changes in both women's and men's household work over the last few decades. In particular, although women continue to perform more household work than men, women spend fewer hours performing housework than in 1965, while men spend more hours involved in family care than they did in the mid-1960s (Robinson and Godbey 1997). Longitudinal research by Bianchi et al. (2000) (shown in Figure 5.2) shows further evidence of this trend. Their data show that women in 1965 averaged more than 6 times the hours men spent in housework, while in 1995, this had dropped to 1.8 times the number of hours spent by men. The decreasing gender gap in housework hours is due to steep declines in the number of hours women spend doing housework, not because men have begun to

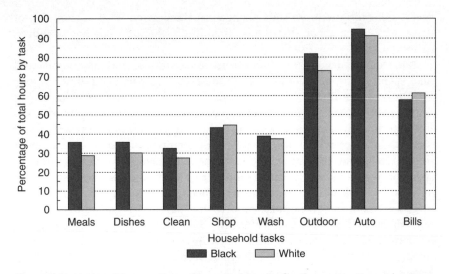

Figure 5.1 Husbands' percentage of household tasks, for those reporting at least one hour

Source: Bart Lanary (2002), *Black Working Wives: Pioneers of the American Family Revolution* (Berkeley, CA: University of California Press), p. 158.

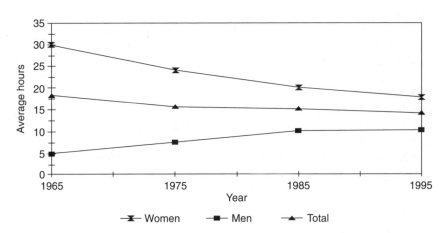

Figure 5.2 Average hours of housework for men and women

Source: Reprinted from *Social Forces* 79 (2000): 191–228, "Is Anyone Doing the Housework? Trends in the Gender Division of Household Labor," by Suzanne M. Bianchi, Melissa A. Milkie, Liana C. Sayer, and John P. Robinson. Copyright © The University of North Carolina Press.

spend substantially more time engaged in these activities. On the basis of these data, some argue that the household division of labor has stabilized to some extent.

What factors have contributed to these changes in the time women and men spend doing household work? One factor, in particular, deserves our attention: women's rising rates of labor-force participation (see Chapter 4). Women who work for pay perform fewer hours of household work than full-time homemakers, and women employed part-time do less household work than those with full-time jobs. Higher rates of female employment thus have been accompanied by a decline in the hours women are able to spend doing housework. Interestingly, this decline in women's hours of household work does not extend to childcare. As Robinson and Godbey observe: "Contrary to popular reports that parents are spending less time with their children (Mattox, 1990), the data . . . show that both employed and nonemployed women in 1985 spent just as much time in child care as those in the 1960s . . ." (1997: 104). It seems that women may be doing less of some kinds of housework than they did in the 1960s, but are not any less involved in childcare.

Increases in women's labor-force participation undoubtedly are also responsible for men's increasing involvement in household work. There are several reasons why this is the case. First, employed wives may simply have less time to perform all the tasks necessary to running a home, forcing men to pick up the slack. In addition, both women's and men's conceptions of themselves and their responsibilities to their families may be altered when women participate in the paid labor force. One way to illustrate this point is to compare white and African-American husbands' involvement in household work. Historically, financial need often compelled African-American wives and mothers to work for pay. These women faced less disapproval for working from friends and families than white women, and were often encouraged to work by their husbands (Landry 2000). This legacy of labor-force participation and supportive families among African-Americans has been used to account for African-American husbands' greater involvement than white husbands in household work (Landry 2000). This implies that greater equality of participation in one sphere – such as the workplace – may eventually contribute to more equitable arrangements in others.

Despite women's increasing rates of labor-force participation and the many other changes that have accompanied this shift, however, employed women continue to perform more household work than their male counterparts. In her 1989 book on dual-earner households, Arlie Hochschild captured this difference by concluding that employed women have a **second shift** at home after their paid work is done. Hochschild (1989) estimated that employed women spend roughly 15 hours per week longer than men

at these tasks, resulting in women working an extra mo\
per year.

Women and men also perform different kinds of ac\
Household work, like paid work, is sex-segregated, w\
each performing tasks typically associated with the\
perform outdoor tasks, such as mowing the lawn or w\
while women do cleaning and care for children) (Berk 1985; Blair anu
Lichter 1991). Robinson and Godbey (1997) found that women perform
almost 80 percent of all childcare, a figure that has not changed substantially since the 1960s. The amount of care provided by mothers and fathers
evens out somewhat as children age, but even among school-age children,
mothers have more caregiving responsibilities than fathers.

The tasks typically performed by women and men diverge in other
respects as well. Household tasks performed by men involve greater personal discretion than those women perform, are more likely to have a fixed
beginning and end, and are more likely to involve a leisure component
(Hochschild 1989). As Robinson and Godbey note: "most of the time men
spend with the children is in the form of 'interactive activities,' such as play
or helping with homework, rather than the 'custodial' cleaning and feeding
that is the mother's domain" (1997: 104). In contrast to Parsons's view of
the household as an expressive realm, these studies indicate that household
members perform a significant amount of "instrumental" family work –
cleaning, cooking meals, shopping, etc. Although the total number of hours
devoted to household work has declined over time, these tasks continue to
be performed primarily by women (England and Farkas 1986).

Other studies extend this research by examining the factors that influence women's and men's participation in housework. Researchers have been
especially interested in the conditions associated with more egalitarian
household divisions of labor. Some theorists argue that the **relative resources**
of husband and wife explain the amount of time each devotes to household
work (Brines 1994; England and Farkas 1986). Because earnings are one
important resource in marriage, this perspective suggests that husbands'
performance of household work should respond to changes in wives' relative wages. Studies have found some support for this argument. Wives do
less housework and men do more as the proportion of family income contributed by the wife increases (Bianchi et al. 2000). Similarly, when wives
are the same age as their husbands, they do less housework and husbands
do more than when wives are two or more years younger than their spouse.

Others argue that time availability, as affected by such factors as children or the time demands of paid employment, explain sex differences in
the household division of labor. In support of this view, studies suggest that
the hours both spouses spend performing housework are influenced by the
hours each spends in paid employment and having children, especially

unger children. Children increase the hours women spend performing housework much more than men's housework hours, however (Bianchi et al. 2000). Researchers thus conclude that men's participation in housework increases when their wives are unavailable to perform these activities.

In addition to this research, there is some evidence that the household division of labor is shaped by factors such as marital status and family type. For example, according to studies cited by Shelton and John (1996), married women perform more household work than cohabiting women, other factors being equal, though there are no differences between married and cohabiting men. Studies of gay and lesbian households suggest that these couples are somewhat more egalitarian in their sharing of household tasks than heterosexual couples (Blumstein and Schwartz 1983). Other attempts to account for sex differences in the household division of labor focus on women's and men's **gender ideologies**. These studies explore how women's and, to a lesser extent, men's gender attitudes influence the type and amount of household work each performs. The results of this research are mixed. Although some conclude that gender ideologies are unrelated to husbands' and wives' performance of household work, others find greater support for this argument (England and Farkas 1986). Hochschild (1989) offers a more complex perspective of the relations between gender ideologies and the household division of labor. She suggests that while gender ideologies shape women's and men's conceptions of their family roles and the "gender strategies" they pursue to enact those roles, there may be an inconsistency between the form each spouse believes the division of labor "should" take and its actual expression. Couples may develop what she calls "family myths" to manage this tension between their gender ideologies and the realities of the household division of labor.

The meanings of housework and parenthood: interactionist views

In addition to research on housework as physical labor, other studies explore the symbolic meanings associated with household work and people's experience of motherhood or fatherhood. These investigators argue that to truly understand housework and childcare, we must explore the meanings people give to these activities and the ways these meanings develop within social interaction (Ferree 1990). This approach to studying household work thus draws heavily from interactionist views of gender. From an interactionist perspective, the performance of household work results in both the production of goods and services (e.g., meals, clean laundry, etc.) *and* the production of gender (Berk 1985; West and Fenstermaker 1993). In West and Fenstermaker's words: "Our claim is not simply that household labor is regarded as women's work, but that for a woman to do it and a man not to do it draws on and affirms what people conceive to be the essential nature of each" (1993: 162).

In her study of "feeding the family," DeVault (1991) draws on these ideas to explore how family caregiving activities, such as cooking and preparing family meals, are understood by those who perform them. DeVault (1991: 10) explains that it was difficult for some people in her study to describe their experiences:

> They talked about feeding as something other than work in the conventional sense, trying to explain how their activities are embedded in family relations. Some, for example, talked of this work in terms of family ties. They described feeding as part of being a parent: "I feel like, you know, when I decided to have children it was a commitment, and raising them included feeding them." Or as part of being a wife: "I like to cook for him. That's what a wife is for, right?"

For DeVault, the vocabulary of paid work is insufficient to describe how people doing family work think about their activities.

On a more general level, Coltrane (1989: 473) explores how women's and men's performance of household labor "provides the opportunity for expressing, confirming, and sometimes transforming the meaning of gender." He shows that parents in families where household work and childcare are shared are more likely to view women and men as similar than those in households with less equitable arrangements. For Coltrane (1989), however, family members' conceptions of gender are the product, rather than the source, of the household division of labor. In other words, participation in the everyday activities associated with household work produces family members' beliefs about women and men.

Engendering motherhood and fatherhood

No mother's or father's experience is exactly the same. Parenthood brings joy and stress, good times and frustration. The qualities of their children also play a role in parents' experiences. Despite the fact that parents and children are unique in some important ways, motherhood and fatherhood are socially organized; people in similar kinds of circumstances often report similar kinds of feelings and experiences.

In American society, motherhood is sometimes said to be "compulsory" for women. **Compulsory motherhood** refers to a set of cultural beliefs prescribing that "women should find total fulfillment in having children and taking care of them" (Coltrane 1998: 91). The reality may be quite different. For example, some women find their opportunities to be mothers and to care for their children restricted by social policies (such as welfare laws that reduce or limit benefits when additional children are born, or laws that make it difficult for gay and lesbian parents to adopt) or poverty. Compulsory motherhood, then, is probably best understood as a set of cultural beliefs most often applied to heterosexual, married women who are not poor. Even among this group, however, not all women are mothers or want to be mothers. Although many women do have children and find it fulfilling, motherhood is demanding and not always as intensely satisfying as the ideology of compulsory motherhood suggests. In addition, only a small proportion of mothers today are involved in that role full-time. As we saw in the previous chapter, most mothers – even mothers of infants – are employed for pay at least some hours a week.

Compulsory motherhood should be understood as less a description of how women *are* than a set of expectations about how (heterosexual, married) women are *expected* to be. As we saw in Chapter 4, a gendered institutions perspective has been useful for understanding how these cultural expectations emerged and became so powerful. In particular, researchers in this tradition have examined several interlocking historical developments – namely, industrialization, urbanization, and the "doctrine of separate spheres" – that reshaped families in the late nineteenth and early twentieth century (Williams 2000). These changes redefined the relations between work and home, and, in the process, produced new understandings of women's and men's roles in the family. Children's lives and societal expectations about childhood were also altered. Children were assumed to require mothers' intensive nurturing and mothers were seen as the morally pure guardians of the home and community. Fathers' responsibilities to the family were to be fulfilled through his role as breadwinner.

Then, as now, these expectations for mothers, fathers, and children were social-class specific. Only middle-class families could afford a life where women and children remained at home. Poor and working-class families, whose ranks included new immigrants, racial-ethnic minorities, and women without husbands, were unable to achieve the culturally exalted, middle-class ideal and thus often found themselves stigmatized and the subject of various social reforms attempting to control their sexuality or "protect" their children (McMahon 1995).

Social class differences in the meaning and experience of motherhood have not disappeared. Differences between white working-class and middle-class mothers were the subject of McMahon's 1995 book, *Engendering Motherhood*. The author interviewed 59 employed, first-time mothers, approximately half of whom were working class and the others middle class. Some of the women she interviewed were married or had a male or female partner, while others were single. McMahon uses an interactionist approach to explore her topic: "I analyze motherhood as a gendered and engendering experience. That is, the analysis goes beyond conceptualizing motherhood simply as an expression of female identity, to expose the ways in which the experience of motherhood *produces* a gendered sense of self in women" (1995: 3; emphasis in original).

McMahon (1995) argues that while motherhood is a gendered and engendering experience, this meant different things in the lives of her working-class and middle-class respondents. The working-class women in her sample had generally positive views of motherhood prior to pregnancy; they embraced motherhood in part because it showed that they had "grown up" and achieved adult womanhood. By contrast, the middle-class women in McMahon's study began thinking about motherhood only after they felt mature and accomplished. As McMahon explains: "When middle-class women talked about having their first children they frequently put forward their claims to maternal identities as achieved social accomplishments . . . Borrowing from middle-class masculinist models of the individual, these middle-class women constructed personal achievement, not "womanhood," as a precondition for having children" (1995: 265–6).

Not surprisingly, these social class differences in the way women approached motherhood reflected other differences in the women's lives. Working-class women, with fewer opportunities for careers and meaning-ful work, tended to become mothers in their early 20s, and pregnancy was often unplanned. Middle-class women, on the other hand, viewed career success as a precondition for motherhood and thus had children later in life after this goal was accomplished. For both groups of women in this study, however, motherhood transformed their sense of themselves as women. In McMahon's words:

> What women chose in becoming mothers (and many did not choose) was not the role of mother in the way we often think of that role. They did not choose to take on the romanticized cultural image of mother, be it saint, self-sacrificer, or morally transformed person. Rather, through a wide variety of routes, women took on the behavior or outcome of having a child . . . [However,] once women stepped into the situation of being a mother, the social relationships and cultural definition of the situation, along with women's own responses, acted together to make participants feel they were morally trans-formed persons. Although they did not set out to achieve this identity, women came to claim for themselves the romanticized identity of mother. (1995: 275)

As McMahon shows, motherhood remains laden with cultural meanings that still resonate with women, regardless of social class, sexual orienta-tion, or employment status. Though women who become mothers may not even be conscious of their impact, women draw on these taken-for-granted meanings to make sense of their experiences and gain a feminized sense of themselves as mature adults. This process of drawing on deeply ingrained cultural beliefs about mothers and motherhood illustrates how gendered institutions shape people's lives and sense of self.

Lesbian and gay families rewriting parenthood

Research on lesbian and gay parents offers another way to understand families as gendered institutions and see the power of gender in shaping people's experiences of themselves as mothers and fathers. Lesbian and gay couples can become parents by giving birth themselves (in the case of lesbians), by adoption, or through a previous heterosexual relationship. Regardless of how children join lesbian or gay households, the law does not automatically recognize both partners as parents, as it does in the case of married, heterosexual couples who give birth or adopt. Instead, in most cases, the law recognizes one person as the mother or father (biological or adoptive), and the partner must petition the court to be granted co-parenting status. Thus, for lesbian and gay couples, becoming a two-parent family requires that they work around the dominant cultural understanding of the family as a heterosexual unit.

In heterosexual families, the duties, expectations, and obligations associated with parenting are strongly gendered, and these, in turn, are closely linked to sex category: Women become mothers and men become fathers. What happens in gay and lesbian households with two co-parenting women or men? Dalton and Bielby's (2000) research on lesbian families shows that these households are not immune from the gendered expectations attached to mothering. Instead, in lesbian families, mothering is likely to be shared, with both partners embracing the duties and responsibilities of this highly gendered role. By adhering to conventional gender expectations regarding mothering, lesbian parents reinforced traditional cultural understandings of motherhood.

In many other respects, of course, lesbian families challenged what Dalton and Bielby call "heteronormative conceptions of the family" (2000: 57). For example, while marriage signifies heterosexual couples' commitment to family, lesbians and gays are legally prevented from taking this step. Several of the lesbian couples in Dalton and Bielby's study participated in commitment ceremonies to publicly identify themselves as families. On the one hand, these ceremonies acknowledge the role of marriage as a means of demonstrating commitment to family. On the other, these same efforts challenge those forces that restrict the link between marriage and family to heterosexuals.

As this discussion shows, the power of a social institution like the family extends both to those who conform to traditional understandings and to those who do not conform. This underscores the power of institutions and the necessity of looking beyond individuals when seeking to understand gender's role in social life.

MARRIAGE, FAMILIES, AND THEIR CONSEQUENCES FOR WOMEN AND MEN

Why are researchers so concerned with understanding the household division of labor? What are the implications of one set of household arrangements as opposed to another? In fact, the organization of family life has important consequences for women's and men's lives both within and outside of the family. These consequences have been explored in depth by researchers. First, let us consider how marriage and the household division of labor affect women's and men's experiences in the labor market. In her 1977 classic, *Men and Women of the Corporation*, Rosabeth Moss Kanter cited what used to be, and perhaps still is, a common belief about the effects of marriage on men's and women's value as employees: "Married men bring two people to the job, while married women bring less than one." This suggests that married men are more productive employees than married women. Married men are assumed to benefit at work from the fact that they have a spouse. The spouse's efforts on behalf of the family and, in particular, the husband, are assumed to enhance his work performance. Because she cleans, cooks, and runs the household, he can devote his time and energies to work. The situation is different for married women. Marriage – and the household responsibilities it entails – are assumed to interfere with married women's abilities to be successful on the job. Because they have responsibilities at home, they have less time and energy to commit to the paid workplace. A married woman is seen as less than one "full" worker.

Consistent with this view, Williams (1995) suggests that the ideal worker in the eyes of most employers is one who does not have any non-work responsibilities. Because women typically have more responsibilities than men for housework and child care, this is not a gender-neutral preference. As a result, men more than women embody the ideal worker. Work organizations reflect this preference as well. They contain "built-in advantages for men that are often unnoticed; indeed, they seem like natural or inevitable characteristics of all organizations" (Williams 1995: 9).

Current research suggests that marriage is a different kind of "signal" to employers for men than it is for women. By "signal," I am referring to marriage as an indicator of a person's qualities and responsibilities. Marriage, for men, signals many positive qualities to employers, such as maturity and responsibility. In addition, married men may be seen as having a helpmate at home, a source of emotional support and a person to perform household chores. Marriage for women, on the other hand, may send employers a different kind of signal. Rather than being seen as more committed, they may be viewed as a greater risk for an employer, especially in jobs that require extensive training and those where workers are costly to replace.

Does marriage pay?

What evidence is there that employers actually hold such views of married men and women? Is there any evidence that marriage differentially affects men's and women's job performance and orientation to work? The first question is best answered somewhat indirectly since many people – employers included – would hesitate to directly express the kinds of attitudes described above. Given this, another way to assess how married women and men are viewed in the labor market is to examine whether marriage "pays" for each sex, and whether it pays differently for women and men. Marriage pays if it can be shown that being married results in a net economic benefit, such as a higher salary, for married people as compared to the unmarried.

In fact, there is some evidence that this is the case for men. In a 1992 study of almost 4,000 male college professors, Bellas (1992) found that never-married men had the lowest salaries, followed by men with employed wives; the highest salaries were found among men with nonemployed wives. Differences between each group of men in terms of job characteristics and achievement levels (e.g., educational degree, rank, and productivity) partly explained these salary differences. Married men with nonemployed wives had the highest salaries and achievement levels. Nevertheless, even when these job and achievement characteristics were held constant (i.e., when comparing men with roughly equivalent levels of achievement and similar employment characteristics), Bellas (1992) found that men with employed wives earned about $1,000 a year more than never-married men, and men with nonemployed wives earned approximately $2,000 a year more than men who never married. This study suggests that marriage – especially to a nonemployed spouse – has an economic pay-off for this group of male workers. Marriage for men may "signal" positive qualities to employers and, as Bellas's (1992) research suggests, wives – especially those who are nonemployed – may contribute to their husbands' careers. For example, by caring for children and the home, nonemployed wives may make it possible for their husbands to devote more time and energy to work. Wives may be an important source of social and emotional support as well, or may perform other tasks, such as entertaining, that may help their husbands' career advancement.

If married men benefit from marriage, do married women suffer a wage penalty at work, as compared to unmarried women? The answer to this question appears to be that employed women are not penalized for marriage and may even derive a wage advantage, relative to other women, all else being equal (Budig and England 2001). The finding that employed women overall are not economically penalized by marriage must be qualified in one – important – respect, however: Mothers – regardless of marital status – earn less than non-mothers. Budig and England (2001) estimate that mothers experience a wage penalty of about 7 percent per child.

Several factors could explain this pattern. First, because women have primary responsibility for children – especially young children – women may lose work experience and seniority when they become mothers. The birth of a child may lead some women to change jobs or decrease the time they spend at work, both of which are associated with lower wages. Perhaps mothers continue to work for pay, but become less productive and devote less effort to their jobs, relative to non-mothers. This, too, would reduce their wages. The motherhood wage penalty may also reflect mothers' tendency to seek employment in "mother-friendly" jobs, such as those with flexible schedules, on-site childcare, or reduced work hours. Some economists would argue that the "mother-friendliness" of these jobs compensates for the job's lower wages. In this view, mothers trade off higher wages for the opportunity to have a job that can be combined with their childcare responsibilities.

Finally, it may be that employers discriminate against mothers by restricting them to lower-paying jobs. Just as marriage for men may "signal" positive qualities to employers, motherhood for women may send negative signals. Regardless of how mothers actually perform relative to non-mothers, employers may *believe* that mothers will perform less well. Employers who act on these beliefs by refusing to promote mothers or hire them into high-paying jobs are engaging in discrimination – differential treatment of a group on the basis of motherhood.

Which explanation is correct? In a sophisticated statistical analysis of these arguments, Budig and England (2001) concluded that about one-third of the 7 percent motherhood wage penalty could be explained by mothers having less work experience and seniority than non-mothers. When women become mothers, their involvement in the paid work force lessens somewhat, and this partly explains their decreased earnings. Nevertheless, two-thirds of the motherhood wage penalty remains even after accounting for differences in work experience and seniority: Among women with similar levels of experience and seniority, mothers earn roughly 4 percent less than non-mothers. This may reflect differences between the productivity levels of the two groups, or it may indicate that employers are discriminating against mothers. In any case, as Budig and England (2001) observe, the wage costs of motherhood are born primarily by mothers themselves.

"His" marriage and "her" marriage

The employment effects of marriage and the household division of labor are only part of the story. It is also important to examine women's and men's marital and psychological well-being as these are affected by family arrangements. To address these questions, we start with the classic work of sociologist Jesse Bernard. In her 1972 book, *The Future of Marriage*, Bernard argued that researchers had overlooked an important point about marriage; they had ignored the fact that marriage was gendered. In Bernard's view, marriage had to be understood from the perspective of "his" and "hers." Women and men, she argued, experienced marriage differently, in part due to their differing life situations prior to marriage and in part due to their roles and responsibilities in marriage.

Bernard (1972: 41) explained these differences with what she called a **"shock theory of marriage."** Specifically, Bernard claimed that marriage was more of a "shock" for women than men. As a result, she argued that married women were generally more psychologically distressed than single women and married men. Although married life is a change for all involved, Bernard believed that married women had to make greater adjustments than their partners. One of the most obvious ways that this occurs is when a woman takes her husband's name at marriage and gives up her own. The shift from Miss to Mrs. may also signify a loss of independence for a woman, who is now identified in terms of her relationship to her husband. As we have seen, married women may find themselves having to take on more of the household work – even when both wife and husband are employed. Regardless of whether both are employed or only the husband is employed, it is likely that his job will have the greatest influence on the couple's lifestyle, including where they live and how often they move. Bielby and Bielby (1992), for example, found that women were much more likely to accommodate their jobs and careers to their husband's than vice versa.

The differential adjustments each gender makes to marriage reflect a larger truth about relationships – even intimate relationships: Those with greater resources tend to have more power in the relationship. Unequal resources imply unequal power and dependence. Because men's economic contribution to the family is greater than women's, on average, men typically have more power in the household. By this logic, full-time homemakers are most dependent on their spouses and have the least amount of power in the relationship. When Bernard proposed the shock theory of marriage, she was thinking most about the situation of the full-time homemaker.

Marriage reassessed

Is Bernard's (1973) description of marriage still accurate today? To answer this question we need to consider some of the changes that have occurred in family life during the past few decades. There are far fewer full-time homemakers today than in the 1970s, suggesting that women's economic dependence on men has lessened. Fewer women than ever take their husband's name at marriage and some men take their wife's name, or adopt a combination of both. More people are cohabiting and, for many, this is a transition to marriage (Coltrane 1998). In addition, Bernard may have overlooked some of the positive effects of marriage for women and may have understated some of the negative effects of paid employment.

In their recent book, Waite and Gallagher (2000) argue that marriage today is overwhelmingly positive for women. Married women, they contend, are happier with their lives, report fewer mental health problems, have more satisfying sexual relations, are less likely to be victims of domestic abuse, and are better off financially than their unmarried or cohabiting counterparts. Despite these apparent benefits, the health benefits of marriage nevertheless seem to be greater for men than for women (Waite and Gallagher 2000). This is because single men, in general, are much worse off than single women. For example, single men are more likely than single women *and* married men to engage in risky and unhealthy behaviors, such as excessive drinking. Single women are more likely to care for their health than single men; married men receive this care and attention from their wives. Single women also have closer ties to family and friends and this lesser social isolation improves their health relative to that of single men.

Given this, it is not easy to make an overall assessment of the relative benefits of marriage for women and men (England 2001). Clearly, marriage is a social institution that provides both partners with important social and financial resources. And, despite high divorce rates, births outside of marriage, and other trends, the USA has the highest marriage rate of any industrialized country (Skolnick 2001). At the same time, this arrangement works out somewhat differently for women and men. In this respect, Bernard's contention that marriage should be understood in terms of "his" and "her" marriage continues to capture an important aspect of this gendered institution.

Lesbian and gay relationships

Although most studies on families and marriage focus on heterosexual couples, there are some important exceptions to this pattern. One is

Blumstein and Schwartz's 1983 book *American Couples*. Blumstein and Schwartz were interested in how gay and lesbian couples compared to heterosexual couples with respect to issues such as the household of division of labor, compatibility, and sexual satisfaction. These researchers not only found some differences between heterosexual and nonheterosexual couples, but they also found that gay and lesbian couples differ in some important ways. For example, gay and lesbian couples tended to spend more time together and share more interests than heterosexual couples. Later research, reported by Kurdek (1995), found that gay and lesbian couples were more likely than heterosexual couples to relate to each other as best friends and aspire to an egalitarian relationship. Research also suggests that the household division of labor in gay and lesbian households tends to be more egalitarian than in heterosexual households; Blumstein and Schwartz (1983) found that lesbian couples were most likely to share tasks equally. These differences between heterosexual and gay and lesbian couples are not the whole story, however, as research has found some significant differences between gay and lesbian couples. The majority of lesbian and heterosexual couples in Blumstein and Schwartz's sample, for example, tended to be monogamous, while gay men tended to prefer more sexually open relationships (see also Kurdek 1995).

As Blumstein and Schwartz (1983) (see also Stacey 1996) suggest, these patterns can be best understood by thinking about *gender* and *gender roles*, not *sexual orientation*. In other words, people's expectations about and behavior in relationships depend more on their gender than their sexual orientation. Similarly, what people expect of their partner depends more on the partner's gender than his or her sexual orientation. As we have seen in earlier chapters, those with an essentialist orientation to gender emphasize the ways that gender shapes people and the choices they make. This is especially true with respect to people's choices and behavior in relationships, as both are influenced by growing up male or female.

Returning to the household division of labor may help to illustrate this point about the importance of gender in both heterosexual and gay and lesbian couples. As Blumstein and Schwartz note, "An extremely important effect of having one male and one female in heterosexual couples is that each gender is automatically assigned certain duties and privileges . . . For heterosexual couples, gender provides a shortcut and avoids the decision-making process . . . Same-sex couples cannot, obviously, rely on gender to guide their decisions about who will do what in the relationship" (1983: 324). Heterosexual couples may find themselves conforming to a household division of labor like that described earlier – women do routine, day-to-day tasks, while men are likely to do tasks involving more discretion. These patterns stem less from conscious choices as from people's reliance on tradition, social norms, and personal experiences growing up. Same-sex couples cannot rely on these clues about how to behave and are likely to rely more on trial and error as a basis for organizing and dividing household work. The household division of labor is more "scripted" for heterosexual couples and may be more difficult to alter or challenge than for same-sex couples. At the same time, same-sex couples may have more flexibility in organizing their lives as a couple, but lack the traditions and models that guide heterosexual couples.

This discussion of gay and lesbian couples is not meant to suggest that these relationships are free of conflict and inequality. Some of the problems faced by gay and lesbian couples are similar to those found in any intimate relationship, regardless of sexual orientation. For example, both kinds of couples confront issues associated with balancing the demands of work with personal and family life (Dunne 1998).

Other issues may be unique to gay and lesbian couples, just as heterosexual couples may face challenges that are unique for them. Blumstein and Schwartz observed that: "Gay [and lesbian] couples face problems that arise from 'sameness of gender'; these give us an indication of where it might be wise for partners to be different. Heterosexuals face problems that arise from their 'differentness'; these give us guidance about where it might be better for two partners to be more alike" (1983: 330). Differentness, for example, may be a liability for heterosexual couples interested in creating an egalitarian household division of labor. Men and women may have distinct preferences and skills, and different expectations regarding roles and responsibilities. At the same time, similarity may create problems for gay and lesbian couples. As Blumstein and Schwartz explain, "Same-sex couples understand each other better and share similar sexual goals, but roadblocks may arise when neither partner wants to take on behavior that seems inappropriate to his or her gender" (1983: 305).

Gay and lesbian couples also confront several other obstacles to maintaining close relationships and building families. These couples are legally prevented from marriage, which limits the rights and obligations of gay and lesbian family members. Many states explicitly prohibit same-sex marriage and in 1996 Congress passed the "Defense of Marriage Act," a federal prohibition against same-sex marriage. The issue of same-sex marriage is hotly debated among gays and lesbians. While believing that the opportunity to marry is a civil right denied them as a result of sex discrimination and homophobia, some gays and lesbians do not wish to model their relationships on the heterosexual standard. They prefer the freedom and flexibility to form intimate relationships and families without having to conform to the norms, laws, and institutions that govern heterosexual marriage (Stacey 1996). Others feel differently and have agitated strongly for the legal right to marry, arguing that this right would strengthen families, encourage long-term, committed relationships, and protect the children of gay and lesbian parents.

CHAPTER SUMMARY

Socialization is one process through which people become gendered. They learn what is expected of them because they are female or male and how to display these characteristics. Gender socialization has an especially central role to play in individualist understandings of gender, as these approaches emphasize the ways that gender is embodied in people. Parents (especially fathers) do seem to interact differently with their male and female children, but these differences in parental treatment are confined to certain limited areas, such as toy choice and method of punishment. Children are actively involved in the socialization process, learning to apply gender stereotypes to themselves and others. Peers are also an important source for gender-related information, especially as children get older.

While socialization is important, many sociologists have criticized research that relies exclusively on socialization as an explanation for gender differences. Critics argue that this type of explanation falsely creates a view of women and men as homogeneous groups, possessing internally consistent and unchanging motives, behavioral dispositions, etc. (Gerson 1985, 1993; see also Epstein 1988). In the section on peer groups, I showed how an interactionist approach that takes into account features of the social context can help us understand the creation of gender distinctions.

Like other areas of gender research, studies of the household division of labor draw upon diverse conceptions of gender and pursue different objectives. While some examine gender differences in the type and amount of women's and men's household work, others want to uncover the meanings associated with these activities and the ways these meanings are produced. The former topics generally reflect an individualist view of gender, while the latter derive from an interactionist approach. Although men are performing more chores around the house than they used to, researchers still find that women have primary responsibility for housework and childcare. From an interactionist perspective, "doing" household work and caring for children are not merely activities one performs; rather, these activities help to create people's gendered sense of themselves.

Are some kinds of families (or relationships) better or worse for their participants than others? What role does gender play in all this? Researchers employing individualist and interactionist approaches have helped us explore some of these questions, keeping in mind, however, that they are extremely difficult questions to answer. Remember too that research can only tell us about general patterns and trends, which may or may not be true for a particular person or couple. Although sociologists cannot predict the success or happiness of any particular individual, we can say something about how people are affected by the kinds of intimate bonds they form (or do not form) and the kinds of factors that seem to matter.

Marriage has different consequences for women and men. Economically speaking, being married "pays off" for men. Employers seem to view married men as more responsible and productive workers. Women are not economically penalized by marriage, but married women – especially those with children – are sometimes assumed to be less committed to their jobs than women without family obligations. The psychological rewards of marriage also differ by sex. Bernard's "shock theory of marriage" posits that marriage requires women to accommodate more to men than vice versa, although evidence suggests that this may have changed somewhat. Lesbian and gay families are on the rise. These couples face some of the same issues faced by heterosexual couples, but also confront unique challenges.

FURTHER READING

Bianchi, Suzanne M., Milkie, Melissa A., Sayer, Liana C., and Robinson, John P. 2000. "Is Anyone Doing the Housework? Trends in the Gender Division of Household Labor." *Social Forces* 79: 191–228.

Coltrane, Scott. 1997. *Family Man: Fatherhood, Housework, and Gender Equity.* New York: Oxford University Press.

Hochschild, Arlie. 1989. *The Second Shift: Working Parents and the Revolution at Home.* New York: Viking Penguin.

Maccoby, Eleanor E. 1998. *The Two Sexes: Growing Up Apart, Coming Together.* Cambridge, MA: Harvard University Press.

McMahon, Martha. 1995. *Engendering Motherhood: Identity and Self-Transformation in Women's Lives.* Toronto: Guilford Press.

A CLOSER LOOK

Reading 1: Raising Gender-Aschematic Children

Sandra Lipsitz Bem

Feminist parents who wish to raise gender-aschematic children in a gender-schematic world are like any parents who wish to inculcate their children with beliefs and values that deviate from those of the dominant culture. Their major option is to try to undermine the dominant ideology before it can undermine theirs. Feminist parents are thus in a difficult situation. They cannot simply ignore gender in their child rearing as they might prefer to

From "Gender Schema Theory and Its Implications for Child Development: Raising Gender-aschematic Children in a Gender-schematic Society," *Signs* 8 (1983): 598–616.

do, because the society will then have free rein to teach their children the lessons about gender that it teaches all other children. Rather, they must manage somehow to inoculate their children against gender-schematic processing.

Two strategies are suggested here. First, parents can enable their children to learn about sex differences initially without their also learning the culture's sex-linked associative network by simultaneously retarding their children's knowledge of sex's cultural correlates and advancing their children's knowledge of sex's biological correlates. Second, parents can provide alternative or "subversive" schemata that their children can use to interpret the culture's sex-linked associative network whey they do learn it. This step is essential if children are not simply to learn gender-schematic processing somewhat later than their counterparts from more traditional homes. Whether one is a child or an adult, such alternative schemata "build up one's resistance" to the lessons of the dominant culture and thereby enable one to remain gender-aschematic even while living in a gender-schematic society.

TEACHING CHILDREN ABOUT SEX DIFFERENCES

Cultural correlates of sex. Children typically learn that gender is a sprawling associative network with ubiquitous functional importance through their observation of the many cultural correlates of sex existing in their society. Accordingly, the first step parents can take to retard the development of gender-schematic processing is to retard the child's knowledge of these cultural message about gender. Less crudely put, parents can attempt to attenuate sex-linked correlations within the child's social environment, thereby altering the basic data upon which the child will construct his or her own concepts of maleness and femaleness.

In part, parents can do this by eliminating sex stereotyping from their own behavior and from the alternatives that they provide for their children, just as many feminist parents are already doing. Among other things, for example, they can take turns making dinner, bathing the children, and driving the car; they can ensure that all their children – regardless of sex – have both trucks and dolls, both pink and blue clothing, and both male and female playmates; and they can arrange for their children to see women and men in nontraditional occupations.

When children are quite young, parents can further inhibit cultural messages about gender by actually censoring books and television programs whose explicit or implicit message is that the sexes differ on nonbiological dimensions. At present, this tactic will eliminate many children's books and most television programming. Ironically, it will also temporarily eliminate a number of feminist books designed to overcome sex stereotypes; even a book which insists that it is wrong for William not to be allowed to have a doll by implication teaches a child who has not yet learned the associative network that boys and dolls do not normally go together.

To compensate for this censorship, parents will need to seek out – and to create – materials that do not teach sex stereotypes. With our own children, my husband and I got into the habit of doctoring books whenever possible so as to remove all sex-linked correlations. We did this, among other ways, by changing the sex of the main character; by drawing longer hair and the outline of breasts onto illustrations of previously male truck drivers, physicians, pilots, and the like; and by deleting or altering sections of the text that described females or males in a sex-stereotyped manner. When reading children's picture books aloud, we also chose pronouns that avoided the ubiquitous implication that all characters without dresses or pink bows must necessarily be male: "And what is this little piggy doing? Why, he or she seems to be building a bridge."

All of these practices are designed to permit very young children to dwell temporarily in a social environment where, if the parents are lucky, the cultural correlations with sex will be attenuated from, say, .96 to .43. According to gender schema theory, this attenuation should retard the formation of the sex-linked associative network that will itself form the basis of the gender schema. By themselves, however, these practices teach children only what sex is not. But children must also be taught what sex is.

Biological correlates of sex. What remains when all of the cultural correlates of sex are attenuated or eliminated, of course, are two of the undisputed biological correlates of sex: anatomy and reproduction. Accordingly, parents can make these the definitional attributes of femaleness and maleness. By teaching their children that the genitalia constitute the definitive attributes of females and males, parents help them to apprehend the merely probabilistic nature of sex's cultural correlates and thereby restrict sex's associative sprawl. By teaching their children that whether one is female or male makes a difference only in the context of reproduction, parents limit sex's functional significance and thereby retard gender-schematic processing. Because children taught these lessons have been provided with an explicit and clear-cut rule about what sex is and when sex matters, they should be predisposed to construct their own concepts of femaleness and maleness based on biology, rather than on the cultural correlates to which they have been exposed. And to the extent that young children tend to interpret rules and categories rigidly rather than flexibly, this tendency will serve to enhance their belief that sex is to be narrowly defined in terms of anatomy and reproduction rather than to enhance a traditional belief that every arbitrary gender rule must be strictly obeyed and enforced. Thus there may be an irony, but there is no inconsistency, in the fact that an emphasis on the biological differences between the sexes should here be advocated as the basis for feminist child rearing.

The liberation that comes from having an unambiguous genital definition of sex and the imprisonment that comes from not having such a definition are nicely illustrated by the story of what happened to our son Jeremy, then age four, the day he decided to wear barrettes to nursery school. Several times that day, another little boy told Jeremy that he, Jeremy, must be a girl because "only girls wear barrettes." After trying to explain to this child that "wearing barrettes doesn't matter" and that "being a boy means having a penis and testicles," Jeremy finally pulled down his pants as a way of making his point more convincingly. The other child was not impressed. He simply said. "Everybody has a penis; only girls wear barrettes."

In the American context, children do not typically learn to define sex in terms of anatomy and reproduction until quite late, and, as a result, they – like the child in the example above – mistakenly treat many of the cultural correlates of sex as definitional. This confusion is facilitated, of course, by the fact that the genitalia themselves are not usually visible and hence cannot be relied on as a way of identifying someone's sex.

Accordingly, when our children asked whether someone was male or female, we frequently denied certain knowledge of the person's sex, emphasizing that without being able to see whether there was a penis or a vagina under the person's clothes, we had no definitive information. Moreover, when our children themselves began to utilize nonbiological markers as a way of identifying sex, we gently teased them about that strategy to remind them that the genitalia – and only the genitalia – consitute the definition of sex: "What do you mean that you can tell Chris is a girl because Chris has long hair? Does Chris's hair have a vagina?"

We found Stephanie Waxman's picture book *What is a Girl? What is a Boy?* to be a superb teaching aid in this context.[1] Each page displays a vivid and attractive photograph of a boy or a girl engaged in some behavior stereotyped as more typical of or more appropriate for the other sex. The accompanying text says such things as, "Some people say a girl is someone with jewelry, but Barry is wearing a necklace and he's a boy." The book ends with nude photographs of both children and adults, and it explicitly defines sex in terms of anatomy.

These particular lessons about what sex is, what sex is not, and when sex matters are designed to make young children far more naive than their peers about the cultural aspects of gender and far more sophisticated than their peers about the biological aspects of sex. Eventually, of course, their naiveté will begin to fade, and they too will begin to learn the culture's sprawling network of sex-linked associations. At that point, parents must take steps to prevent that associative network from itself becoming a cognitive schema.

PROVIDING ALTERNATIVE SCHEMATA

Let us presume that the feminist parent has successfully produced a child who defines sex in terms of anatomy and reproduction. How is such a child to understand the many sex-linked correlations that will inevitably begin to intrude upon his or her awareness? What alternative schemata can substitute for the gender schema in helping the child to organize and to assimilate gender-related information?

Individual differences schema. The first alternative schema is simply a child's version of the time-honored liberal truism used to counter stereotypic thinking in general, namely, that there is remarkable variability of individuals within groups as compared with the small mean differences between groups. To the child who says that girls do not like to play baseball, the feminist parent can thus point out that although it is true that some girls do not like to play baseball, it is also true that some girls do (e.g., your Aunt Beverly and Alissa who lives across the street) and that some boys do not (e.g., your dad and Alissa's brother Jimmy). It is, of course, useful for parents to supply themselves with a long list of counterexamples well in advance of such occasions.

This individual differences schema is designed to prevent children from interpreting individual differences as sex differences, from assimilating perceived differences among people to a gender schema. Simultaneously, it should also encourage children to treat as a given that the sexes are basically similar to one another and, hence, to view all glib assertions about sex differences as inherently suspect. And it is with this skepticism that feminist consciousness begins.

Cultural relativism schema. As the child's knowledge and awareness grow, he or she will gradually begin to realize that his or her family's beliefs and attitudes about gender are at variance with those of the dominant culture. Accordingly, the child needs some rationale for not simply accepting the majority view as the more valid. One possible rationale is cultural relativism, the notion that "different people believe different things" and that the coexistence of even contradictory beliefs is the rule in society rather than the exception.

Children can (and should) be introduced to the schema of cultural relativism long before it is pertinent to the domain of gender. For example, our children needed the rationale that "different people believe different things" in order to understand why they, but not the children next door, had to wear seat belts; why our family, but not the family next door, was casual about nudity in the home. The general principle that contradictory beliefs frequently coexist seems now to have become a readily available schema for our children, a schema that permits them to accept with relative equanimity that they have different beliefs from many of their peers with respect to gender.

Finally, the cultural relativism schema can solve one of the primary dilemmas of the liberal feminist parent: how to give one's children access to the riches of classical literature – as well as to the lesser riches of the mass media – without abandoning them to the forces that promote gender-schematic processing. Happily, the censorship of sex-stereotyped materials that is necessary to retard the initial growth of the sex-linked associative network when children are young can end once children have learned the critical lesson that cultural messages reflect the beliefs and attitudes of the person or persons who created those messages.

Accordingly, before we read our daughter her first volume of fairy tales, we discussed with her the cultural beliefs and attitudes about men and women that the tales would reflect, and while reading the tales, we frequently made such comments as, "Isn't it interesting that the person who wrote this story seems to think that girls always need to be rescued?" If such discussions are not too heavy-handed, they can provide a background of understanding against which the child can thoroughly enjoy the stories themselves, while still learning to discount the sex stereotypes within them as irrelevant both to their own beliefs and to truth. The cultural relativism schema thus brings children an awareness that fairy tales are fairy tales in more than one sense.

Sexism schema. Cultural relativism is fine in its place, but feminist parents will not and should not be satisfied to pretend that they think all ideas – particularly those about gender – are equally valid. At some point, they will feel compelled to declare that the view of women and men conveyed by fairy tales, by the mass media – and by the next-door neighbors – is not only different, but wrong. It is time to teach one's children about sexism.

Moreover, it is only by giving children a sexism schema, a coherent and organized understanding of the historical roots and the contemporaneous consequences of sex discrimination, that they will truly be able to comprehend why the sexes appear to be so different in our society: why, for example, there has never been a female president of the United Sates; why fathers do not stay home with their children; and why so many people believe these sex differences to be the natural consequence of biology. The child who has developed a readiness to encode and to organize information in terms of an evolving sexism schema is a child who is prepared to oppose actively the gender-related constraints that those with a gender schema will inevitably seek to impose.

The development of a sexism schema is nicely illustrated by our daughter Emily's response to Norma Klein's book *Girls Can Be Anything.*[2]

One of the characters is Adam Sobel, who insists that "girls are always nurses and boys are always doctors" and that "girls can't be pilots, . . . they have to be stewardesses." After reading this book, our daughter, then age four, spontaneously began to label with contempt anyone who voiced stereotyped beliefs about gender an "Adam Sobel." Adam Sobel thus became for her the nucleus of an envolving sexism schema, a schema that enables her now to perceive – and also to become morally outraged by and to oppose – whatever sex discrimination she meets in daily life.

As feminist parents, we wish it could have been possible to raise our children with neither a gender schema nor a sexism schema. At this historical moment, however, that is not an option. Rather we must choose either to have our children become gender schematic and hence sex typed, or to have our children become sexism schematic and hence feminists. We have chosen the latter.

NOTES

1 Stephanie Waxman, *What is a Girl? What is a Boy?* (Culver City, CA: Peace Press. 1976).
2 Norma Klein, *Girls Can Be Anything* (New York: E. P. Dutton. 1973).

> Does Bem believe it is possible to raise gender-aschematic children? In your view, should children be raised in a gender-aschematic way? What is the meaning of Bem's distinction between gender-schematic and sexism-schematic?

Reading 2: *The Meaning of Motherhood in Black Culture*

Patricia Hill Collins

BLOODMOTHERS, OTHERMOTHERS, AND WOMEN-CENTERED NETWORKS

In African American communities, the boundaries distinguishing biological mothers of children from other women who care for children are often fluid

From *Black Feminist Thought: Knowledge, Consciousness, and the Politics of Empowerment* (Boston, MA: Unwin Hyman, 1990).

LIVERPOOL JOHN MOORES UNIVERSITY
LEARNING SERVICES

and changing. Biological mothers or bloodmothers are expected to care for their children. But African and African American communities have also recognized that vesting one person with full responsibility for mothering a child may not be wise or possible. As a result, "othermothers," women who assist bloodmothers by sharing mothering responsibilities, traditionally have been central to the institution of Black motherhood.[1]

The centrality of women in African American extended families is well known.[2] Organized, resilient, women-centered networks of bloodmothers and othermothers are key in understanding this centrality: Grandmothers, sisters, aunts, or cousins acted as othermothers by taking on child care responsibilities for each other's children. When needed, temporary child-care arrangements turned into long-term care or informal adoption.[3]

In African American communities, these women-centered networks of community-based child care often extend beyond the boundaries of bio-logically related extended families to support "fictive kin."[4] Civil rights activist Ella Baker describes how informal adoption by othermothers func-tioned in the Southern, rural community of her childhood:

> My aunt who had thirteen children of her own raised three more. She had become a midwife, and a child was born who was covered with sores. Nobody was particularly wanting the child, so she took the child and raised him . . . and another mother decided she didn't want to be bothered with two children. So my aunt took one and raised him . . . they were part of the family.[5]

Even when relationships were not between kin or fictive kin, African American community norms were such that neighbors cared for each other's children. In the following passage, Sara Brooks, a Southern domestic worker, describes the importance of the community-based child care that a neighbor offered her daughter. In doing so, she also shows how the African American cultural value placed on cooperative child care found institutional support in the adverse conditions under which so many Black women mothered.

> She kept Vivian and she didn't charge me nothin either. You see, people used to look after each other, but now it's not that way. I reckon it's because we all was poor, and I guess they put theirself in the place of the person that they was helpin.[6]

Othermothers were key not only in supporting children but also in sup-porting bloodmothers who, for whatever reason, were ill-prepared or had little desire to care for their children. Given the pressures from the larger political economy, the emphasis placed on community-based child care and the respect given to othermothers who assume the responsibilities of child care have served a critical function in African American communities. Children orphaned by sale or death of their parents under slavery; children conceived through rape; children of young mothers; children born into extreme poverty; or children, who for other reasons have been rejected by their bloodmothers, have all been supported by othermothers who, like Ella Baker's aunt, took in additional children, even when they had enough of their own.

PROVIDING AS PART OF MOTHERING

The work done by African American women in providing the economic resources essential to Black family well-being affects motherhood in a contradictory fashion. On the one hand, African American women have long integrated their activities as economic providers into their mothering relationships. In contrast to the cult of true womanhood where work is defined as being in opposition to and incompatible with motherhood, work for Black women has been an important and valued dimension of Afro-centric definitions of Black motherhood. On the other hand, African American women's experiences as mothers under oppression were such that the type and purpose of work Black women forced to do greatly impacted on the type of mothering relationships bloodmothers and othermothers had with Black children.

While slavery both disrupted West African patterns and exposed enslaved Africans to the gender ideologies and practices of slaveowners, it simultaneously made it impossible, had they wanted to do so, for enslaved Africans to implement slaveowner's ideologies. Thus, the separate spheres of providing as a male domain and affective nurturing as a female domain did not develop within African American families.[7] Providing for Black children's physical survival and attending to their affective, emotional needs continued as interdependent dimensions of an Afrocentric ideology of motherhood. However, by changing the conditions under which Black women worked and the purpose of the work itself, slavery introduced the problem of how best to continue traditional Afrocentric values under oppressive conditions. Institutions of community-based child care, informal adoption, greater reliance on othermothers, all emerge as adaptations to the exigencies of combining exploitative work with nurturing children.

In spite of the change in political status brought on by emancipation, the majority of African American women remained exploited agricultural workers. However, their placement in southern political economies allowed them to combine child care with field labor. Sara Brooks describes how strong the links between providing and caring for others were for her:

When I was about nine I was nursin my sister Sally – I'm about seven or eight years older than Sally. And when I would put her to sleep, instead of me goin somewhere and sit down and play, I'd get my little old hoe and get out there and work right in the field around the house.[8]

Black women's shift from southern agriculture to domestic work in southern and northern towns and cities represented a change in the type of work done, but not in the meaning of work to women and their families. Whether they wanted to or not, the majority of African American women had to work and could not afford the luxury of motherhood as a non-economically productive, female "occupation."

COMMUNITY OTHERMOTHERS AND SOCIAL ACTIVISM

Black women's experiences as othermothers have provided a foundation for Black women's social activism. Black women's feelings of responsibility for nurturing the children in their own extended family network have stimulated a more generalized ethic of care where Black women feel accountable to all the Black community's children.

This notion of Black women as community othermothers for all Black children traditionally allowed Black women to treat biologically unrelated children as if they were members of their own families. For example, sociologist Karen Fields describes how her grandmother, Mamie Garvin Fields, draws on her power as a community othermother when dealing with unfamiliar children.

She will say to a child on the street who looks up to no good, picking out a name at random, "Aren't you Miz Pinckney's boy?" in that same reproving tone. If the reply is, "No, ma'am, my mother is Miz Gadsden," whatever threat there was dissipates.[9]

The use of family language in referring to members of the Black community also illustrates this dimension of Black motherhood. For example, Mamie Garvin Fields describes how she became active in surveying the poor housing conditions of Black people in Charleston.

I was one of the volunteers they got to make a survey of the places where we were paying extortious rents for indescribable property. I said "we," although it wasn't Bob and me. We had our own home, and so did many of the Federated Women. Yet we still felt like it really was "we" living in those terrible places, and it was up to us to do something about them.[10]

To take another example, while describing her increasingly successful efforts to teach a boy who had given other teachers problems, my daughter's kindergarten teacher stated, "You know how it can be – the majority of the children in the learning disabled classes are *our children*. I know he didn't belong there, so I volunteered to take him." In these statements, both women invoke the language of family to describe the ties that bind them as Black women to their responsibilities to other members of the Black community as family.

Sociologist Cheryl Gilkes suggests that community othermother relationships are sometimes behind Black women's decisions to become community activists.[11] Gilkes notes that many of the Black women community activists in her study became involved in community organizing in response to the needs of their own children and of those in their communities. The following comment is typical of how many of the Black women in Gilkes' study relate to Black children: "There were a lot of summer programs springing up for kids, but they were exclusive . . . and I found that most of *our kids* (emphasis mine) were excluded."[12] For many women, what began as the daily expression of their obligations as community othermothers, as was the case for the kindergarten teacher, developed into full-fledged roles as community leaders.

NOTES

1   The terms used in this section appear in Rosalie Riegle Troester, "Turbulence and Tenderness: Mothers, Daughters, and Othermothers" in Paule Marshall's *Brown Girl, Brownstones," SAGE: A Scholarly Journal on Black Women* 1 (Fall 1984): 13–16.

2   See Tanner's discussion of matrifocality in Nancy Tanner, "Matrifocality in Indonesia and Africa among Black Americans," in *Woman, Culture, and Society*, ed. Michelle Z. Rosaldo and Louise Lamphere (Stanford, CA: Stanford University Press, 1974), pp. 125–56; see also Carrie Allen McCray, "The Black Women and Family Roles," in *The Black Woman*, ed. LaFrances Rogers-Rose (Beverly Hill, CA: Sage, 1980), pp. 67–78; Elmer Martin and Joanne Mitchell Martin, *The Black Extended Family* (Chicago: University of Chicago, 1978); Joyce Aschenbrenner, *Lifelines: Black Families in Chicago* (Prospect Heights, IL: Waveland, 1975); and Carol B. Stack, *All Our Kin* (New York: Harper & Row, 1974).

3   Martin and Martin, *The Black Extended Family*; Stack, *All Our Kin*; and Virginia Young, "Family and Childhood in a Southern Negro Community," *American Anthropologist* 72 (1970): 269–88.

4   Stack, *All Our Kin*.

5   Ellen Cantarow, *Moving the Mountain: Women Working for Social Change* (Old Westbury, NY: Feminist Press, 1980), p. 59.

6   Thordis Simonsen, ed., *You May Plow Here: The Narrative of Sara Brooks* (New York: Touchstone, 1986), p. 81.

7   Deborah White, *Arn't I a Woman? Female Slaves in the Plantation South* (New York: W. W. Norton, 1984); Bonnie Thornton Dill, "Our Mothers' Grief: Racial Ethnic Women and the Maintenance of Families," Research Paper 4, Center for Research on Women (Memphis, TN: Memphis State University, 1986); Leith Mullings, "Uneven Development: Class, Race and Gender in the United States before 1900," in *Women's Work, Development and the Division of Labor by Gender*, eds. Eleanor Leacock and Helen Safa (South Hadley, MA: Bergin & Garvey, 1986), pp. 41–57.

8   Simonsen, *You May Plow Here*, p. 86.

9   Mamie Garvin Fields and Karen Fields, *Lemon Swamp and Other Places: A Carolina Memoir* (New York: Free Press, 1983), p. xvii.

10 Ibid., p. 195.

11 Cheryl Gilkes, "'Holding Back the Ocean with a Broom,' Black Women and Community Work," in Rogers-Rose, *The Black Woman*, pp. 217–31; "Going Up for the Oppressed: The Career Mobility of Black Women Community Workers," *Journal of Social Issues* 39 (1983): 115–39.

12 Gilkes, "'Holding Back,'" p. 219.

What are "othermothers"? How does Collins link the importance of othermothers to the social organization of black family life?

Reading 3: The Wage Penalty for Motherhood

Michelle J. Budig and Paula England

[. . .]

We find a wage penalty for motherhood of approximately 7 percent per child among young American women. Roughly one-third of the penalty is explained by years of past job experience and seniority, including whether past work was part-time. That is, for some women, motherhood leads to employment breaks, part-time employment, and the accumulation of fewer years of experience and seniority, all of which diminish future earning. However, it is striking that about two-thirds of the child penalty remains after controlling for elaborate measures of work experience.

We added numerous job characteristics to models to assess whether mothers earn less because their jobs are less demanding or because they offer mother-friendly characteristics. These factors had only a small effect in explaining the child penalty, and about half of the effect came from a

From "The Wage Penalty for Motherhood," *American Sociological Review* 66 (2001): 204–25.

single job characteristic – whether the current job is part-time. Most job characteristics had no effect on the motherhood penalty – either because the characteristics don't affect pay or because motherhood does not affect whether women hold these jobs.

In what social locations are motherhood penalties the steepest? Black women and Latinas have smaller penalties, but only for the third and subsequent births. Never-married women have lower child penalties than married or divorced women. Second children reduce wages more than a first child, especially for married women. There is no evidence that penalties are proportionately greater for women in more demanding or high-level jobs, or "male" jobs, or for more educated women, although the penalties are higher for women who work full-time and already have more work experience.

Our use of fixed-effects modeling gives us some confidence that the effects of motherhood identified here are causal rather than spurious. Further, our detailed measures of work experience assure us that no more than one-third of the motherhood penalty arises because motherhood interrupts women's employment, leading to breaks, more par-time work, and fewer years of experience and seniority. Finally, we find that little of the child penalty is explained by mothers' placement in jobs with characteristics associated with low pay. However, we did not have direct measures of many job characteristics that would make jobs easier to combine with parenting. Thus, we may have underestimated the importance of this particular factor. For future research to be able to answer this question and generalize to the nation as a whole, we need the inclusion of questions about job characteristics that accommodate parenting on national surveys using probability sampling, preferably panels.

What explains the approximately two-thirds of the 7-percent-per-child penalty not explained by the reductions motherhood makes in women's job experience, if little of it is from working in less demanding or mother-friendly job? The remaining motherhood penalty of about 4 percent per child may arise from effects of motherhood on productivity and/or from employer discrimination. A weakness of social science research is that direct measures of either productivity or discrimination are rarely available. Thus, new approaches to measuring productivity or discrimination would be a welcome contribution. In the meantime, our analyses provide indirect evidence that at least part of the child penalty may result from mothers being less productive in a given hour of paid work because they are more exhausted or distracted. Net of human capital variables, women earn less with each subsequent child, and children reduce women's pay more if the mothers are married or divorced than if they are never-married. Employers may discriminate against all women by treating them all like mothers, or they may discriminate against all mothers relative to other women. But is it plausible that employers discriminate by number of children, and discriminate more against married mothers than single mothers (but give a premium for marriage when women have no child or one child)? This seems far fetched. This does *not* mean that *none* of the child penalty is discriminatory. It may be that a base amount is discriminatory, and that the portion that is related to productivity is the portion that varies by number of children and marital status, because those factors affect decisions about how time and energy is allocated between child rearing and jobs.

How should public policy respond to wage penalties for motherhood? Because distinguishing between discriminatory and non-discriminatory differences by race and sex is institutionalized in our legal system, it is tempting to conclude that a motherhood penalty is not of public concern unless it results from employers' discrimination. We don't know how much of the penalty arises from discrimination in the form of "differential treatment" of equivalently qualified and productive mothers and non-mothers. Nor do we know how many policies that have a disparate impact on mothers would fail the legal standard of being a "business necessity." But we think there is a serious equity problem, *even if* the penalty were found to be entirely explained by mothers having less work experience, lower productivity, and choosing mother-friendly jobs, and *even if* employers' policies had the intent and effect only of maximizing output relative to costs. In short, we think there is a serious equity problem when we all free ride on the benefits of mother's labor, while mothers bear much of the costs of rearing children. At this point we depart from the narrow scientific analysis, and articulate our findings with a normatively based notion of equity.

Reducing the extent to which mothers bear the costs of rearing children is a worthy goal, in our view. Broadening the concept of discrimination to include anything about how jobs are structured or what is rewarded that has a disparate impact on mothers, and making employers change such policies, would be one way to approach this. But should employers have to get rid to *any* policy that penalizes mothers? We suspect that this would reduce the net output of organizations because policies that reward experienced workers and workers who can work long hours when needed by the employer would need to be changed. Of course, the net effect on output is an empirical question; in some cases the productivity gains resulting from increased morale and continuity of mothers' employment would offset costs.

But if there are costs to employers of restructuring work to eliminate the motherhood penalty, deciding who should pay them is part of the larger question of who should bear the costs of raising the next generation. A general equity principle is that those who receive benefits should share in the costs. As Marxist feminists pointed out in the 1970s, capitalist employers benefit from the unpaid work of mothers, who raise the next generation of workers. But employers are not the only ones who benefit when children are well reared – we all free ride on mothers' labor. Thus, mandating that employers share in these costs makes sense only as part of a broader redistribution of the costs of child rearing.

Those who rear children deserve public support precisely because the benefits of child rearing diffuse to other members of society. Indeed, child rearing (whether unpaid or paid), broadly construed, creates more diffuse social benefits do than most kinds of work. In our view, the equitable solution would be to collectivize the costs of child rearing broadly – to be paid not just by employers but by all citizens – because the benefits diffuse broadly. While most US mothers today are employed, mothers continue also to bear the lion's share of the costs of rearing children. Yet other industrial democracies have collectivized the costs to a much greater extent than has the United States (albeit often with other, pronatalist, motivations). Costs can be socialized through family allowances, child care, and medical care that are financed by progressive taxes. Adopting such policies in the United States would not eliminate the fact that motherhood lowers wages, although it might reduce some of the gross effect if the presence of subsidized child care increased women's employment. Such policies would put a floor under the poverty of families with mothers, and would redistribute resources toward those who now pay a disproportionate share of the costs of rearing children. In a period when most mothers are employed, when welfare mothers are being required to take jobs, and when the economy is generating budget surpluses unthinkable a decade ago, there may be a political opening for creative proposals that would increase equity for mothers while also helping children.

Should public policy respond to the motherhood wage penalty? What is Budig and England's argument? Do you agree?

6

Gendered Jobs and Gendered Workers

CHAPTER OBJECTIVES

- Explain and critically evaluate alternative explanations for sex segregation

- Discuss the ways that jobs, occupations, and work hierarchies are gender-typed

- Explain how wages are determined and how gender enters into the wage-setting process

Classical sociologists Karl Marx and Max Weber had much to say about the industrial capitalist workplace. For Marx, capitalist means of production unleashed tremendous productivity, but the social relations of work were exploitative and alienating for workers. Weber called attention to the forces of bureaucratization that were transforming all institutions, including the institution of work. Marx and Weber's observations have long served as the foundation for sociological analyses of the workplace.

Neither theorist, however, had much to say about gender. Rather, both seemed to suggest that the processes they described were gender-neutral, meaning that they were somehow generic and general, unaffected by and separate from gender meanings and distinctions. Many have critiqued these understandings of work for their assumption of gender neutrality and suggested that gender is embedded in, not separate from, organizational processes.

This chapter considers three ways in which gender may be incorporated into the workings of employment. First, gender shapes the social organization of work, expressed primarily in the sex segregation of occupations, jobs, and firms. Second, gender shapes the meanings people assign to particular occupations, jobs, and work activities, leading us to see some as more appropriate for women and some as more appropriate for men. Third, gender shapes the "worth" of jobs, leading some jobs to be more valued and paid more than other jobs. As we explore these issues, we will be drawing from individualist, interactionist, and institutional perspectives.

EXPLAINING THE SEX SEGREGATION OF JOBS AND OCCUPATIONS

Recall that sex segregation refers to the concentration of women and men into different jobs, occupations, and firms. In Chapter 5, we looked at the levels of sex segregation over time and place. Here, I shift the focus to understanding the factors that best explain why women and men work in different jobs, occupations, and firms. Individualist, interactionist, and institutional perspectives offer somewhat differ views on this issue. Examining these views allows us to revisit each perspective and look closely at the different ways they approach the study of gender. Because sex segregation does not have a single cause or explanation, each perspective has something to contribute.

The choices of gendered workers: the individualist view

There are several ways we might expect male and female workers' characteristics to contribute to sex segregation. First, it may be that the sex composition of an occupation or job is a function of sex-specific preferences, skills, and abilities. If women and men possess different "bundles" of these characteristics, they may end up in – and be best suited for – different kinds of work. In this view, then, women and men are not really "substitutable" for one another.

While intuitively appealing, however, this argument receives limited empirical support. With the exception of two jobs that can *only* be performed by one particular sex (i.e., wet nurse and sperm donor!), there is scant evidence that women and men are incapable of doing jobs typically performed by the other sex. Historical research on the Second World War, for example, shows that when men were unavailable, women filled many jobs that were performed almost exclusively by men prior to the war. As Milkman (1987: 50) notes, jobs "that had previously been viewed as quintessentially masculine were suddenly endowed with femininity and glamour for the duration. The war mobilization era not only illustrates the resilience of job segregation by sex, but also graphically demonstrates how idioms of sex-typing can be flexibly applied to whatever jobs women and men happen to be doing." Hence, "masculine" jobs that had been filled by men prior to the war were relabeled as appropriate for women during wartime when female workers were in demand.

Gender socialization

The process of gender socialization is another kind of individualist explanation for sex segregation. As we know from earlier chapters, a socialization perspective emphasizes the ways in which men and women develop different traits, abilities, values, and skills. To the extent that this occurs, men and women would be expected to approach work differently, make different kinds of choices, and consequently end up in different kinds of occupations.

Research by Tomaskovic-Devey (1993) sheds light on socialization accounts of employment. He hypothesized that because traditional gender roles have loosened somewhat over time, younger workers would be less likely than older workers to choose more sex-typical occupations. In other words, as socialization practices change, so, too, should occupational choices. Tomaskovic-Devey (1993) found that his hypothesis received support among women, but not among men. Younger women are more likely than older women to be employed in sex-integrated jobs, but this is not the case among men.

While socialization accounts of women's and men's occupational positions are intuitively appealing, they are not completely satisfactory. There are two general kinds of criticisms of these arguments. The first is a straightforward empirical critique: Is the empirical evidence consistent with these explanations? The second critique may be more difficult to grasp, as it challenges the assumptions underlying socialization explanations for behavior.

Empirically, socialization explanations for women's and men's different occupational locations receive very mixed support. For example, while children's occupational aspirations are highly gender-typed, these differences get smaller as children age and enter adulthood. For example, Stroeher's (1994) qualitative study of two kindergartens found that girls preferred traditional female careers. Research on older cohorts, however, finds little evidence for these preferences. Marini and Shu (1998), for example, show that young women's occupational aspirations have changed dramatically over time. Younger women were less likely than older women to aspire to predominantly female occupations and were more likely to aspire to occupations with higher earnings' potential. These changes occurred among all social classes and racial groups, to some extent, though were particularly strong among women from higher socioeconomic backgrounds. Men's occupational aspirations remained relatively stable across the birth cohorts in Shu and Marini's study.

Finally, it is doubtful that the link between young people's aspirations and later employment is a strong one. Research on individual careers also challenges the notion that sex segregation reflects sex differences in capabilities and skills. Jacobs (1989: 186), for example, found that women's and men's aspirations, college majors, and occupations show considerable "sex-type mobility." Moreover, among both women and men who change aspirations, college majors, or occupations, there is only a weak relationship between the sex-type of the original position and the destination position. In other words, while women's and men's occupational aspirations, skills, and choices may be influenced by sex, sex-typed preferences are fluid and not strongly linked to the sex composition of a worker's job (Reskin and Hartmann 1986).

Research by sociologist Kathleen Gerson also supports this claim. Gerson's (1985, 1993) interest in women's and men's work and family decisions led her to explore the role people's childhood experiences played in their lives. Not surprisingly, given our previous discussion, Gerson found that childhood plans and experiences, while not insignificant, explained very little about people's adult lives. Describing a group of men whose lives she explored, Gerson explains: "Among the men whose life paths we will trace, some recreated the patterns of their childhood environment but most did not. Over time, these men had experiences that led them to reassess the meaning of their parents' lives and their own early outlooks. Childhood experiences neither prepared them for the obstacles and challenges of adulthood in a rapidly changing world nor determined how they would react. The childhood context simply provided them with a point of departure" (1993: 61).

Do women and men have different work-related values? Empirical support for sex differences in this domain is weak. In a recent study of this issue, Rowe and Snizek (1995) examined data from twelve national samples of the US population, spanning the years 1973 to 1990. Survey respondents were asked to rank five work values, ranging from most to least preferred in a job. Contrary to predictions from socialization theory, Rowe and Snizek (1995) found that women and men ranked each value in exactly the same order of preference: Feeling of accomplishment, high income, chance for advancement, job security, and short working hours (from most to least preferred). Moreover, these researchers found no real changes over time in the magnitude of sex differences. Work values, as measured in this study, had more to do with factors such as age, education, and occupational prestige than sex. Research by Lefkowitz (1994) also challenges socialization arguments. Lefkowitz examined sex differences in almost 50 job attitudes, work values, and reactions to work. Virtually all of the differences disappeared when income, education, and occupation level were controlled. In other words, differences in job attitudes, values, and reactions to work that some may have attributed to sex can be better understood as differences due to factors such as education and income. Sex itself has little explanatory power as far as job attitudes, values, and reactions are concerned.

Yet another kind of empirical challenge to socialization accounts comes from research on women and men in gender-*atypical* occupations. From a socialization perspective, the different socialization boys and girls receive should lead each sex to make different occupational choices. To the extent that this occurs, sex segregation will result. Obviously, some women and some men do not end up in sex-typical occupations, but rather are employed in occupations where their sex is a minority. Women become engineers, men teach elementary school or become nurses. From a socialization perspective, these outcomes – like more traditional occupational choices – should be the result of early socialization. Have women and men who enter sex-atypical occupations been socialized differently from those who enter more sex-typical occupations? Contrary to a socialization account, however, the answer to this question seems to be "no."

Williams's (1989, 1995) research on female Marines and men employed as nurses, social workers, librarians, and elementary school teachers suggests that factors *other* than childhood socialization explain these sex-atypical careers. Women who joined the Marine Corps, for example, maintained a female gender identity and a sense of themselves as feminine. Most joined the Marines for quite practical and pragmatic reasons, such as a desire for financial security, and very few joined out of a desire to challenge traditional gender roles. In other words, the female Marines Williams studied were very much like other women. Similarly, Williams rejects the claim that men who become nurses or elementary school teachers are less masculine than other men or that they pursue these occupations as a result of childhood socialization. Indeed, she found that men in sex-atypical occupations often did not even consider these fields until college and ended up pursuing them as a result of experiences they had as adults. Williams's research thus challenges the claim that gender socialization during childhood leads women and men into different kinds of occupations as adults.

These empirical challenges to socialization accounts have been accompanied by other critiques of this approach. Socialization theory assumes that people make choices and that these choices are shaped by their prior experiences, particularly those occurring in childhood. While early experience *is* important, sociologists like Gerson, Williams, and others argue that people's occupational choices are formed less by experiences in childhood or adolescence than they are by the circumstances of adulthood. In particular, people respond to opportunities, often pursuing paths never dreamed of years earlier. For example, one of the men interviewed in Williams's (1995) study described his entrance into elementary school teaching in this way:

> My roommate was an education major, and he said there was this class that you would get an A in without doing any homework . . . I was very reluctant to take any courses in the education department . . . I just hated the thought of teaching. But he said this one course . . . you would go out to a school, you sit in the back of the room, you do observation, that's all you have to do. So, I did that. I got sent to a first grade classroom, and fell in love with the miniature furniture and the little kids [laughs] and basically . . . I was pretty much hooked after that. (1995: 55–6)

This man clearly never aspired to teach elementary school, but instead responded to a suggestion from a friend. He discovered that he enjoyed something he had never really thought about pursuing as a career. This example helps explain why the occupational aspirations – especially those formed prior to adulthood – are such poor predictors of later occupational location. People may adjust and change their aspirations as new opportunities present themselves and others are closed off.

Longitudinal studies that examine how the sex composition of occupations has changed over time and identify factors associated with a change from predominantly male to predominantly female (or vice versa) also help us understand the factors that create and sustain sex segregation. In their research on the changing sex composition of occupations, Reskin and Roos (1990) concluded that the sex composition of occupations and jobs has less to do with sex-specific task requirements and more to do with the supply and demand for male and female labor, and with related social forces that are continually altering the relative desirability of jobs and occupations.

Human capital theory

Socialization accounts of occupational choice view these choices as growing out of people's encounters with parents, peers, and others. Economists treat issues of occupational choice and the gendered worker much more narrowly: They argue that people are motivated primarily by an economic calculus, seeking to reduce costs and increase rewards by choosing one occupation over another. To understand how this applies to issues of gender, we must consider the concept of **human capital**. Human capital refers to those things that increase one's productivity. Human capital theorists suggest that people invest in their own human capital – through actions such as going to college or acquiring on-the-job-training – with the expectation that this investment will eventually pay off for them economically. Two people who make different kinds of investments thus will acquire different types and amounts of human capital. Further, these theorists assume that people are economically rational – that is, they will try to avoid bad investments and gravitate toward those where the rewards of the investment outweigh the costs.

Human capital theorists believe that women and men, on average, make different kinds of human capital investments. As a result, men and women are not really "substitutable" for one another in the labor market; they look different to an employer and thus end up working in different kinds of jobs. Why should investments in human capital be differentiated by sex? Human capital theorists trace this to one simple fact: women bear children and men do not. While not all women have children, most do or at least plan on doing so. Human capital theorists believe that this alters women's human capital investment "strategies" by orienting them toward occupations that do not penalize them for child-bearing and rearing (Polachek 1979). However, because men neither bear nor have primary responsibility for children, they make a different sort of human capital investment. In particular, according to Polachek, men choose jobs where their human capital will "appreciate" (or grow in value) over time.

Human capital theory thus provides an explanation for sex segregation that rests on women's and men's choices – particularly their decisions regarding investments in human capital. Like socialization theory, it implies that women and men are different from one another when they enter the labor market. Employers respond to these differences, but do not create them. There are two other implications of this theory that are worth noting. First, this perspective implies that women who neither marry nor bear children would be less likely than other women to work in predominantly female jobs. In other words, these women would be most "like" men in their labor-market behavior. Second, human capital theory implies that predominantly female jobs would be more compatible with childbearing and rearing than other occupations. If women act rationally and seek jobs that facilitate care for children, human capital theorists would predict that jobs filled by women would indeed be more child-friendly than jobs filled mostly by men.

Like socialization accounts, human capital theory provides an intuitively appealing explanation for sex segregation. It is consistent with at least some conventional wisdom suggesting that women's jobs are more compatible with children than jobs occupied by men. Despite its intuitive appeal, however, human capital theory does not provide a satisfactory account of sex segregation. In a series of articles, Paula England (1982, 1984; England

and Farkas 1986) shows that predominantly female jobs are not easier than other jobs to re-enter after leaving the labor force. Challenging another claim of these theorists, Beller (1982) and Tomaskovic-Devey (1993) found that single and childless women were as likely to be employed in predominantly female jobs as married women and women with children. In other words, women who "look like men" (i.e., do not have primary responsibility for children) are no more likely than other women to be employed in a job containing men.

Another challenge to human capital accounts of sex segregation comes from research on jobs and job characteristics that are compatible with bearing and raising children. Contrary to popular belief, women – even those with children – identify job characteristics that are more available in predominantly male as compared to predominantly female jobs as compatible with caring for children. Glass and Camarigg (1992), for example, found that both women and men identified schedule flexibility and ease of job performance as factors reducing their job–family conflict. However, working mothers in their sample were no more likely than others to hold jobs possessing these characteristics, nor were predominantly female jobs more likely than other jobs to possess characteristics believed to reduce job–family conflict.

Finally, a central problem with human capital accounts of sex segregation is the validity of its claims regarding sex differences in levels of human capital. Most researchers recognize years of education as one useful measure of human capital. Even at the highest levels of education, however, the gap between women and men on this measure has closed. In 2000, women received 57 percent of all undergraduate degrees, 58 percent of all master's degrees, and 42 percent of all doctoral degrees (US Department of Education 2001). If differences in human capital explain sex segregation, however, we would have expected sex segregation to decline by a much more significant amount than it has declined. The education gap has closed but women and men continue to work in fields dominated by members of their own sex. Other traditional measures of human capital, such as years of work experience, show similar trends. Women and men are much more alike with respect to the kinds of things that make them productive employees than they were 20 years ago.

In short, there is little evidence to support the claim that sex segregation in paid employment reflects sex differences in job-related preferences, skills, and abilities. Individualist perspectives thus offer only a partial account of this process. This does *not* mean that women's responsibilities for children are unrelated to their experiences in the paid labor market. Rather, the research suggests that these responsibilities are not the cause of sex segregation in paid employment.

The opportunity structure:
interactionist and institutional perspectives

The factors that explain how and why people get the jobs they do may have less to do with workers' choices and more to do with the opportunity structure and employers' actions. In this view, the social relations of work – including encounters between employers and workers, and among workers – and the structure of jobs and firms explain how segregation is perpetuated.

Employers play important roles in creating and maintaining sex segregation because employers – in the form of their personnel managers or other gatekeepers – are the ones who assign workers to jobs. Passage of Title IV in 1964 Civil Rights Act made it illegal to formally reserve some jobs for men and some for women. Nevertheless, segregation can be maintained by employer practices when making job assignments. To understand how this occurs, we must consider the role of sex-based discrimination.

Sex discrimination by employers

Jencks (1992) identifies five types of discrimination: myopic, principled, statistical, consumer-driven, and worker-driven. In Jencks's view, the first two forms of discrimination are usually economically irrational, while the latter three may have economic benefits for employers. With respect to sex, myopic and principled discrimination reflect either employers' short-sightedness (i.e., myopia) or their belief in male (or female) superiority. Jencks argues that, in most cases, employers who practice either form of discrimination (and thereby hire only men or only women) are behaving in economically costly ways. By excluding all members of one sex from consideration for a job, employers are limiting their pool of candidates, thus decreasing supply and potentially driving up the wages they must pay. Jencks and other economists thus predict that these forms of discrimination should only occur among employers that are less sensitive to market considerations.

The three other forms of discrimination discussed by Jencks are more insidious, however, and much more difficult to eliminate. In fact, because these forms of discrimination may produce economic benefits for employers, employers may be motivated to engage in them. Of these three economically rational forms of discrimination, **statistical discrimination** has received the most attention. This form of discrimination occurs when an individual applying for a job is treated as if he or she possesses the qualities and characteristics "typical" for his or her sex. For example, there is a small, average difference between the height of women and men in

American society. As a result, employers who needed to fill a job with people who were at least six feet tall could decide to exclude all women from consideration on the assumption that the average woman is less likely to meet this height requirement than the average man. Employers who used sex as a device to screen prospective employees on height would likely be able to find qualified job candidates. Some men they considered would not be tall enough and they would exclude from consideration some women who met the height requirement. Overall, however, they would not be excluding very many qualified candidates nor including many applicants who were unqualified.

When employers statistically discriminate, they are assumed to be *correctly* assigning group averages to individuals. This distinguishes statistical discrimination from discrimination resulting from employers' use of incorrect, exaggerated, or unsubstantiated stereotypes to hire or assign jobs to workers. The issue of whether or not employers' views are accurate is important. Consider this example (modified from Jencks 1992: 42–3):

> Suppose a bank has found over the years that its [female] tellers make slightly more mistakes than its [male] tellers. Suppose that when all else is equal [men] with four years of college perform as well as [women] with two years of college, while [men] with two years of college perform as well as [female] high-school graduates. If this were the bank's experience, an economically rational policy would be to hire only [men] only if they had at least two more years of schooling than otherwise similar [women.] Statistical discrimination of this kind would be illegal, but it might nonetheless make economic sense from the bank's viewpoint.

As this example makes clear, employers sometimes discover on their own, or learn about from other sources, the existence of average group differences in performance or other job-related characteristics. This information can then be used to make hiring decisions. Group characteristics, such as sex or age, thus become screening devices used by employers to identify qualified workers and to exclude those less qualified. For instance, the bank in the above example could decide to exclude all men from teller positions and hire only women. If, as statistical discrimination accounts suggest, employers like the bank have correct information about group differences, then a decision to screen out all members of a particular sex is economically rational. (That is, employers engaging in this practice will, on average, be considering workers who are qualified and excluding those who are less so.)

How does this argument apply to sex? Most important, research suggests that women are most likely to be excluded from jobs that require a large employer investment in on-the-job training. Employers hiring for these positions may correctly conclude that women are more likely than men to have primary responsibility for childcare, to take parental leave, and to leave their job when a spouse's job requires a move. Employers may therefore conclude that women will be more costly to employ in these positions than men, and thus may exclude all or most women from such jobs. Of course, any individual woman may or may not be different from any individual man regarding intent to remain with the employer for an extended time. Employers who fail to determine this on an individual basis may be guilty of sex discrimination.

Research suggests that statistical discrimination does help explain women's low representation in certain types of jobs. In their study of California work establishments, Bielby and Baron (1986) found that women were more likely than men to be employed in jobs involving finger dexterity, while jobs requiring spatial skills, nonrepetitive tasks, and eye-hand–foot coordination were more likely to be assigned to men. Bielby and Baron (1986) suggest that these differences in job assignment are consistent with employers' views of women's and men's abilities, turnover costs, and work orientations.

As long as employers are correct about the average difference between the sexes, statistical discrimination is economically rational. This does not mean that it is legal or has positive social consequences. Rather, the fact that it is economically beneficial provides a strong motivation for it to continue and helps us understand why sex segregation persists.

The two other forms of economically rational discrimination can be understood with a similar logic. **Consumer-driven discrimination** occurs when employers believe that they will lose customers if they hire a woman or a man for a job typically performed by the other sex. For example, if the manager of an electronics store believed that customers preferred to buy computer equipment from men, women might be excluded from any computer sales positions. If this employer were correct about his or her customers' beliefs, the decision not to hire women makes economic (though not legal or social) sense. Similarly, if an employer believed that already-employed workers would resist working with a person of another sex, that employer might decide that the exclusion of women (or men) was worth the loss in productivity that might occur if these workers were hired.

To reiterate, the fact that some forms of discrimination are economically beneficial (or, at least, are believed to be so) by employers creates a powerful motive for sex segregation. However, just because these forms of discrimination can be economically advantageous for employers, does *not* mean that they are socially beneficial. Indeed, the costs of these forms of discrimination fall mainly on individual members of the excluded group, who are prevented from competing for jobs for which they may be highly qualified.

Institutionalized barriers

Thus far we have focused on factors influencing hiring and job assignment and implied that employers make these assignments based on their perceptions of sex differences in performance. Barriers between predominantly male and predominantly female jobs may also be maintained by more institutionalized forces. Workplace practices or policies that have become institutionalized are those that require little effort to maintain. Institutionalized barriers that maintain sex segregation have a life of their own in part because they are built into the formal structure of work organizations. As Reskin and Hartmann explain: "These institutionalized barriers may have had their origin in prejudice or may be the by-products of administrative rules and procedures that were established for other reasons . . . However, once they are incorporated in an organization's structure, they persist regardless of the lack of any discriminatory intent, unless they are altered" (1986: 51).

The structure of internal labor markets is one such factor that may help perpetuate sex segregation. **Internal labor markets,** more frequent in large firms, refer to structured opportunities for advancement that are made available to those already employed. While entry-level positions may be filled from the external labor market, competition for promotions after hiring is restricted to those already employed. Internal labor markets are often very complicated, however, governed by seniority systems and other complex rules for promotion. These factors may make it difficult for people who begin their careers in a sex-segregated entry-level job to transfer to a less-segregated position later. In this way, internal labor markets can institutionalize sex segregation within a firm.

Other examples of institutionalized barriers include the tools or technologies used in the job. Tools designed to be used by men may be more difficult for a woman to operate, thus limiting the numbers of women who are likely to be hired for that position. Reskin and Hartmann (1986: 53) cite women's experience at AT&T to illustrate this point: "women in outdoor jobs had higher accident rates than men until lighter-weight and more mobile equipment was introduced. Although it is unlikely that the intent to exclude women consciously influenced decisions about machine design or equipment, the decisions may nonetheless be exclusionary in effect." Can you think of any other examples of tools or technologies that may be designed in such a way that one sex or the other is effectively excluded from their use?

Formal barriers that maintain distinctions between predominantly male and predominantly female jobs are only one part of the story, however. Many informal workplace practices and policies also contribute to sex segregation. Take employer hiring practices, for example. Research on job searches lends strong support to the conventional wisdom that people get jobs based in large part on who they know (Granovetter 1974). Our social networks thus play important roles both in job search and hiring. Because those social networks are likely to be sex-segregated, however, job information is exchanged between people of the same sex. If people learn about jobs from people like themselves, they are likely to get jobs where similar people predominate. This process is compounded by employers' behavior. Employers often rely on employee referrals. While current employees are quite reliable sources for these referrals, they are likely to refer people like themselves. If men exchange job information with other men and women rely on other women for this information, jobs are likely to be filled by people of the same sex as those already employed. Think about your own social network: Who are you most likely to discuss jobs and careers with? Are your social networks sex-segregated or not?

As this discussion reveals, men and women end up in different jobs as a result of a number of social processes. The story is not fully complete, however, until we examine the roles that co-workers play in maintaining segregation and look more closely at the social relations of work and interactions patterns on the job.

Social closure

Under what conditions do men (and, to a lesser extent, women) have an interest in excluding the other gender from their occupations or jobs? Does sex segregation in paid employment – and sex (and gender) distinctions more generally – enable men to separate themselves from women and to monopolize more desirable positions for themselves? Because men disproportionately benefit from sex segregation, some argue that men seek to preserve these arrangements. Others suggest that both men and women perpetuate sex segregation – and sex (and gender) distinctions more generally.

These arguments treat women and men as social groups competing with one another for resources and rewards. Drawing on the work of the classical sociologist Max Weber, some researchers argue that men engage in **social closure** as a means to insure that their advantages over women will be preserved. Social closure represents the processes through which a group closes off – or monopolizes – desirable positions for themselves (Murphy 1988; Tilly 1998; Weber 1994). Social closure thus is a process of exclusion as well as segregation.

Tomaskovic-Devey (1993) provides the most detailed empirical investigation of social closure as an explanation for sex segregation. He argues that male workers' motives for, and capacity to engage in, sex-based social closure will vary depending upon several factors. In particular, social closure will be more likely when the job is more desirable and attractive to men. Women thus should be concentrated in more undesirable jobs (e.g., highly fragmented and routinized, offering few opportunities for advancement, low skill, etc.) while better jobs should be reserved for men. Certain organizational arrangements may mitigate social closure, however. For example, highly formalized, bureaucratic hiring practices make it more difficult to enforce sex segregation because these practices require accountability in the decision-making process (Tomaskovic-Devey 1993).

This research suggests that men engage in social closure as a means to acquire tangible job benefits. The exclusion and segregation of women thus results in better jobs for men. Others argue that the motives behind sex-based social closure are not purely economic. For example, as we saw in Chapter 3, similarity is a powerful source of interpersonal attraction. *Ascribed* characteristics, such as sex, race, and age, are among the characteristics most often used to infer similarity (or dissimilarity) with another. Recall that ascribed characteristics are relatively immutable and, for most, not voluntarily chosen. Sex, race, and age are important ascribed characteristics in social life because they are so easily observed and difficult to hide. The power of these characteristics also derives from the fact that sex, race, and age are highly institutionalized statuses and, hence, each is laden with layers of social meaning. This increases their value as "proxies" for similarity and dissimilarity since they are believed to be reliably associated with particular characteristics.

The similarity-attraction hypothesis implies that being a member of a sex-segregated group (that is, a group containing all men or all women) would be preferable to being in a more sex-integrated group (other factors being equal). In other words, people should prefer to interact with others like themselves and feel uncomfortable, threatened, and less committed when they are in more heterogeneous groups. Perhaps you can understand now how these dynamics may help to reproduce sex segregation. When men or women enter an occupation, job, or work setting that has been previously dominated by the other sex, discomfort – even hostility – may ensue. Those already employed may resent the newcomer and be unsure about how to relate to him or her. Group norms may have to be renegotiated and miscommunication may occur. The newcomer is likely to feel equally uncomfortable, cautious and unsure about how or where she or he fits in. The discomfort on both sides may produce conflict. The newcomer may not have much incentive or desire to stay.

As our previous discussion implies, however, the dynamics surrounding women who enter jobs traditionally held by men may be very different than those occurring when men enter predominantly female jobs. Men in predominantly male jobs may perceive women as a threat to their power and status and thus may be motivated to drive them out. This resistance may range from attempts to make women uncomfortable or to refuse assistance and support to more serious expressions of hostility and harassment, including sexual harassment.

Williams's (1989, 1994) research on men employed in predominantly female occupations, such as nursing and elementary school teaching, tells a different story. She shows that while relatively few men seek out predominantly female occupations, those who do are likely to be successful and more highly economically rewarded than their female co-workers (Williams 1994). Williams attributes this to several factors: Because femaleness is less highly valued than maleness, women entering predominantly male occupations must struggle to fit in and demonstrate their competence. Men entering predominantly female occupations, on the other hand, carry no such burden. Maleness is positively regarded, in general, and thus men in predominantly female occupations may strive to demonstrate these qualities and preserve their distinctiveness from women.

Men are not necessarily strategic and conscious of these efforts to "do masculinity." Indeed, Williams believes that men's motives to preserve gender distinctions stem in part from deep-seated psychological processes. Nevertheless, men are likely to benefit from their token status in ways that women do not. While female tokens must prove themselves capable of doing "men's work," male tokens often find themselves on **glass escalators**, invisible and sometimes even unwanted pressures to move up in the workplace (Williams 1992).

Psychoanalytic theorists such as Christine Williams thus argue that men have an emotional incentive to differentiate themselves from women. In the workplace, this incentive will be expressed through social closure and, when social closure cannot be obtained, through other kinds of practices that create and maintain sex-based distinctions in the workplace. As Williams explains: "Job segregation by sex allows men to maintain their masculinity in contradistinction to femininity. Men have historically used the occupational realm not only to secure economic advantages over women, but also to establish their essential difference from – and personal sense of superiority over – women" (1989: 133).

As we have seen, it is difficult to test this psychoanalytic argument using conventional social science methodologies. Nevertheless, this perspective is consistent with the pattern I have described. Sex segregation is a persistent feature of the workplace and seems to be continually reproduced. When women enter occupations traditionally dominated by men, men begin to avoid those fields, thus leading to a resegregation of that occupation as one dominated by women. When occupations or jobs integrate by sex, as we have seen, other kinds of sex distinctions often emerge.

The arguments presented thus far emphasize men's means and motives for sex segregation, but say little about women's role in these practices.

Indeed, social closure explanations imply that men gain more from sex seg-regation than women and thus have a much stronger stake in its perpetu-ation. Men protect their access to more desirable jobs and are able to satisfy deeply rooted psychological needs for separation. What is women's role in these processes? Are both sexes motivated to participate in the reproduc-tion of sex segregation?

Psychoanalytic theorists' response to these questions is to assert that both men and women are, at some level, motivated to behave in ways consistent with their gender identity. In this respect, then, both sexes seek opportun-ities to enact their gender in the workplace. Psychoanalytic theorists argue, however, that women are less likely than men to believe that this requires sex segregation, or other forms of separation and differentiation from the other gender. Hence, women may have a weaker motive than men to main-tain segregation, because women do not experience integration as a threat to their gender identity. This difference in orientation has been used to account for women's and men's different experiences when employed in jobs populated by the other gender (Williams 1989).

Women's stake in sex segregation may also be influenced by issues of status and economics. As we have seen, jobs held by men tend to be more highly valued and compensated than those containing large numbers of women. When men enter predominantly female jobs, they are in danger of losing status and income, while women who cross gender boundaries stand to improve their situation (Wharton and Baron 1987, 1991). These differ-ences in motivation help to explain why women have entered jobs tradi-tionally held by men in much larger numbers than men have entered jobs traditionally held by women (Williams 1994).

Workforce diversity in the twenty-first century

As the twenty-first century begins, the US labor force is more diverse than ever. Given these changes, it has become even more important to under-stand the consequences of "being different" for both numerical minorities and majorities in the workplace. One line of research examines the effects of diversity on workers and work organizations. Firmly rooted in an inter-actionist perspective, these studies examine how the demographic compo-sition of work groups shapes interaction and behavior (Chemers et al. 1995; Tsui and Gukek 1999). Diversity researchers, however, are not exclusively or even primarily concerned with the sex composition of groups, but are also interested in how other kinds of differences shape people's interactions on the job and their responses to work.

A most important finding emerging from these studies is that differences between people – such as those deriving from gender or race – are not always salient in the workplace. A salient characteristic is one that influences a person's perceptions and behavior in a situation, and it is one that shapes how others respond to that person (Turner 1987). While sex category is probably more salient in more situations than many other attributes of a person, diversity research suggests that it is not always the most central factor in workplace social relations. For example, Chatman et al. (1998) found that a more collectivistic organizational culture that emphasizes teamwork and encourages people's sense of a shared fate can create cohesiveness even among diverse groups. Diversity researchers challenge employers in the twenty-first century to create workplaces where people who are different can work together.

GENDER-TYPING OF JOBS, OCCUPATIONS, AND HIERARCHIES

In the previous section, we looked at how women and men end up in different jobs, occupations, and firms. We now turn to the gender-typing of tasks and activities and the gender meanings attached to different kinds of work. These issues have been taken up almost exclusively by gender scholars employing interactionist and institutional perspectives.

A gender-typed job or occupation is one that is seen to require distinctly feminine or distinctly masculine characteristics. Examples of gender-typed occupations are everywhere. For instance, when asked to describe the qualifications for being a nurse, many would list characteristics assumed to be much more typical of women than men, such as nurturance and caretaking ability. Similarly, many would say that jobs presumed to require aggression and competitiveness, such as prosecutor, are more appropriate for men than for women.

✴ One way in which jobs and occupations become gendered is as a result of their sex composition. In other words, jobs take on the characteristics of those who typically perform them. Nursing is an example of that process. As it came to be filled disproportionately by women, it was viewed as an occupation that demanded "feminine" qualities, such as empathy. This assumption, in turn, helps perpetuate the traditional sex composition of nursing since it implies that women as a group are inherently better suited than men for this occupation. Hence, a job's sex composition will shape its gender type and its gender type will perpetuate its sex composition.

That jobs dominated by a particular sex come to be seen as most appropriate for that sex may seem unproblematic and inevitable, but this association is produced through a complex process of social construction. As Reskin and Roos note, virtually any occupation can be understood as being more appropriate for one sex or another "because most jobs contain both stereotypical male and stereotypical female elements" (1990: 51). Hence, the creation of a link between an occupation's sex composition and its gender type necessarily involves processes of selection and deselection. Certain aspects of occupations may be emphasized as particularly important or essential, while others may be downplayed. Nursing, for example, requires workers to be skilled in the use of complex medical technologies. Emphasizing the caring aspects of this occupation, however, allows it to be cast as an occupation particularly appropriate for women.

✔Most jobs and occupations contain enough different kinds of characteristics that they can be construed as appropriate for *either* women or men. The gender type of an occupation thus can be altered relatively easily, as occurred during the Second World War when it was necessary to quickly fill jobs traditionally dominated by men with women workers (Milkman 1987). Historical research on the feminization of clerical work and public school teaching provides further examples of the ways that changes in sex composition produce changes in a job's gender type. These studies thus show the mutually reinforcing relations between the gender type of an occupation and its sex composition.

Gender and emotional labor

One increasingly important way in which occupations, jobs, and work tasks are gender typed is through the kinds of **emotional labor** they require. Service economies like the United States produce many jobs that require workers to interact directly with clients or customers. Employers who hire workers for these interactive service jobs often expect them to present a particular emotional demeanor as part of performing the job. For example, flight attendants and other workers whose jobs involve contact with customers are expected to be friendly and helpful, and can be disciplined if they fail to display these qualities. Other types of jobs require less pleasurable emotional demeanors. For example, litigators are expected to be aggressive (Pierce 1995) and bill collectors are required to be hostile and confrontational with debtors (Sutton 1991). Emotional labor refers to the effort involved in displaying these characteristics. More specifically, emotional labor refers to "the management of feeling to create a publicly observable facial and bodily display" (Hochschild 1983: 7).

Emotional labor is a distinctive form of labor, different from physical or mental effort. Emotional labor does not involve primarily the body or mind, but rather the worker's subjectivity – that is, her sense of self. Jobs that require emotional labor ask a worker to be a certain kind of person on the job and to display certain qualities when interacting with others. As a result of these connections between workers' subjectivity and job requirements, jobs that involve emotional labor may be more gender-typed than others and jobs that are gender-typed may be more likely than other jobs to require emotional labor.

When jobs are gender-typed as feminine, they are likely to require different kinds of emotional labor than jobs gender-typed as appropriate for males. For example, the occupation of flight attendant – a field traditionally filled by women, but one that has seen increasing numbers of men – requires workers to be sociable and outgoing (Hochschild 1979). Many service jobs are viewed as much more appropriate for women than men, largely as a result of being associated with this kind of emotional labor. Macdonald and Sirianni (1996: 3) use the term "emotional proletariat" to refer to the low-paying, low-skill service jobs that require workers to display friendliness and deference to customers. These occupations, while not exclusively female, are often gender-typed as such. Jobs such as waiting tables or receptionist are examples of jobs that require, among other qualifications, that workers display attentiveness to others' needs and concerns.

Not all jobs that require emotional labor are gender-typed as female, however. Many professional and managerial jobs, for example, require a self-presentation designed to convey and wield authority. Workers in these occupations, in contrast to those in the "emotional proletariat," exercise authority over those they interact with, rather than having to display deference. For example, doctors and lawyers provide guidance and advice to their patients and clients, and are assumed to have more expertise in the areas of medicine or law than those to whom this guidance and advice is provided. Although consumer movements have challenged these professionals' authority in certain respects, neither doctors nor lawyers operate strictly on the principle of "the customer is always right."

From a sociological perspective, one of the features of professions that distinguishes them from other occupations is their capacity to exercise authority over clients and patients (Hodson and Sullivan 1995). That professionals are viewed as entitled to this authority stems from widespread acceptance of the legitimacy of their expertise. Tannen observes that in our society, "[i]mages of authority come drenched in gender . . . [t]he very notion of authority is associated with maleness" (1994: 166–7). Jobs involving authority, such as law or medicine, thus are often gender-typed as masculine; they are seen as more appropriate for men than women, and men are seen as more qualified to perform the job requirements.

Managerial jobs provide a second example of a position gendered as male. A simple exercise may illustrate this point. Make a list of the most important characteristics of a good manager. Next, choose the three characteristics on this list deemed "most important" and the three that are "least important." Assume that you went to a busy street in a large city and asked a hundred, randomly selected people the following question in relation to each characteristic: "Is this characteristic more typical of women, men, or neither sex?" What do you think you would find? In studies conducted by Powell (1993), members of both sexes described good managers as possessing stereotypical masculine characteristics.

As this discussion of the links between emotional labor and the gender-typing of occupations makes clear, gender is incorporated into our understanding of job requirements and characteristics. Also demonstrated in this discussion, however, is that the gender-typing of occupations, jobs, and work tasks is not a random process. In particular, we have seen that low-status jobs containing low amounts of power and control over others are much more likely to be gendered female than high-status jobs requiring the exercise of authority. Deference – the capacity to place oneself in a "one down" position *vis-[ag]-vis* others – is a characteristic demanded of low-status social groups in many circumstances. This capacity may also be expressed as "niceness" or the ability to "get along." It is not surprising that when this capacity is a job requirement, women will be viewed as better qualified than men. Moreover, even when deference may not be a formal job requirement, jobs containing large numbers of women are likely to contain an informal job requirement that encourages this behavior. Conversely, jobs involving the display of authority are more likely to be gendered as male, at least in part because authority in the context of the USA is seen as a masculine characteristic. Hence, when jobs require emotional labor – either as deference or authority – they are likely to also be gendered.

Bureaucracy and gendered hierarchies

Gender-typing shapes particular jobs (and occupations) and it also enters into our understanding of the relations between jobs, especially hierarchical relations. In his writings on bureaucracy, the classical sociologist Max Weber provided one of the definitive sociological understandings of work hierarchies. For Weber, bureaucratic work arrangements were necessarily hierarchical and involved specialization, a fixed division of labor, and meritocratic rules and regulations (Weber 1946). He viewed the advantages of this system of organization as far outweighing its disadvantages.

One of bureaucracy's primary advantages, in Weber's view, was that it depersonalized organizations. Because bureaucratic authority, in principle, rests in positions, not people, and is encoded in rules and administrative regulations, bureaucracies are not dependent on the knowledge, expertise, or characteristics of any particular person. In addition, rules, regulations, and offices help insure that the organization's business can be conducted regardless of the nature of the personal ties between organizational members. Weber's faith in bureaucratic systems of administration thus rested heavily on his belief that rules and regulations specifying both the nature of official duties and the relations between positions in the hierarchy increased organizational control over its members' actions.

Weber emphasized the formal aspects of organization and focused on bureaucracy as an "ideal type." By contrast, later scholars turned their attention to the informal workings of bureaucracy and the ways these organizations functioned in fact, rather than in theory. For example, as many have noted, while bureaucracies are notorious for their reliance on rules and regulations, organizations would be less efficient bureaucratically if all members followed all of the rules all of the time. In fact, "working to rule" is an age-old strategy for resisting bureaucratic authority. Studies of informal organization thus have helped complement Weber's analysis of bureaucracy.

A gendered institutions view brings gender into these arguments in two ways. First, some argue that gender is an aspect of bureaucracy itself; that is, gender is embedded in this formal system of organization. A second argument treats gender as entering into the informal aspects of organization. In the former view, bureaucracy is gendered, while in the latter, bureaucracies are expressed in gendered ways. We will consider each view in turn.

For Weber, bureaucracy was a gender-neutral form whose effectiveness stemmed from its decidedly depersonalized character. Gender scholars take issue with this argument, calling attention to the ways that gender shapes patterns of hierarchy and authority in organizations. Women have made inroads into managerial occupations in recent years, yet they remain much less likely than men to have jobs requiring the exercise of authority over resources and/or people. This lack of access to authority is referred to as a **glass ceiling**.

The glass ceiling can be seen in several areas. First, within managerial occupations, women's progress to the top levels of organizational decision-making has been slow. In 2001, for example, there were only five women employed as CEOs in the largest 500 corporations (Padavic and Reskin 2002). Women also have less authority than men in other occupations, including professions, the military, and labor unions. In a systematic study of the glass ceiling among white and African-American women and men, Cotter et al. (2001) found strong evidence of this effect for both groups of women. Similarly, Smith and Elliott's (2002) study of workers in three large cities found that women were less likely than men to exercise authority on the job, regardless of their race or ethnicity: "White men had a decided advantage in every case: They were four times more likely to hold positions that provided authority than were black and Hispanic women, and three times more likely than Asian women, twice as likely as black or Hispanic men, and slightly more likely than Asian men to hold positions that conferred authority" (Padavic and Reskin 2002: 105).

Research on the glass ceiling typically focuses on women's exclusion from the formal exercise of authority on the job. In these studies, the emphasis is on women's blocked access to jobs that have the exercise of authority as a job requirement. Gender is also more informally embedded within bureaucratic relations. This latter issue has long been of interest to sociologists. Indeed, in a 1949 article on restaurants, William Foote Whyte noted how gender entered into workers' relations with one another on the job and affected the flow of work. Whyte speculated that because most men grow up expecting to be in positions of authority over women, they are uncomfortable when their work requires them to receive orders from women. In his research on restaurants, Whyte identified several strategies male "countermen" (i.e., cooks) used to avoid having to take an order directly from a female waitress. This study helped initiate a line of research on the ways that gender enters into the social relations of the workplace.

This issue has received an increasing amount of attention over the years. For example, in her classic case study of a large corporation, Kanter (1977) described how women in secretarial positions were expected to function as "office wives." What Kanter referred to as "the marriage metaphor" provided an apt description of the boss – secretary relationship, which included such elements as "greater privileges and less work for women attached to high-status men"; "expectations of personal service, including office 'housework'"; and "an emotional division of labor in which the woman plays the emotional role and the man the providing role" (1977: 89).

The "marriage metaphor," as described by Kanter, may have a less powerful hold on relations between men and women in the workplace now than before. Yet, gender continues to structure these relations. In her research on law firms, for example, Pierce (1995) explored the relations between lawyers (mostly male) and paralegals, a predominantly female occupation. Although the lawyers and paralegals she studied engaged in some of the same kinds of tasks (e.g., legal research and writing) and were very interdependent in many respects, the relations between these positions were highly gendered. As Pierce states: "Structurally, paralegal positions are specifically designed for women to support high-status men, and the content of paralegal work is consistent with our cultural conceptions of appropriate behavior for traditional wives and mothers" (1995: 86). Paralegals thus are expected to defer to and serve lawyers, who, in turn, rely on paralegals to perform this caretaking labor.

On a broader level, the gender division of labor described above parallels the way relations between women and men are often characterized in other spheres of life, outside the workplace. This division of labor in many ways reflects the "doctrine of separate spheres" (Chapter 4), in which men are expected to engage in productive labor, while women are to provide care and support. The parallels between gender relations outside and inside the workplace led Nieva and Gutek (1981) to propose the concept of "sex role spillover" as a means to explain the gender typing of work relations. "Spillover" is the process whereby gender expectations for behavior emerging outside the workplace creep over into work relations. Spillover thus provides another kind of explanation for gender typing.

Spillover has also been used to account for **sexual harassment** (Gutek and Morasch 1982; Welsh 1999). As a legal matter, sexual harassment is a form of sex discrimination, defined in terms of two types of behavior. Quid pro quo harassment involves using sexual threats as a condition of employment or as a basis for a job decision (e.g., a promotion); hostile environment harassment refers to behaviors that create a hostile or offensive work environment, thus interfering with a person's ability to perform his or her job (Welsh 1999). While both women and men can be victims of sexual harassment, research suggests that women are far more likely to experience this than men (Padavic and Reskin 2002).

The concept of spillover links sexual harassment to the gendered organization of work. For example, work settings containing highly feminized jobs that require workers to provide care and support to male superiors (e.g., secretaries and male bosses) create the conditions for quid pro quo harassment. Harassment may also be engendered by other kinds of highly feminized work situations, where informal work norms require that women be physically appealing to men or where highly sexualized interaction is tolerated or encouraged. For example, consider this description of a catering manager's expectations for her female assistants:

> She "expected" women workers to be able to cope with sexual behavior and attention from men customers as "part of the job." She said that if "the women catering assistants complain, or say things like they can't cope, I tell them it happens all the time and not to worry about it . . . it's part of the job . . . if they can't handle it then they're not up to working here." (Adkins 1995: 130, cited in Williams et al. 1999: 77)

While the manager was not necessarily condoning the sexual harassment of her workers, she certainly expected them to tolerate behaviors that could have been viewed in this way.

At the other extreme, highly masculinized work settings containing few women may create the conditions for sexual harassment as well. By emphasizing women's status as women rather than as workers, some men may use sexual harassment as a tool to put women "in their place." A common element of all of these instances is that women's "femaleness" takes precedence over their other characteristics. Sexual harassment thus can be understood as at least partly a function of the gendered organization of work and the norms that surround it.

The Wages of Gender

Another aspect of work as a gendered institution is gender's influence on the relative values attached to different kinds of work. Societies placing a higher value on males than females carry over this assessment into other institutions. Activities performed by women tend to be viewed as worth less than those performed by men. In the workplace, the relative worth of activities can be assessed economically – in the form of wages – and symbolically – in the form of status and prestige. On both counts, men and masculine activities are more highly valued than women and feminine activities.

The gender pay gap: an overview

Women earn less than men. This has been true ever since the USA began keeping track of the relative earnings of women and men. Moreover, this wage disparity persists "regardless of how you define earnings (e.g., annual vs. weekly, mean vs. median), in all race/ethnic groups, across educational categories, over the life cycle, within detailed occupational categories, and across cultures" (Roos and Gatta 1999: 95). The **gender wage gap** is most often expressed as a ratio of women's earnings to men's earnings. Typically, this ratio is measured in terms of the median earnings of women and men who work full-time, year-round. In 2000, the gender wage gap was about .72, meaning that the average woman employed full-time, year-round earned slightly less than three-quarters of the average full-time, year-round employed man (Padavic and Reskin 2002). Figure 6.1 shows that the gender wage gap has fluctuated somewhat over time, declining since the mid-1970s, but rising between 1995 and 2000.

This decline in the gender wage gap has occurred among African-Americans and Hispanics as well. For example, in 1970 African-American women working full-time, year-round earned 66.9 percent of what African-American men earned; this ratio had risen to 81.0 percent by 1990 (Roos and Gatta 1999). A similar trend can be seen among Hispanics and whites. In the past five years, however, all racial-gender groups have lost ground relative to white men, who continue to have the highest earnings of any group.

The gender wage gap varies somewhat by age. In general, the earnings of younger women are closer to the earnings of younger men than is the case among older workers. In 1990, for instance, women between the ages of 25 and 29 (employed full-time, year-round) earned 81.8 percent of what men in this age group earned; by contrast, the gender wage gap among

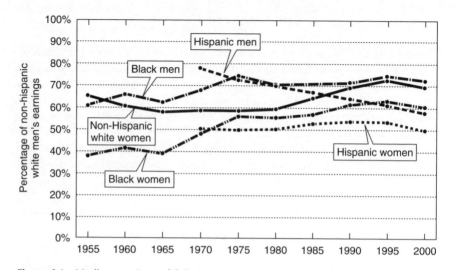

Figure 6.1 Median earnings of full-time, year-round workers as a percentage of non-Hispanic white men's earnings, by sex, race, and Hispanicity, 1955–2000
Note: 2000 figures are averages of 1998, 1999, and 2000 Current Population Survey data.
Source: Irene Padaric and Barbara Reskin (2002), *Women and Men at Work* (Thousand Oaks, CA: Pine Forge Press), exhibit 6.3. Reprinted by permission of Sage Publications Inc.

those 45–49 was 57.8. Researchers suggest two reasons to explain why the gender wage gap varies by age (Roos and Gatta 1999). The first involves cohort differences; younger workers are beginning their careers in a more gender-equal world than the one in which older workers began theirs. In addition, these variations in the gender wage gap in part reflect life cycle differences in women's and men's careers. Women's and men's earnings may be more similar at the beginning of their careers than later in adulthood after other life events – such as marriage and child-bearing – have taken place. Together, these explanations imply that, while gender-based wage discrimination may have decreased, women's and men's earnings continue to be differentially affected by changes over the life course. ✔

As Table 6.1 shows, women earn less than men in almost every occupation, including those containing high percentages of women. In a recent study, Budig shows that, even with comparable qualifications, men earn more than women within occupations. Men's advantage with respect to both wages and wage growth is roughly uniform across occupations, regardless of the occupation's sex composition (Budig 2002).

Table 6.1 Percentage female and median earnings ratios for selected occupations, year-round/full-time workers, 1990

1980 Occupational Title (code)	% Female	Year-round/full-time median earnings ratio
Executive, Administrative and Managerial Occupations		
Financial Managers (007)	46.0	58.5
Personnel and Labor Relations Managers (008)	49.2	68.8
Managers, Marketing, Advertising and Public Relations (013)	31.8	60.0
Accountants and Auditors (023)	52.6	65.5
Personnel, Training and Labor Relations Specialists (027)	57.3	71.3
Professional Specialty Occupations		
Computer Systems Analysts and Scientists (064)	30.8	82.8
Physicians (084)	20.7	51.5
Registered Nurses (095)	94.4	88.2
Pharmacists (096)	36.3	87.5
Teachers, Elementary School (156)	78.4	79.9
Librarians (164)	80.3	81.3
Social Workers (174)	68.8	84.6
Clergy (176)	10.1	86.6
Lawyers (178)	24.2	66.9
Editors and Reporters (195)	51.0	78.1
Public Relations Specialists (197)	58.5	68.8
Technical Occupations		
Dental Hygienists (204)	98.3	79.1
Licensed Practical Nurses (207)	93.6	87.1
Electrical and Electronic Technicians (213)	14.5	79.4
Air Traffic Controllers (227)	22.6	66.7
Computer Programmers (229)	32.4	83.3
Legal Assistants (234)	76.6	83.0
Sales Occupations		
Insurance Sales Occupations (253)	35.1	56.7
Real Estate Sales Occupations (254)	50.4	71.7
Sales Workers – Apparel (264)	81.2	60.0
Sales Workers – Radio, TV, Hi-Fi, and Appliances (267)	28.5	79.7
Cashiers (276)	78.5	67.3
Administrative Support Occupations		
Computer Operators (308)	60.9	69.2
Secretaries (313)	98.7	90.0
Telephone Operators (348)	87.0	75.0
Mail Carriers, Postal Service (355)	26.5	93.3

Table 6.1 *Continued*

1980 Occupational Title (code)	% Female	Year-round/full-time median earnings ratio
Insurance Adjusters, Examiners and Investigators (375)	70.9	66.7
Bank Tellers (383)	90.0	81.5
Private Household and Protective Service Occupations		
Child Care, Private Household (406)	97.2	90.0
Firefighting Occupations (417)	2.5	75.0
Police and Detectives, Public Service (418)	11.8	84.0
Other Service Occupations		
Bartenders (434)	48.9	73.3
Waiters and Waitresses (435)	80.0	66.7
Cooks, including Short Order (436/437)	47.5	74.1
Janitors and Cleaners (453)	30.7	68.8
Farming		
Farmers, except Horticultural (473)	12.9	44.9
Farm Workers (479)	18.5	71.3
Fishers (498)	5.9	63.9
Precision Production, Craft and Repair Occupations		
Automobile Mechanics, except Apprentices (505)	1.9	90.0
Electricians, except Apprentices (575)	2.6	74.6
Plumbers, Pipefitters and Steamfitters, except Apprentices (585)	1.4	88.5
Cabinet Makers and Bench Carpenters (657)	6.1	76.9
Dressmakers (666)	93.3	71.4
Bakers (687)	45.3	67.3
Operators, Fabricators and Laborers		
Typesetters and Compositors (736)	69.2	67.3
Textile Sewing Machine Operators (744)	88.1	68.8
Truck Drivers – Heavy and Light (804/805)	5.8	66.7
Bus Drivers (808)	47.9	62.5
Handlers, Equipment Cleaners, Helpers and Laborers		
Garbage Collectors (875)	3.4	78.9
Stock Handlers and Baggers (877)	29.5	76.5
Laborers, except Construction (889)	21.6	72.1

Source: Patricia A. Roos and Mary Elizabeth Gatta, "The Gender Gap in Earnings," in Gary N. Powell (ed.), *Handbook of Gender and Work* (Thousand Oaks, CA: Sage Publications, 1999), pp. 103–4. Reprinted by permission of the publisher.

The gender wage gap varies across countries (Table 6.2). In 1997, for example, women in Sweden earned 89 percent of what men earned, as compared to Greece and the Netherlands where the gender wage gap was around 71 percent (Van Der Lippe and Van Dijk 2001). These patterns reflect several factors: these include cross-national differences in levels and types of sex segregation, government policies, occupational structures, and cultural beliefs.

Determining the worth of jobs

Why do women earn less than men? Sociologists' and economists' interest in this question reflects a desire to know what determines the "worth" of jobs and why some jobs pay more than others. Understanding how wages are attached to jobs is a complicated topic and there are many different approaches to this issue (see England 1992). For our purposes, however, the relevant question is how gender enters into the wage-determination process.

Sociologists argue that the wages attached to jobs are a function of several kinds of characteristics. One important set of characteristics includes the skill level of the job. For neo-classical economists, skill reflects productivity, in that more skilled workers add more value to the firm than those with fewer skills. Workers acquire skills by investing in activities that make them more productive. While this investment may be costly initially, it is done for the sake of a future pay-off. The portfolio of skills that workers acquire through these means represents their human capital. As discussed earlier, human capital theoretically consists of anything that increases a worker's productivity. The most common measures of human capital, however, include easily measured investments, such as years of schooling and various types of on-the-job-training. According to the theory of human capital, then, jobs requiring more investment by workers (e.g., college education, technical training, etc.) pay more than other jobs because otherwise workers would not invest in the required training. Higher pay for these jobs thus is a means to compensate workers for their investment. At the same time, employers can also benefit from workers' human capital because these workers are assumed to be more productive than workers with less human capital.

Compensating workers for their investments in human capital is undoubtedly important to employers' assessments, but this is not the only consideration. Employers may also consider other factors when setting wages. In particular, they must consider the relative supply of workers available at a given skill level. For any particular job at a given skill level, supply is "affected by opportunities outside this job for people with the same skills

Table 6.2 Inequality between men and women in the labor market by country

| | Sector of activity (1997) | | | | | | Share of women in total employment by sector (1997) | | | Female administrators and managers (1995) | Income gap[a] (1997) |
| | Women | | | Men | | | | | | | |
	agr.	industry	services	agr.	ind.	serv.	agr.	ind.	serv.		
Belgium	2.1	13.2	84.7	3.0	37.4	59.6	32.3	19.5	49.3	18.8	88
Denmark	1.7	14.5	83.8	5.5	36.0	58.6	20.0	25.1	54.3	19.2	85
Germany	2.6	18.9	78.5	3.2	46.5	50.3	37.2	23.4	54.0	25.8	83
Greece	23.1	13.4	63.5	17.9	27.7	54.3	42.7	21.9	40.4	22.0	71
Spain	6.1	13.6	80.2	9.5	38.7	51.8	26.0	16.1	45.7	31.9	80
France	3.4	14.5	82.2	5.7	36.3	58.0	32.4	24.2	53.1	9.4	82
Ireland	3.5	17.2	79.3	15.6	35.8	48.5	12.8	23.5	51.0	22.6	
Italy	5.9	21.4	72.7	6.9	37.5	55.6	32.7	24.3	42.4	53.3	86
Luxemburg	1.2	6.6	92.1	3.0	33.3	63.7	25.0	10.3	34.3	8.6	82
Netherlands	2.4	9.4	88.3	4.6	32.1	63.3	25.9	16.6	48.8	20.3	71
Austria	7.7	14.6	77.6	6.2	41.2	52.5	49.0	21.5	53.3	23.9	
Portugal	15.2	20.3	64.5	11.7	39.8	48.5	51.6	29.4	52.0	31.0	
Finland	5.3	13.9	80.8	10.0	39.6	55.5	32.3	24.0	59.0	25.3	83
Sweden	1.7	11.7	86.6	4.7	38.2	57.1	24.4	21.9	58.8	38.9	89

Country											
UK	1.1	13.2	85.7	2.5	38.0	59.5	25.4	22.1	54.0	32.9	76
Poland	28	25	48	27	45	28	44.5	34.8	55.0[b]	34.7	
Slovenia	6	39	54	5	52	43	48.1	39.4	56.0[b]	28.2	
Hungary	11	32	57	19	42	39	24.8[c]	38.6[c]	52.6[b,c]	33.8	
Bulgaria										28.9	
Czech Republic	9	36	55	13	54	33	32.7	37.5	54.4[b]	26.9	
Slovakia	9	31	60	14	36	50	31.3	38.2	57.3[b]	27.4	
Romania	28	40	32	21	53	26					
United States	1.1[c]	12.6	86.3	3.3	36.0	60.7	25.3	26.3	59.3	42.7	74[d]
Canada	2	11	78	5	29	57				42.2	
Australia	4	13	80	7	34	57				43.3	

[a] Income gap: hourly earnings of women as percentage of men's, full-time.
[b] Private sector not included.
[c] Figures refer to 1996.
[d] Figures refer to 1996 and to men and women 25 and over.

Source: Tanja van der Lippe and Liset van Dijk (2001), "Introduction: Women's Employment in a Comparative Perspective," in Tanja van der Lippe and Liset van Dijk (eds.), *Women's Employment in a Comparative Perspective* (New York: Aldine de Gruyter), pp. 6–7. Reprinted by permission of the publisher.

(e.g., wages of alternative jobs), by how much investment in training a job requires, and by whether the . . . worker finds doing the work in the job a 'disamenity' – an unpleasantness – or an amenity" (England 1992: 50). Regarding the latter point, employers may decide that jobs workers perceive as particularly onerous or unpleasant require higher wages than otherwise comparable jobs involving more desirable working conditions. Otherwise, workers will prefer the jobs with more desirable working conditions.

All employers must decide the relative worth of the jobs they offer to workers. Human capital theory offers a general understanding of the relations between skill and wage-setting that can help us delve more deeply into this process. Human capital theory's emphasis on employers' roles in assessing the skill level of jobs and their relative value is our starting point. Sociologists argue that the processes through which employers make these assessments and the resulting wages offered reflect social as well as economic considerations. In this view, skill is socially constructed. This implies that which jobs are defined as skilled and hence higher-paying is more than a technical exercise. In addition, the ways in which employers understand and respond to forces of labor supply also reflect the influence of social processes. Hence, while human capital theory provides a starting point for understanding wage-setting, economic arguments overlook the many ways in which social factors enter into this process.

Job evaluation and the social construction of skill

Human capital theorists define skill in terms of productivity-enhancing investments. Jobs that require more skill thus should receive more pay than those requiring less skill. How employers decide upon the skill requirements of jobs and assess the other kinds of factors necessary to set pay levels is a subject which has received considerable attention from researchers. In particular, studies examine the ways in which employers use job evaluation techniques. **Job evaluation** is a method used to determine how pay is assigned to jobs and to justify (or critique) relative pay rates. Employers use job evaluation in order to decide how to compensate different jobs and feminists have used it to demonstrate gender bias in wage-setting. Hence, one way to illustrate how actual processes of wage-setting depart from the tenets of human capital theory is to examine the process of job evaluation.

England provides a useful account of job evaluation: "In all methods of job evaluation, it is the requirements of the *job* that are evaluated, not the performance of a given *individual* within the job. It is taken for granted that within any one job, different individuals are paid different amounts because of differences in merit or seniority. However, each job generally has a pay range within which such individual variation is confined" (1992: 190; emphasis in original). Jobs can be evaluated according to several different methods, ranging from a simple ranking of "payworthiness" to more sophisticated systems that assign wages based on a point system (England 1992). All of these methods are based on the belief that it is possible to objectively rank jobs according to their worth to an employer. This ranking may be done by employers or their managers, by outside consulting firms, or by unions and worker representatives.

Although job evaluation is a technique long used by employers, it gradually began to be used by those interested in identifying and correcting gender bias in wage setting. State of Washington employees were among some of the first to use job evaluation in this manner. A job evaluation study conducted by an outside consulting firm for the state found that predominantly female jobs were systematically paid less than male jobs, even when they received the same number of evaluation points (England 1992). When the state failed to rectify this situation, the union representing state employees filed a lawsuit against the state alleging sex discrimination. Though the union eventually lost their case in the courts, the state agreed to an out-of-court settlement that resulted in higher wages for predominantly female jobs.

Job evaluation techniques have been used in other state and local settings as well, including Oregon, New York State, and the city of San Jose, California (Acker 1989; Blum 1991; Steinberg and Haignere 1987). In all these cases, this technique was proposed as a way to correct perceived sex biases in the ways wages were attached to jobs. Most notably, job evaluation showed that jobs evaluated as comparable in terms of their skill requirements, working conditions, and the like were often compensated at different levels depending upon their sex composition. Predominantly female jobs tended to be devalued relative to jobs of comparable skill filled by men. These results called into question the notion that wages were set according to sex-neutral processes and instead revealed an important source of sex bias. In fact, as England notes: "if a single job evaluation plan is used to set pay throughout a firm or government, *it nearly always gives women's jobs higher wages relative to men's than most employers pay*" (1992: 205; emphasis in original).

That jobs filled with women receive lower average wages than comparable jobs filled by men has become a well-established research finding (Padavic and Reskin 2002; Roos and Gatta 1999; Tomaskovic-Devey 1993). Note that the effect of the sex composition of jobs is net of other factors that could contribute to wage differences between women and men, such as differences in human capital, job characteristics and skill requirements, and firm resources. Moreover, both women *and* men suffer wage penalties when they work in predominantly female jobs and the wages of both sexes benefit from employment in jobs held predominantly by men (Tomaskovic-Devey 1993). This implies that it is the *jobs* themselves that are valued more or less depending upon their sex composition.

Job evaluation helped reveal an important source of sex bias in wage setting. In recent years, however, these methods themselves have been found to contain their own sources of bias (Acker 1989; England 1992). Researchers thus have begun to question whether it is possible to objectively measure the worth of jobs. One potential source of bias in job evaluation occurs when predominantly female jobs are given fewer points than they merit, while predominantly male jobs are given a boost in ranking. One example cited by England illustrates the point: "attendants at dog pounds and parking lots (usually men) were rated more highly than nursery school teachers, and zookeepers more highly than day care workers" (1992: 199; see also Steinberg and Haignere 1987). In this instance, the sex composition of the job likely influenced its ranking by evaluators.

As this discussion makes clear, sex bias may enter into wage-setting through numerous subtle and unintended ways. Even the practice of job evaluation – intended to identify and correct sources of sex bias – may inadvertently contribute to the devaluing of predominantly female jobs. Why should jobs filled predominantly by women receive less pay than comparable jobs filled by men?

The devaluation of predominantly female jobs

A job's wages are determined by a number of factors. The job's skill requirements and the market forces of supply and demand for that type of labor are certainly among the most important. At the same time, however, this discussion has shown that wage-setting is also influenced by other forces. In particular, the individuals and groups who set wages are influenced by cultural understandings of the "worth" of jobs and the values that should be given to various kinds of skills. In societies that have traditionally placed higher value on male achievements and masculinity than on the achievements of women and femininity, it is not surprising that, insofar as cultural values enter into wage-setting, they will result in a higher value being placed on jobs and activities associated with men, all else being equal (England and Folbre 1999). Once these biases have been incorporated into the wage-setting process, they become institutionalized and persist over time.

While employers and their representatives play important roles in wage-setting, their motives and capacity to devalue jobs held by women and minorities vary across jobs and organizations. Baron and Newman (1990), for example, found that the tendency for jobs held by women and minorities to be devalued is greater in larger, "generic" jobs than in those that are more idiosyncratic and in jobs where performance criteria are more ambiguous. The efforts of workers and their organizations also influence the wages of many kinds of jobs. The more powerful the workers, the more likely they are to successfully influence the wages their jobs receive. Historically, male workers have been better organized and thus a more powerful force in negotiating wages with employers than women. Although women have a long history of labor activism, for example, craft unions representing skilled workers in predominantly male manufacturing jobs have been among the most powerful throughout the twentieth century. As a result, some argue that men – particularly white men – have been better able to organize for and demand higher wages than their female counterparts, regardless of skill level and market forces. In recent years, women and racial minorities have had more opportunities to engage in collective action in the public sector. Hence, it is not surprising that public-sector unions have been among the strongest supporters of pay equity.

CHAPTER SUMMARY

The pervasive and resilient nature of sex segregation demand explanation, and I have tried to suggest some of the factors that may contribute to these arrangements. Proponents of an individualist account of gender emphasize how workers' and employers' choices create gender segregation. Interactionists stress the ways that social interaction on the job makes gender integration easy or more difficult. From a gendered institutions perspective, gender segregation stems from institutionalized barriers between "male" and "female" jobs.

Gender enters the workplace not only through sex segregation, but through the process of gender-typing. Jobs, occupations, work roles, and work relations are laden with gender meanings. In this way, specific work roles, jobs, and occupations come to be seen as more appropriate for one gender than another. Gender-typing results from the social processes through which meaning is collectively generated and reinforced. It is external to individuals and imposes itself on them by establishing certain work roles, jobs, and occupations as appropriate for one sex and off-limits to another. It establishes the "way things are," or a set of conventional understandings of who should engage in what type of work. Gender-typing thus represents one aspect of work as a gendered institution.

In addition to shaping the meanings attached to jobs, gender shapes the relative values attached to different kinds of work. The relative worth of jobs can be assessed economically – in the form of wages – and symbolically – in the form of status and prestige. On both counts, gender-typing privileges men and masculine activities and penalizes women and feminine activities.

:arn less than men, on average, although women from all racial groups have made progress relative to white men's wages in 's. Studies of wage-setting reveal how gender shapes the "worth" ,d the power of workers to demand and receive high wages. Jobs held ʋ, ⁄omen are seen as worth less than jobs held by men. Societies that place a higher value on males than females thus carry over this assessment into other institutions. Activities performed by women tend to be viewed as worth less than those performed by men.

The gendered aspects of work described in this chapter are often unintended, taken for granted, and operate so subtly that they rarely are scrutinized. In this respect, gender is a highly institutionalized feature of the modern workplace.

FURTHER READING

England, Paula. 1992. *Comparable Worth: Theories and Evidence*. New York: Aldine de Gruyter.

Gerson, Kathleen. 1993. *No Man's Land: Men's Changing Commitments to Family and York*. New York: Basic Books.

Lippe, Tanya van der and Liset van Dijk, eds. 2001. *Women's Employment in a Comparative Perspective*. New York: Aldine de Gruyter.

Padavic, Irene and Barbara Reskin. 2002. *Women and Men at Work*. Thousand Oaks, Ca: Pine Forge Press.

Williams, Christine. 1989. *Gender Differences at Work: Women and Men in Nontraditional Occupations*. Berkeley, CA: University of California Press.

Williams, Christine. 1995. *Still a Man's World*. Berkeley, CA: University of California.

A CLOSER LOOK

Reading 1: Women as Emotion Managers

Arlie Russell Hochschild

Middle-class American women, tradition suggests, feel emotion more than men do. The definitions of "emotional" and "cogitation" in the *Random House Dictionary of the English Language* reflect a deeply rooted cultural

From *The Managed Heart: The Commercialization of Human Feeling* (Berkeley, CA: University of California Press, 1983), pp. 164–70.

idea. Yet women are also thought to command "feminine wiles," to have the capacity to premeditate a sigh, an outburst of tears, or a flight of joy. In general, they are thought to *manage* expression and feeling not only better but more often than men do. How much the conscious feelings of women and men may differ is an issue I leave aside here. However, the evidence seems clear that women do *more* emotion managing than men. And because the well-managed feeling has an outside resemblance to spontaneous feeling, it is possible to confuse the condition of being more "easily affected by emotion" with the action of willfully managing emotion when the occasion calls for it.

Especially in the American middle class, women tend to manage feeling more because in general they depend on men for money, and one of the various ways of repaying their debt is to do extra emotion work – *especially emotion work that affirms, enhances, and celebrates the well-being and status of others*. When the emotional skills that children learn and practice at home move into the marketplace, the emotional labor of women becomes more prominent because men in general have not been trained to make their emotions a resource and are therefore less likely to develop their capacity for managing felling.

There is also a difference in the kind of emotion work that men and women tend to do. Many studies have told us that women adapt more to the needs of others and cooperate more than men do. These studies often imply the existence of gender-specific characteristics that are inevitable if not innate. But do these characteristics simply exist passively in women? Or are they signs of a social work that women *do* – the work of affirming, enhancing, and celebrating the well-being and status of others? I believe that much of the time, the adaptive, cooperative woman is actively working at showing deference. This deference requires her to make an outward display of what Leslie Fiedler has called the "seriously" good girl in her and to support this effort by evoking feelings that make the "nice" display seem natural. Women who want to put their own feelings less at the service of others must still confront the idea that if they do so, they will be considered less "feminine."

What it takes to be more "adaptive" is suggested in a study of college students by William Kephart (1967). Students were asked: "If a boy or girl had all the other qualities you desire, would you marry this person if you were not in love with him/her?" In response, 64 percent of the men but only 24 percent of the women said No. Most of the women answered that they "did not know." As one put it: "I don't know, if he were that good, maybe I could *bring myself around* to loving him." In my own study (1975), women more often than men described themselves as "trying to make myself love," "talking myself into not caring," or "trying to convince myself." A content analysis of 260 protocols showed that more women than men (33 percent versus 18 percent) spontaneously used the language of emotion work to describe their emotions. The image of women as "more emotional," more subject to uncontrolled feelings, has also been challenged by a study of 250 students at UCLA, in which only 20 percent of the men but 45 percent of the women said that they deliberately show emotion to get their way. As one woman put it: "I pout, frown, and say something to make the other person feel bad, such as 'You don't love me, you don't care what happens to me.' I'm not the type to come right out with what I want; I'll usually hint around. It's all hope and a lot of beating around the bush."[1]

The emotional arts that women have cultivated are analogous to the art of feigning that Lionel Trilling has noted among those whose wishes outdistance their opportunities for class advancement. As for many others of lower status, it has been in the woman's interest to be the better actor. As the psychologists would say, the techniques of deep acting have unusually high "secondary gains." Yet these skills have long been mislabeled "natural," a part of woman's "being" rather than something of her own making.

Sensitivity to nonverbal communication and to the micro-political significance of feeling gives women something like an ethnic language, which men can speak too, but on the whole less well. It is a language women share offstage in their talk "about feelings." This talk is not, as it is for men offstage, the score-keeping of conquistadors. It is the talk of the artful prey, the language of tips on how to make him want her, how to psyche him out, how to put him on or turn him off. Within the traditional female subculture, subordination at close quarters is understood, especially in adolescence, as a "fact of life." Women accommodate, then, but not passively. They actively adapt feeling to a need or a purpose at hand, and they do it so that it *seems* to express a passive state of agreement, the chance occurrence of coinciding needs. Being becomes a way of doing. Acting is the needed art, and emotion work is the tool.

The emotion work of enhancing the status and well-being of others is a form of what Ivan Illich has called "shadow labor," an unseen effort, which, like housework, does not quite count as labor but is nevertheless crucial to getting other things done. As with doing housework well, the trick is to erase any evidence of effort, to offer only the clean house and the welcoming smile.

We have a simple word for the product of this shadow labor: "nice." Niceness is a necessary and important lubricant to any civil exchange, and men make themselves nice, too. It keeps the social wheels turning. As one flight attendant said, "I'll make comments like 'Nice jacket you have on' – that sort of thing, something to make them feel good. Or I'll laugh at their jokes. It makes them feel relaxed and amusing." Beyond the smaller niceties are the larger ones of doing a favor, offering a service. Finally, there is the moral or spiritual sense of being seriously nice, in which we embrace the needs of another person as more important than our own.

Each way of being "nice" adds a dimension to deference. Deference is more than the offering of cold respect, the formal bow of submission, the distant smile of politeness; it can also have a warm face and offer gestures small and large that show support for the well-being and status of others.

Almost everyone does the emotion work that produces what we might, broadly speaking, call deference. But women are expected to do more of it. A study by Wikler (1976) comparing male with female university professors found that students expected women professors to be warmer and more supportive than male professors; given these expectations, proportionally more women professors were perceived as cold. In another study, Broverman, Broverman, and Clarkson (1970) asked clinically trained psychologists, psychiatrists, and social workers to match various characteristics with "normal adult men" and "normal adult women"; they more often associated "very tactful, very gentle, and very aware of feelings of others" with their ideas of the normal adult women. In being adaptive, cooperative, and helpful, the woman is on a private stage behind the public stage, and as a consequence she is often seen as less good at arguing, telling jokes, and teaching than she is at expressing appreciation of these activities. She is the conversational cheerleader. She actively enhances other people – usually men, but also other women to whom she plays woman. The more she seems natural at it, the more her labor does not show as labor, the more successfully it is disguised as the *absence* of other, more prized qualities. As a *woman* she may be praised for out-enhancing the best enhancer, but as a *person* in comparison with comics, teachers, and argument-builders, she usually lives outside the climate of enhancement that men tend to inhabit. Men, of course, pay court to certain other men and women and thus also do the emotion work that keeps deference sincere. The difference between men and women is a difference in the psychological effects of having or not having power.

Racism and sexism share this general pattern, but the two systems differ in the avenues available for the translation of economic inequality into private terms. The white manager and the black factory worker leave work and go home, one to a generally white neighborhood and family and the other to a generally black neighborhood and family. But in the case of women and men, the larger economic inequality is filtered into the intimate daily exchanges between wife and husband. Unlike other subordinates, women seek *primary* ties with a supplier. In marriage, the principle of reciprocity applies to wider arenas of each self: there is more to choose from in how we pay and are paid, and the paying between economically unequal parties goes on morning, noon, and night. The larger inequities find intimate expression.

Wherever it goes, the bargain of wages-for-other-things travels in disguise. Marriage both bridges and obscures the gap between the resources available to men and those available to women. Because men and women do try to love one another – to cooperate in making love, making babies, and making a life together – the very closeness of the bond they accept calls for some disguise of subordination. There will be talk in the "we" mode, joint bank accounts and joint decisions, and the idea among women that they are equal in the ways that "really count." But underlying this pattern will be *different potential futures outside the marriage* and the effect of that on the patterning of life. The woman may thus become especially assertive about certain secondary decisions, or especially active in certain limited domains, in order to experience a sense of equality that is missing from the overall relationship.

Women who understand their ultimate disadvantage and feel that their position cannot change may jealously guard the covertness of their traditional emotional resources, in the understandable fear that if the secret were told, their immediate situation would get worse. For to confess that their social charms are the product of secret work might make them less valuable, just as the sexual revolution has made sexual contact less "valuable" by lowering its bargaining power without promoting the advance of women into better-paying jobs. In fact, of course, when we redefine "adaptability" and "cooperativeness" as a form of shadow labor, we are pointing to a hidden cost for which some recompense is due and suggesting that a general reordering of female–male relationships is desirable.

There is one further reason why women may offer more emotion work of this sort than men: more women at all class levels do unpaid labor of a highly interpersonal sort. They nurture, manage, and befriend children. More "adaptive" and "cooperative," they address themselves better to the needs of those who are not yet able to adapt and cooperate much themselves. Then, according to Jourard (1968), because they are seen as members of the category from which mothers come, women in general are asked to look out for psychological needs more than men are. The world turns to women for mothering, and this fact silently attaches itself to many a job description.

NOTE

1   Johnson and Goodchilds, "How Women Get Their Way," p. 69.

REFERENCES
REFERENCES

REFERENCES

Broverman, Inge K., Donald M. Broverman, and Frank E. Clarkson. 1970. "Sex Role Stereotypes and Clinical Judgments of Mental Health." *Journal of Consulting and Clinical Psychology* 34: 1–7.

Fiedler, Leslie A. 1960. "Good Good Girls and Good Bad Boys: Clarissa as a Juvenile." In Leslie A. Fiedler, *Love and Death in the American Novel*. New York: Criterion, pp. 254–72.

Hochschild, Arlie. 1975. "The Sociology of Feeling and Emotion: Selected Possibilities." In Marcia Millman and Rosabeth Kanter (eds.), *Another Voice*. Garden City, NY: Anchor, pp. 280–304.

Johnson, Paula B., and Jacqueline D. Goodchilds. 1976. "How Women Get Their Way." *Psychology Today* 10: 69–70.

Jourard, S. M. 1968. *Disclosing Man to Himself*. Princeton, NJ: Van Nostrand.

Kephart, William. 1967. "Some Correlates of Romantic Love." *Journal of Marriage and the Family* 29: 470–4.

Wikler, Norma. 1976. "Sexism in the Classroom." Paper presented at the annual meeting of the American Sociological Association, New York.

> How is "niceness" a form of emotion work, according to Hochschild? How does this form of emotion work express itself on the job? Do you agree with Hochschild's claim that "mothering . . . silently attaches itself to many a job description?"

Reading 2: Hegemonic Masculinity in Female Occupations

Christine L. Williams

Waiting for a scheduled interview with a librarian, I had a chance to peruse the various clippings and announcements posted on his office door. In the center was a cartoon drawing of an enormous, brutish, muscular man labeled "Conan the Librarian" (a takeoff on "Conan the Barbarian"). There was to be little doubt that the man behind the door was masculine.

Men use several different strategies to "maintain" hegemonic masculinity in female occupations. Men distinguish themselves from women in the

From *Still a Man's World: Men Who Do Women's Work* (Berkeley, CA: University of California Press, 1995), pp. 123–41.

workplace by segregating themselves into certain male-identified specialties, emphasizing the masculine elements of the job, pursuing higher administrative positions, and disassociating from their work altogether. Each of these strategies enables men to maintain a sense of themselves as different from and better than women – thus contributing to the gender system that divides men from women in a way that privileges men.

SEX SEGREGATION

[. . .]

It is more common to find male nurses in hospital emergency rooms and psychiatric wards than in obstetrical wards. Men are more likely to teach in the higher grades in elementary schools, whereas 98 percent of kindergarten teachers are women. School librarianship is also an overwhelmingly female specialty (over 95 percent female), but men make up over a third of all academic librarians. And caseworkers in social-work agencies are mostly women, while administrators and managers in those agencies are mostly men.[1]

Several of the men I interviewed claimed that they entered their particular specialties precisely because they contained more men. For example, one man left his job as a school social worker to work in a methadone drug treatment program because "I think there was some macho shit there [in myself], to tell you the truth, because I remember feeling a little uncomfortable there . . . ; it didn't feel right to me." Another social worker told me, "I think one of the reasons personally for me that I moved to corrections – and I think it was real unconscious – was the conflict [over masculinity]. I think corrections . . . is a little more macho than like if I worked in a child guidance clinic like I used to." For both of these men, specializing in "male-identified" areas helped them resolve inner conflicts about masculinity caused by being male in a predominantly female occupation.

The social workers I interviewed seemed much more self-consciously aware of specialization as a strategy for maintaining masculinity than members of the other professional groups (probably as a result of their professional training). Other men in the study were not quite so articulate in describing their psychological needs to differentiate from women, but they often made it clear during the course of the interviews that their specialties were chosen in part because they felt they were more appropriate for men. For instance, a psychiatric nurse chose his specialty "because psych is pretty easy for me. That's what I scored the highest in on the boards. And there's a lot more males, I think, in psych than on the floors. . . ." And this sixth grade teacher explained his preference for teaching the upper grades:

I felt I had a little more of an affinity for that age level. I could go down to fifth, but below fifth, they're just a little too cutesy, a little too young, and I get a little tired of explaining things seven or eight times. . . . I did [substitute teaching in] second grade three different times, and after that I said, "No more primaries." I think it was like that movie with Arnold Schwarzenegger, *Kindergarten Cop*: You think you have everything under control and things just fall apart. . . . I think at that age, the kids relate more effectively to a woman, you know, the mother figure. Cause that's more of a significant person in their lives at that age. That's the way I see it. And I think, I assume that that's why you don't see so many men teaching those grades.

It is significant that this teacher identifies with Arnold Schwarzenegger, an emblem of masculinity in our culture. This is how hegemonic masculinity works: It is not necessarily what men are, but a symbolic form that men are motivated to support. Arnold Schwarzenegger is a physically strong, stoic, and unambiguously heterosexual movie star. By identifying with him and his inability to control a kindergarten class, this teacher establishes a sense of himself as powerful and in control since he teaches the *sixth* grade – even though this is also a traditionally female occupation.

Stratification within these professions is due in part to the "glass escalator": Men are channeled into specialties considered more legitimate for men, and many of them are complicit with this process. Internal stratification is due to a combination of organizational pressures and individual motives. This point was nicely summarized in an interview with a female social worker. When asked if her agency assigned men and women to different jobs, she quipped, "They'd never give some big buck a juvenile job unless he wants it. And if he wants it, he wouldn't say it anyways."

EMPHASIZING THE MASCULINE

Specializing in male-identified areas is perhaps the most obvious way that men can differentiate themselves from women. However, even those who work in the more "traditional" female specialties can distinguish the work they do from "women's work" by highlighting the masculine aspects of their specialties.[2] School and public librarians, for example, can identify with automating the library catalogue and other computer work that they do. One public librarian specializing in cataloging believes that advanced technology was the key to attracting him as well as other men to the profession:

After automation became part of the profession, more and more men are coming. I think that men are looking more for prestigious careers, and automation has given that to the profession. Not just organizing books, but applying technology in the process.

Another approach to emphasizing the masculine is to focus on the prestige of one's workplace. A California teacher who described his institution as "the top flight elementary school in the country" said,

> It makes you feel good about your job. It makes you, as a male, feel like it's okay to be a teacher, because this is a highly prestigious institution in the world of private schools.

Other men focused on the power and authority of their particular job specialties. Describing a previous job in Children's Protective Services (a heavily female specialty), this Arizona social worker said,

> Child welfare is an area in social work where you balance a helping role with a social control role. Going out to people's homes, I almost wore two hats: a social worker and an authority figure, someone with some enforcement power. . . . I carried a certain amount of professional and legal authority with me. . . . I literally had the authority to take people's kids out of their homes.

In addition, a few men emphasized the physical aspects of their work. A former teacher at a school for autistic children explained that men were needed for "restraining" the children, some of whom were "very, very violent." And a public librarian specializing in children's collections described a distinctive reading style he observed among the few male storytellers in town:

> I guess you could say, maybe in some sense, we're real physical in our story-times, you know, the way we interact with the kids. I don't mean . . . I mean, these days, you have to be very careful touching children, of course. . . . I don't mean real touchy-feely, but I mean . . . you just get a real physical sense of the story.

Thus, men can identify with the technical or physical aspects of their jobs, or emphasize the special prestige or power that accrue to them because of their specific institutions. In all of these ways, men can highlight the components of their jobs that are consistent with hegemonic masculinity, thus maintaining a sense of themselves as "masculine" even though they work in nontraditional occupations.

[. . .]

ADMINISTRATION AND HIGHER EDUCATIONAL CREDENTIALS

A third distancing strategy is to define the present occupation as a way station for future jobs that are more lucrative, prestigious, or challenging (and thus more legitimate for men). Men who use this strategy do not identify with their current jobs, but see them as laying the groundwork for future jobs. For instance, a teacher told me that he chose to start his career in elementary school to "learn the basics of human nature," and then move up to junior high, and ultimately high school (where there is a much larger proportion of men). Others saw their professions as "springboards" to other careers. An Arizona nurse, for example, who saw "nursing as a backup," hoped in the future to work in the biomedical engineering profession.

Aspiring to the top rungs of the profession was an especially common distancing strategy. Men described future plans to become "director of a branch library" (children's librarian), "director of a home for the aged" (floor nurse), or a "principal of a school" (fourth grade teacher). These areas were all explicitly defined as more appropriate for men, and they are also viewed as more prestigious and powerful than rank-and-file jobs.

As is the case in most professions, advancement to these top positions often requires higher educational preparation beyond the entry-level credential. Men are more likely than women to seek postgraduate degrees in these occupations. The higher the educational credential, the higher the proportion of men earning the degree. Indeed, men received nearly half of the doctorates awarded in education and library science in 1988.

This discrepancy in the representation of men and women in post-credential degree programs is due to a number of factors. First, men are often encouraged to "aim high" by mentors simply because they are men. A Massachusetts nurse was told by his first clinical instructor in his associate degree (ADN) program,

> "You've got to go on. You *have* to go on . . . past the ADN," she said. "You have to; you are a man." She said, "You have to get more men into the profession; we need men."

Thus, men may receive more encouragement than women to reach the top of their professions.

A second reason for men's overrepresentation among higher degree recipients and administrative officeholders involves men's and women's different family obligations. Women often shoulder the primary responsibility for household care, even when they are employed full-time. This frees up married men to dedicate themselves more exclusively to pursuing higher educational credentials and higher administrative positions.[3] I interviewed three men whose spouses were in the same profession as they, and each had a higher degree than his wife. A doctoral student in library science, who met his wife in the master's degree program, explained why he pursued an advanced degree and she did not:

I realized that I have the responsibility to become the provider at home. . . . She thought that if she were comfortable, if she found a nice [work] environment, she didn't need to go further [with her education]. She didn't have to push harder. . . . And during the time we were in college, the family was growing. So the demand for her to stay at home and care for the kids was growing, too.

Overall, women are far more likely than men to drop out of the labor force. Nearly half of all women in the work force drop out for at least one six-month period, compared to 13 percent of all men.[4] And when women do drop out, it is usually for family reasons: In 1990, 62 percent of the women who had left the labor force for an extended period claimed that they were "keeping house"; only 3 percent of the men who dropped out gave the same reason.[5]

The fact that women drop out of the labor force to care for their children is frequently cited as the main reason why men predominate in the upper echelons of these professions. For instance, the nursing director of a hospital emergency room (ER) explained why men are overrepresented in the top positions:

The men sometimes tend to be a little more stable than the women. A lot of the men who work in the ER have really been here for quite a while. They're married. Most have kids. But when it's time to have a baby, they're not the ones who take off. It's the same problem, it's not a lot different than a lot of other professions. . . . All the men [nurses] we've got here who are married to nurses and have children, without exception, it's been their wives that have taken the flex options and the men have stayed working forty hours.

Professions tend to reward those who follow a specific pattern of career development: early training, continuous employment, technical as opposed to interpersonal skill acquisition, few competing family responsibilities. Men conform more easily to this pattern in part because of the widespread cultural expectation that men should prioritize their career interests over their family roles. As Catharine MacKinnon has argued, professional standards are not "gender neutral," but rather, "[men's] socially designed biographies define workplace expectations and successful career patterns."[6] Of course, this doesn't mean that women are incapable of following this "male" career pattern by, for example, forgoing marriage and family to escape competing obligations. But women are disadvantaged as a group because the criteria for success and promotion even in these predominantly female occupations favor the male model of labor force participation.

[. . .]

DISASSOCIATION

The final distancing strategy used by the men in this study was disassociation from their work. Some men feel little or no connection to their jobs: They either fell into their professions with little forethought or planning, or they became gravely disaffected by their work once they began their careers.[7] For example, a public librarian explained why he chose his profession:

> I sort of thought that it wouldn't be too stressful, it wouldn't be too hard. You could go anywhere in the country you wanted to and get a job. To a small town or something, which certainly has an appeal. Since there's a lot of women, you could do things like take a year off and come back, and people wouldn't look at your résumé and say, "What is that? What is this year off?" And you wouldn't be required to climb a career ladder.

This man described himself as entirely lacking in ambition and enthusiasm for the librarianship profession, and mocked others who took their jobs more seriously.

Similarly, a teacher told me that he got his teaching certificate in college because "it was always something I figured I could fall back on. Or if I moved, I could always get a teaching position if something else didn't work out." Currently he is working on a second degree to become an exercise physiologist, and he plans to continue teaching "only as long as it takes me to get out of there."

Part of this disassociation strategy is to condemn or deride others who are in the profession – particularly other men. A public librarian described his male co-workers as "a bit old ladyish because they've worked in reference a long time. I don't know if that's because of their personality or working in a job so many years. Just being sort of nervous." He explained that he has remained in the same position for nineteen years only because he loves living in Cambridge – not because of his job. And a social worker who periodically leaves his profession to pursue other interests (including a yearlong stint as a car dealer in Atlantic City), described his male colleagues in less-than-glowing terms:

> I grew up in the world of work, business, the bottom line. There is not that kind of accountability in social work. My stereotype of men coming into social work is maybe this is easier, they don't want to face the real world where you're going to be held accountable.

By condemning the profession – and the other men in it – men can distance themselves from their work, and preserve a sense of themselves as different and better than those employed in these professions.

Sometimes this disassociation strategy is directed toward gay men in these professions. Some straight men deride their gay colleagues, blaming them for the poor status of their work. In an interview study of male nurses by Joel Heikes, several men expressed extremely homophobic attitudes.[8] I did not find ample evidence of homophobia in my interviews, perhaps because men are less comfortable expressing anti-gay sentiments to a woman interviewer. However, several of the men I interviewed did make it perfectly clear that they were straight, apparently to distinguish themselves from their gay colleagues (and the gay stereotype about men who work in these professions). Since heterosexuality is a key component of hegemonic masculinity, this disassociation strategy allows men to maintain a sense of themselves as appropriately masculine even though they work in predominantly female jobs.

Thus, men can use several strategies to maintain their masculinity in these female occupations: They can differentiate themselves from women by specializing in certain male-identified areas, by emphasizing masculine components of their jobs, by aspiring to higher administrative positions, and by disassociating from their professions altogether. Each of these strategies entails establishing difference from and superiority over women. Thus, paradoxically, men in nontraditional occupations can and do actually support hegemonic masculinity, and end up posing little threat to the social organization of gender.

NOTES

1   Howard S. Rowland (ed.), *The Nurses' Almanac*, 2d edn. (Rockville, MD: Aspen Systems Corp., 1984), p. 153; King Research, Inc., *Library Human Resources: A Study of Supply and Demand* (Chicago: American Library Association, 1983), p. 41; Reginald O. York, H. Carl Henley, and Dorothy N. Gamble, "Sexual Discrimination in Social Work: Is it Salary or Advancement?" *Social Work* 32 (1987): 336–40; Nancy W. Veeder and Joellen W. Hawkins, "Women in 'Women's Professions': Quiet Knowledge Builders," *Sociological Practice Review* 2 (1991): 264–74.

2   Laurel Davis discusses how male cheerleaders emphasize the masculine elements of their "work" by focusing on tumbling and stunts. See "Male Cheerleaders and the Naturalization of Gender," in *Sport, Men and the Gender Order*, ed. Michael Messner and Donald Sabo (Champaign, IL: Human Kinetics Books, 1990), pp. 153–61.

3   This is the finding of Janet Gans, who studied a national sample of over 5,000 nursing directors: She found that married female nurses were significantly less likely than unmarried female nurses to pursue higher educational credentials. Men's pursuit of these degrees was not affected by their marital status. Gans, "The Mobile Minority: Men's Success in a Woman's Profession," Ph.D. disser-

tation, University of Massachusetts, 1984. I discuss this study in Williams, *Gender Differences at Work* (Berkeley, CA: University of California Press, 1989), pp. 95–98.

4   Sara E. Rix (ed.), *The American Woman, 1988–1989: A Status Report* (New York: W. W. Norton, 1988), p. 343.

5   US Department of Labor, Bureau of Labor Statistics, *Employment and Earnings* 38, no. 1 (January 1991): 18.

6   Catharine MacKinnon, *Toward a Feminist Theory of the State* (Cambridge, MA: Harvard University Press, 1990), p. 224.

7   L. Susan Williams and Wayne J. Villemez argue that a good proportion of men who work in predominantly female occupations enter their jobs through a "trap door": They intended to pursue more traditional lines of work but for some reason ended up in "female" jobs. This probably applies less to those in the predominantly female professions compared to those in unskilled jobs since a substantial amount of planning is required to enter the professions. But some respondents who disassociate from their work did describe the "trap door" phenomenon. See Williams and Villemez, "Seekers and Finders: Male Entry and Exit in Female-Dominated Jobs," in *Doing "Women's Work": Men in Nontraditional Occupations*, ed. Christine L. Williams (Newbury Park, CA: Sage, 1993), pp. 64–90.

8   We compared our interview findings in Christine L. Williams and E. Joel Heikes, "The Importance of Researcher's Gender in the In-Depth Interview: Evidence from Two Case Studies of Male Nurses," *Gender & Society* 7 (1993): 280–91.

Why is it important for men to emphasize their masculinity when they are employed in a predominately female job? Can you think of any other strategies men might use?

Part III

Epilogue

7

Deconstructing Gender Differences and Inequalities

CHAPTER OBJECTIVES

- Review the book's major themes
- Explain the processes of institutionalization and legitimation as they relate to gender inequality
- Examine how the ideologies of deference and paternalism have helped to justify gender inequality
- Explore what is meant by a "degendered" society and consider the prospects for achieving this

The future of gender differences is intimately tied to the future of gender inequality.

Michael S. Kimmel, *The Gendered Society*, p. 264

This book was premised on the position that gender matters. Gender is a multilevel system of social practices that produces distinctions between women and men, and organizes inequality on the basis of those distinctions. It is a powerful principle of social life that is visible throughout the social world. In this book, I have highlighted three primary levels on which gender operates:

- First, gender is produced at the individual level. Though scholars disagree about the exact processes through which this occurs, and the durability of the distinctions that are created, they acknowledge that people are gendered beings.

- Second, gender distinctions and inequalities are produced through social relations and interaction. In this view, gender can best be observed when features of the social context are taken into account.

- Third, gender is produced through organizational arrangements and institutions. To understand gender from this vantage point requires attention to social structure and the policies and practices that sustain it.

In Part I, I discussed these three approaches, beginning with the social practices that produce the gendered person (Chapter 2). In Chapter 3, the focus shifted to interactional and institutional approaches. In Part II, I examined work and family as gendered institutions. Chapter 4 focused on the "big picture," examining these institutions as they have evolved historically, as well as looking at their composition and social organization today. Chapters 5 and 6 moved "inside" families and workplaces, exploring how both are structured by gender distinctions and inequalities.

In these final pages, I want to reiterate the book's goals and offer some thoughts about the *de*construction of the gender system. My primary goal in writing this book was to provide readers with theoretical and conceptual tools that can help them make sense of gender as it operates in social life. This is a tall order because gender is everywhere, and because gender scholars have provided many vantage points from which to examine this issue. I have stressed tools and frameworks rather than specific topic areas, and I have not tried to describe all the ways that gender matters in social life. That would be a very long book indeed. Instead, my goal was more circumscribed: I aimed to show how sociologists have conceptualized gender, focusing particular attention on the different ways they have gone about this task and the different emphases they have placed on various aspects of social life. While the views presented here do not necessarily agree on "where the action is" as far as gender is concerned, together they reinforce the notion that gender is a multilevel system.

With these conceptual tools in hand, the book focused on two important social institutions: family and work. The list could have been expanded to include health, religion, crime, sports, and more, and I urge readers to examine gender in these and other areas of life. Ideally, the conceptual tools acquired here can be used to analyze any area of the gendered world. Can these tools also be used to deconstruct gender and to dismantle gender hierarchies and distinctions? This is the last issue we will explore.

GENDER DISTINCTIONS AND GENDER INEQUALITIES

As we have seen, the gender system involves two sorts of processes – the creation of distinctions *and* inequalities based on these distinctions. The previous chapters have described both processes. Regarding gender distinctions, for example, we have seen how forces operating at the individual, interactional, and institutional levels produce a gender-differentiated world. For example, at the individual level, "sex difference" approaches aim to systematically document differences between women and men. For some researchers in this tradition, at least a few of these differences are presumed to have biological or genetic origins. Gender distinctions are also produced through social interaction, as the ethnomethodological approaches discussed in Chapter 3 explain. The structures and practices of institutions play a role in the production of gender distinctions as well.

Gender distinctions are inextricably linked to gender inequality. This link is evident at all levels of the social world. In the simplest terms, this can be illustrated by the greater societal value and worth attached to maleness *and* to all things masculine, relative to femaleness and things deemed feminine. At the individual level, "traits" and characteristics associated with men and masculinity are accorded more social value than those associated with women and femininity. From an interactionist perspective, as we saw in Chapter 3, the production of difference simultaneously involves the creation of gender hierarchies. Even at the level of organizations and institutions, worth, status, and resources are differentially assigned on the basis of gender. Hence, regardless of the vantage point from which gender distinctions are examined, they provide the underpinnings for inequality.

While most gender scholarship focuses on a single level of analysis, it is important to understand that gender distinctions and inequalities are produced and reproduced at all levels of the social world. Because it is a multilevel system, the gender order has been particularly resistant to change. Gender distinctions and inequalities produced at one level of the social world are often reinforced by social processes operating at other levels.

In order to assess the possibilities for dismantling – or at least systematically challenging – the gender order, we must first look more carefully at how gender is reproduced. I focus on the reproduction of gender *inequality*, but keep in mind that gender distinctions and gender inequalities are interconnected.

THE REPRODUCTION OF GENDER INEQUALITY

Gender inequality is reproduced through two interrelated processes: institutionalization and legitimation. As we explore these processes, we will consider gender inequality in comparison to other kinds of unequal social relations. This comparison helps shed light on why gender inequality has been so difficult to dislodge, and it reveals some of the unique features of gender relations relative to other forms of inequality.

Institutionalizing gender inequality

In Chapter 3, I introduced the concept of gendered institutions. Recall that institutions are comprised of social structures and practices, and they include symbols and beliefs (Friedland and Alford 1991). They are features of social life that seem so regular, so ongoing, and so permanent that they are often accepted as "the way things are." Now, I want to extend this idea by thinking about institutionalization as a *process* that could affect virtually any social relationship or area of social life.

Institutionalization refers to the processes through which social relationships take on the qualities of an institution. From this perspective, we can see that some social relationships are more institutionalized than others. Marriage is an example of a highly institutionalized social relationship (though some would argue that this is less true today than in the past). Though marriage is sometimes referred to as just "a piece of paper" or as a strictly private matter, it is much more powerful than that. Almost everyone expects to marry, and there are widely shared beliefs about the meaning and significance of this social arrangement. In addition, marriage is a legal contract that is recognized by many other important institutions, such as employers, religion, and the government.

Relationships that are highly institutionalized seem to almost reproduce themselves (Berger and Luckmann 1967). They persist without conscious intervention and effort. This means that it is much more difficult to alter something that is highly institutionalized than it is to perpetuate it. As a result, highly institutionalized arrangements do not require coercion to sustain them, making participation appear voluntary and easily justifiable. We can again use the example of marriage to illustrate these qualities: Most people get married and, if their marriage fails, they are likely to get married again. While people may have to justify their choice of a particular marriage partner, adults rarely find themselves having to explain why they are married. *Never married* adults, however, may face questions about their status and have to account for their circumstances.

Social inequalities can also be institutionalized to a greater or lesser degree. Slavery, for example, was a highly institutionalized form of inequality in the United States, enshrined in law and enforced by the state. While slavery has disappeared, this has not meant the end of institutionalized inequalities. Though very different from slavery, gender inequality, along with inequalities based on social class and race, are also highly institution-alized. They are long-term, entrenched, and "durable" (Tilly 1998). They are embedded in the structures and practices of organizations, including workplaces, families, schools, and so on.

Long-term, institutionalized inequalities – like those based on gender, race, and social class – are significantly different from other kinds of unequal social relations in the ways they are experienced and understood (Jackman 1994). These differences affect members of both the dominant and the subordinate groups. Most important, institutionalized inequalities are invisible and "depersonalized" to some extent: "When a relationship [of inequality] is regularized and institutionalized, it is simply a case of 'c'est la vie'" (Jackman 1994: 8). This may be true both for the subordinate group and for those who benefit from the inequality. Dominant group members not only may fail to acknowledge that inequality exists, but are also unlikely to feel personally responsible or guilty. Subordinate group members may also experience institutionalized inequalities as "just the way things are."

Institutionalized inequalities thus are much more likely to endure than those that are not so stable and routine. This long-term stability provides dominant groups with a strong vested interest in maintaining unequal arrangements. In addition, it has the effect of "stacking the deck" in such a way that subordinate groups feel relatively powerless to challenge their position. The dominant group's vested interest in perpetuating inequality, together with the subordinate group's lack of alternatives, shape the ways both groups make sense of their relationship.

Making sense of gender inequality

Inequalities of all kinds persist in part because people view them (and the processes that generate unequal outcomes) as "legitimate." **Legitimation** refers to the processes through which inequalities are justified – that is, they are understood in ways that make them fair and reasonable. Inequal-ities may be taken for granted, seen as acceptable, embraced as desirable, or perhaps merely tolerated. They may be invisible or unrecognized. For example, consider the unequal distribution of wealth in the United States. It is well documented that a small minority owns most of the wealth generated in United States and that this distribution has grown more unequal in recent years (Keister and Moller 2000). Nevertheless, because most people in the United States believe that everyone – including themselves – has the opportunity to get ahead and achieve success, they do not view wealth inequality as unfair or unacceptable (Hochschild 1995).

Americans' views about the availability of economic opportunity and the prospects for achieving success through hard work are part of a powerful ideology commonly understood as "the American Dream." Although not every group in society equally embraces all tenets of this dream, studies show that all segments of society – including the most poor and vulnerable – believe in it to some degree (Hochschild 1995; Kluegel and Smith 1986). Belief in the American Dream thus helps to legitimate social inequality; wealth disparities are seen as the outcome of a system that provides equal opportunities for all to succeed.

The American Dream is an example of an ideology. **Ideology** refers to a dominant, widely shared worldview that reflects people's understanding of the world around them. Ideologies may contain elements of truth or be entirely false. Their role in reproducing inequality depends less on whether they are true and more on how strongly they are embraced. For example, while studies suggest that race shapes people's ability to amass wealth (Keister and Moller 2000), most whites believe that the American Dream is equally open to everyone. This belief helps explain why whites have been generally unenthusiastic supporters of social policies designed to reduce racial barriers in public life (Hochschild 1995; Kluegel and Smith 1986).

Social inequalities of all kinds must be legitimated if they are to remain unchallenged, but the ways this is done vary. As we have seen, institutionalized, long-term relations of inequality, such as those based on gender, give dominant groups a strong, vested interest in maintaining these arrangements. Doing so requires that they construct ideologies that are benign and flattering towards the subordinate group, rather than hostile and antagonistic. The dominant group must offer the subordinate group an interpretation of their relationship that obscures unequal arrangements. The subordinate group must find this ideology persuasive if the dominant group is to protect its interests.

What strategies of persuasion work best to legitimate gender inequality? In her book *The Velvet Glove* (1994), Jackman argues that gender inequality is reproduced through the twin ideologies of paternalism and deference. **Paternalism** referred originally to a traditional father–child relationship, whereby the father cared for and exercised control over his children. In this view, fathers were assumed to love their children, understand their needs, and act in their best interests. Children were seen as less capable and competent than adults and thus were expected to defer to their father's authority and guidance. As Jackman notes, "No arrangement could be more desirable for a group that dominates another" (1994: 10). Paternalism is a powerful ideology because it combines positive feelings for the subordinate group with the exercise of social control. **Deference** implies that these positive feelings are reciprocated by the subordinate group, who see no reason to challenge the dominant group's control over them.

When applied to gender relations, paternalism is an ideology that views women as needing the care, protection, and guidance of men (Rothman 2002). Deference implies women's acceptance of this relationship. Insofar as gender relations are interpreted through the lenses of paternalism (on the part of men), and deference (on the part of women), inequalities will be obscured. Not all men or women embrace these ideologies. Nevertheless, Jackman's (1994) research on gender-related beliefs reveals that a majority of women and men adhere to at least some aspects of these belief systems.

In general, women and men do not view each other as adversaries with conflicting interests. Jackman finds instead an "amicable consensus" in how members of both groups assess the gender-typing of jobs and the traditional gender division of labor in the home (Jackman 1994: 202). For example, roughly two-thirds of her male and female survey respondents saw these arrangements as either positive for the collective, or as benign – neither benefiting nor disadvantaging either group. In addition, her research showed agreement between women and men on each gender's role responsibilities and their support for gender-related social policies. More generally, she found that roughly two-thirds of each gender views the other gender in positive emotional terms; they have warm feelings about the other gender and feel close to them (see also Kleugel and Smith 1986).

Women and men, however, do see each other as *different* in important ways. Both men and women believe that each gender has its own distinctive personality traits. In fact, Jackman (1994) found that only about 12 percent of women and men believe that there are *no* important gender differences. Moreover, women and men generally agree with one another in how they assign these traits; for example, majorities of both genders view women as more talkative and emotional than men. Although both genders believe important differences exist, however, the attributes on which women and men are believed to differ are generally viewed in neutral terms. Women and men generally do not assign positive values to their own group's traits and negative values to those of the other group. Just as in the title of the popular book, *Men are from Mars and Women are from Venus*, women and men tend to regard one another as fundamentally different, but not unequal or differentially valued.

Together, this constellation of beliefs is broadly consistent with the combined ideologies of paternalism and deference: Women and men regard each other positively, agree that each gender has uniquely defined traits and roles, and express relative support for these arrangements. In Jackman's words, "Women are warmly congratulated for their distinctiveness in personal traits that are appropriate to the role they have been assigned" (1994: 374).

To understand the significance of these ideologies, compare the attitudes towards one another of whites and blacks and respondents from different social classes. While there is little outright hostility, paternalism and deference are not significant features of race or social class relations. Blacks and whites feel more estrangement than warmth towards one another, and they disagree over the desirability of government support for race-related social policies (Hochschild 1995; Jackman 1994). More important, whites tend to attribute more positive personal qualities to their own group than to blacks, while blacks reject these labels. These views are in marked contrast to gender relations, which are characterized by consensus among women and men regarding the extent and neutral character of gender differences. The expressions of conflict and division that permeate whites' and blacks' perceptions are less clearly drawn in the case of beliefs about social classes. Even here, however, there is much less paternalism and deference than in people's beliefs about gender.

Jackman suggests that the proximity and frequency of contact between the genders, as compared to black–white contact and contact between members of different social classes, account for these different patterns of beliefs. Women's and men's lives are often bound together in ways that other unequal groups are not. This fact plays a key role in explaining how gender inequality has been legitimated and why it has not provoked divisiveness and hostility among most women and men – especially when compared to inequalities based on race or social class.

Heterosexual women and men share households, marry, and may have children together. The vast majority of people – regardless of their marital status or sexual orientation – have kinship ties to and perhaps even children of the other gender. This proximity, even intimacy, between the genders in households and family life is much less likely to be present between members of other unequal groups. Racial segregation in neighborhoods and schools, for example, remains high (Massey and Denton 1993; Orfield 2001). While social class divisions may exist within families and households, families and households are much less likely to include members of widely divergent social classes – the very rich and the poor – than members of social classes who are closer in social space (e.g., the middle and working class).

Another angle from which to explore these issues is to examine the interrelations of gender and race, as they together shape people's views of gender inequality. In general, studies suggest that African-Americans are more likely than whites to believe that gender inequality exists, and they are more likely than whites to explain this inequality in terms of social rather than biological factors (Kane 2000). African-Americans are also more likely than whites to support social policies and collective action to reduce gender inequality. These patterns hold when analyses are confined only to women. African-American women are more critical of women's place in society than white women and are more supportive of social policies designed to improve women's status (Kane 2000).

Because of their experiences with racism, African-Americans may be more aware of social inequalities of all kinds than whites. In addition, African-Americans may be more predisposed than whites to support collective action and government intervention to reduce social inequality (Kane 2000). This suggests that African-Americans of both genders may be less influenced by the ideologies of paternalism and deference than white women and men.

Institutions and ideologies

Gender inequality is reproduced through the processes of institutionalization and legitimation. As gender inequality becomes institutionalized, it is built into social structures and the everyday routines that sustain them. One consequence of institutionalization is that gender inequality is depersonalized. This depersonalization extends to both women and men. Gender inequality is legitimated through ideological accounts that emphasize women's and men's differences, but downplay the ways in which those differences generate inequalities. Together, these processes make it difficult to reduce gender inequality.

CHALLENGING GENDER INEQUALITY

By focusing on the processes of institutionalization and legitimation we have highlighted the reproduction of gender inequality. These issues are important because much of social life – not just in the realm of gender – is stable, ordered, and changes relatively slowly. Given this, we should not underestimate the difficulties associated with deconstructing gender and reducing gender inequality. At the same time, devoting too much time and energy to issues of reproduction may create the opposite problem: a tendency to downplay the possibilities for individuals and groups to make real change and to be unduly pessimistic about the prospects for gender equality.

Many sociologists have sought to understand how social change occurs within deeply institutionalized social processes. These efforts have produced two key insights worth remembering as we consider the possibilities for reducing gender inequality. First, even highly institutionalized social relationships are not immune to social change. In fact, social change is inevitable and ongoing, and this is especially true in an increasingly diverse, global world. Of course, most changes to highly institutionalized relationships are unplanned, reactive, and incremental. Moreover, there is nothing automatic about change being in the direction of greater equality. In addition to the ubiquity of social change, we should also understand that it is almost always uneven in its impacts and timing: All parts of the social world do not change at the same time or in the same way. This "unevenness" creates conflict, tension, and disruptions, which have often inspired more far-reaching and self-conscious attempts to alter institutionalized arrangements.

As a multilevel system, the gender order is particularly resistant to radical change or disruption. The social processes that create a world of two genders operate simultaneously at the individual, interactional, and institutional levels. It is difficult to imagine the full-scale dismantling of this system – at least in the short-term. Far easier to imagine, however, are openings for smaller-scale, but still significant, challenges to the gender order. These sorts of challenges have already produced change in the direction of greater gender equality and make possible even greater changes to come.

While gender is produced at the individual, interactional, and institutional levels, each level may be somewhat differently impacted by social changes in the larger society. Unevenness of change at these different levels produced significant changes in the gender order during the latter part of the twentieth century. To illustrate how this occurred, consider this example: Many men and women raised during the 1960s and 1970s expected to form families where men were primary breadwinners and women had responsibility for home and children. These expectations were reinforced through socialization and reflected in women's and men's gender identities. Changes at the institutional level in both work and family made these expectations unrealizable for many, however. Instead, women and men often found themselves creating lives quite different from those they had imagined (Gerson 1986). Women worked for pay, and men participated in caring for their children and were expected to shoulder at least some of the work of maintaining a household.

In this instance, gender identities at the individual level were at odds with changed institutional realities. Family and work were being reshaped much faster than socialization practices and the gender identities of individuals. This created disruption and conflict both for individuals and for relationships (Hochschild 1989), but it also helped create the foundation for more far-reaching changes in the gender order. This is because uneven social change is destabilizing. Change in one part of the gender order creates openings for changes at other levels. For example, socialization practices for the next generation adjusted to new realities, and the gender identities of young women and men became less anchored in the traditional dichotomy of the male breadwinner and female mother and wife. While gender equality in the family has not been achieved, women's and men's family lives are quite different today than three decades ago. Women have more bargaining power in relationships with men and men are expected to be more involved with family and children. These are real changes that have produced greater equality in the household division of labor and in women's opportunities in the paid workplace.

In the previous example of uneven social change, institutions took the lead, with individuals and interactions changing more slowly. Sometimes, however, individuals change first and create new kinds of relationships that ultimately pressure institutions to respond. Risman (1998) argues that gay and childless heterosexual couples are examples of intimate relationships that challenge gender at the interactional level. Participants in these relationships have urged institutions to change their policies and practices. For example, employers have been encouraged to offer domestic partner benefits to gay couples. Schools have been pressured to acknowledge students' parents, rather than considering only "mothers and fathers." These changes in institutions are not easily achieved; they require unified, sustained, collective action. But they are far from impossible.

As these examples show, social change may be uneven because it affects one level of the gender order sooner or more deeply than another. Another way to think about uneven social change in relation to gender, however, is to consider its differential impact on the lives of women and men. Kimmel (2000: 267) argues that we began the twenty-first century with a "half-finished revolution." The first half of this revolution involved significant changes in women's lives. "This century," he notes, "has witnessed an unprecedented upheaval in the status of women, possibly the most significant transformation in gender relations in world history." The changes he cites as evidence for this include women gaining the right to vote, as well as the rights to work in virtually all jobs, to be admitted on the same terms as men to all educational institutions and to join the military. On a smaller scale, we see evidence of this half-finished revolution in the dramatic changes that have occurred in women's work and family lives, relative to the lives of men. This half-finished revolution has not been easy for women, Kimmel suggests, but it has paved the way for the second half of the revolution: changes in men's lives.

All of these examples show evidence of uneven social change creating greater rather than less gender equality. Over the past half-century (in the West, at least), changes in the gender order have generally moved us in this direction. Most gender scholars agree that gender inequality at the individual, interactional, and institutional levels has been reduced. As this book has shown, however, we are still a long way from a society where gender inequality has been eliminated. In order for that to occur, many more far-reaching changes would be necessary. What would that society look like?

Making Gender Matter Less

Sociologists have generally written much more on the topic of inequality than equality. In part, this is because inequality is everywhere; equality has proven to be much more elusive. This is also true in the case of gender, where inequality is institutionalized and legitimated, and gender equality seems a long way in the future. While there is no roadmap to gender equality, however, sociologists do agree about some of the necessary stops along the way.

In Chapter 1, I argued that gender matters. The path to gender equality is to make gender matter less. This does not mean that we would live in a science fiction-like world where people were all the same. Instead, it means that gender would be significantly less influential as a factor shaping social life than it is today. In certain respects, this has already begun. For example, the social changes cited earlier as evidence for greater gender equality represent successful attempts to make gender matter less in the areas of voting, employment, and education.

A truly degendered society would extend these changes to all areas of social life. Degendering institutions means that their practices, policies, and structures would be indifferent to gender, organized according to other, yet to be discovered, principles. Degendering interaction means that interaction would not depend upon people being identifiable to one another as male or female. Degendering individuals means that gender would no longer be the primary organizer of people's traits, personalities, and identities. Sex categories would be sufficient acknowledgment of the biological distinctions between males and females; there would be no need or reason to make any more of these characteristics.

To more fully understand what this "degendered" world would look like, reconsider the material discussed in this book. Imagine how personalities and identities would form if gender played a lesser role in shaping what people could become and how they thought of themselves. Consider how social interaction might unfold were people less accountable to gender expectations. Finally, envision families and workplaces as places where gender did not structure the tasks people performed and determine the worth of those activities. For gender equality to be achieved, gender itself must matter less.

These arguments underscore a central theme of this book – the mutually reinforcing ties between gender distinctions and gender inequality. Gender distinctions are the raw material of gender inequality; eroding these distinctions thus is a necessary part of reducing inequality. Reductions in gender inequality, in turn, contribute to a lessening of gender distinctions. As Kimmel (2000) notes, the fact that women and men today are seen as more similar than different reflects not merely a change in people's understanding and perceptions, but rather is a direct consequence of greater gender equality than in the past.

In sum, the forces reproducing gender inequality are deeply entrenched, but this has not prevented some reductions in gender inequality and a lessening of the gender distinctions that support them. By exposing the workings of gender, this book has aimed to help readers analyze its impacts and contribute to its demise.

CHAPTER SUMMARY

Gender is a powerful principle of social life. It is a multilevel system of social practices that produces distinctions between women and men, and organizes inequality on the basis of those distinctions. Gender operates at the individual, interactional, and institutional levels.

Gender is reproduced through the forces of institutionalization and legitimation. Inequalities based on gender, race, and social class are highly institutionalized. This makes them especially difficult to eliminate; they are taken for granted as "just the way things are." All inequalities must be legitimated; ideologies help provide this legitimation by supplying accounts that make inequality seem fair and/or reasonable. Gender inequalities are legitimated through the twin ideologies of paternalism and deference. These ideologies lead men and women to view each other as different in important ways, but they do not necessarily view the other group as an adversary. Gender differences are celebrated, while gender inequalities are downplayed.

Even institutionalized relationships can be changed. These changes are often prompted by changes occurring in the larger society that affect different parts of the gender order in different ways. Uneven social change helps to destabilize the gender system, thus creating the possibility for even more change.

The key to creating gender equality is to make gender a less influential factor in shaping social life than it is today. Reducing the importance of gender will contribute to a lessening of gender inequality. Reducing gender inequality will help reduce gender distinctions.

FURTHER READING

Jackman, Mary R. 1994. *The Velvet Glove: Paternalism and Conflict in Gender, Class, and Race Relations*. Berkeley, CA: University of California Press.
Risman, Barbara J. 1998. *Gender Vertigo*. New Haven, CT: Yale University Press.

A CLOSER LOOK

Reading 1: Privilege as Paradox

Allan G. Johnson

Individuals are the ones who experience privilege or the lack of it, but individuals aren't what is actually privileged. Instead, privilege is defined in relation to a group or social category. In other words, race privilege is more about *white* people than it is about white *people*. I'm not race privileged because of who I am as a person. Whiteness is privileged in this society, and I have access to that privilege only when people identify me as belonging to the category "white." I do or don't receive race privilege based on which category people put me in without their knowing a single other thing about me.

This means that you don't actually have to be white or male or heterosexual to receive the privilege attached to those categories. All you have to do is convince people you belong to the appropriate category. The film *Shakespeare in Love*, for example, is set in Elizabethan England, where acting on the stage was a privilege reserved for men. The character Viola (the woman Shakespeare falls in love with) wants more than anything to act on the stage, and finally realizes her dream not by changing her sex and becoming a man, but by successfully presenting herself as one. That's all that it takes.

In similar ways, you can lose privilege if people think you don't belong to a particular category. My sexual orientation is heterosexual, for example, which entitles me to heterosexual privilege, but only if people identify me as heterosexual. If I were to announce to everyone that I'm gay, I would immediately lose my access to heterosexual privilege (unless people refused to believe me), even though I would still be, in fact, a heterosexual person. As Charlotte Bunch put it, "If you don't have a sense of what privilege is, I suggest that you go home and announce to everybody that you know – a roommate, your family, the people you work with – that you're a queer. Trying being queer for a week."[1] When it comes to privilege, then, it doesn't really matter who we really are. What matters is who other people *think* we are, which is to say, the social categories they put us in.

Several important consequences follow from this paradox of privilege. First, privilege is rooted in societies and organizations as much as it's rooted in people's personalities and how they perceive and react to one another.

From *Privilege, Power, and Difference* (Mountain View, CA: Mayfield, 2001), pp. 34–8.

This means that doing something about the problem of privilege takes more than changing individuals. As Harry Brod wrote about gender privilege:

> We need to be clear that there is no such thing as giving up one's privilege to be "outside" the system. One is always *in* the system. The only question is whether one is part of the system in a way which challenges or strengthens the status quo. Privilege is not something I *take* and which I therefore have the option of *not* taking. It is something that society *gives* me, and unless I change the institutions which give it to me, they will continue to give it, and I will continue to *have* it, however noble and egalitarian my intentions.[2]

Societies and organizations promote privilege in complicated ways. It's important to be aware that we don't have to be special or even feel special in order to have access to privilege, because privilege doesn't derive from who we are or what we've done. It is a social arrangement that depends on which category we happen to be sorted into by other people and how they treat us as a result.

The paradoxical experience of *being* privileged without *feeling* privileged is a second consequence of the fact that privilege is more about social categories than who people are. It has to do primarily with the people we use as standards of comparison – what sociologists call "reference groups." We use reference groups to construct a sense of how good or bad, high or low we are in the scheme of things. To do this, we usually don't look downward in the social hierarchy but to people we identify as being on the same level as or higher level than our own. So pointing out to someone in the United States who lives in poverty that they're better off than impoverished people in India doesn't make them feel much better, because people in the Untied States don't use Indians as a reference group. Instead, they will compare themselves with those who seem like them in key respects and see if they're doing better or worse than *them*.

Since being white is valued in this society, whites will tend to compare themselves with other whites, not with people of color. In the same way, men will tend to compare themselves with other men and not with women. What this means, however, is that whites will tend not to feel privileged *by their race* when they compare themselves with their reference group, because their reference group is also white. In the same way, men won't feel privileged *by their gender* in comparison with other men, because gender doesn't elevate them above other *men*. A partial exception to this is the hierarchy that exists among men between heterosexuals and homosexuals: heterosexual men are more likely to consider themselves "real men" and therefore socially valued above gay men. But even here, the mere fact of being male isn't experienced as a form of privilege, because gay men are also male.

An exception to these patterns can occur for those who are privileged by gender or race but find themselves ranked low in terms of social class. To protect themselves from feeling and being seen as on the bottom of the ladder, they may go out of their way to compare themselves to women or people of color by emphasizing their supposed gender or racial superiority. This can appear as an exaggerated sense of masculinity, for example, or as overt attempts to put women or people of color "in their place," including by harassment, violence, or behavior that is openly contemptuous or demeaning.

A corollary to being privileged without knowing it is to be on the *other* side of privilege without necessarily feeling *that*. For example, I sometimes hear a woman say something like, "I've never been oppressed as a woman." Often this is said to challenge the idea that male privilege exists at all. But this confuses the social position of females and males as social categories with one woman's subjective experience of belonging to one of those categories. They aren't the same. For various reasons – including social-class privilege or an unusual family experience or simply being young – she may have avoided a direct confrontation with many of the consequences of being female in a society that privileges maleness. Or she may have managed to overcome them to a degree that she doesn't feel hampered by them. Or she may be engaging in denial. Or she may be unaware of how she is discriminated against (unaware, perhaps, that being a woman is the reason her professors ignore her in class) or may have so internalized her subordinate status that she doesn't see it as a problem (thinking, perhaps, that women are ignored because they aren't intelligent enough to say anything worth listening to). Regardless of what her experience is based on, it is just that – her experience – and it doesn't have to square with the larger social reality that everyone (including her) must deal with one way or another. It's like living in a rainy climate and somehow avoiding being rained on yourself. It's still a rainy place to be and getting wet is something most people have to deal with.

NOTES

1   Charlotte Bunch, "Not for Lesbians Only," *Quest* 11, no. 2 (Fall 1975).
2   Harry Brod, "Work Clothes and Leisure Suits: The Class Basis and Bias of the Men's Movement," in Michael Kimmel and Michael A. Messner (eds.), *Men's Lives* (New York: Macmillan, 1989), p. 280. Italics in original.

What are the "paradoxes" of privilege to which Johnson refers? How do these paradoxes make privilege more difficult to uproot?

Reading 2: Gender Vertigo

Barbara J. Risman

At this point in history I question the need, indeed the usefulness, of continuing to elaborate on sex category at all. If we are to allow individuals full room to maneuver, to build on their strengths, to create themselves, why shackle any of us with cognitive images that restrict us to gendered notions? Why differentiate at all in the way we socialize girls and boys? Why should sex category matter in determining life chances and social roles, in the family or outside of it?

My answer is that gender should be irrelevant to all aspects of our lives. I am not denying biology. Women give birth and lactate. But in the interests of equity we might create social norms that take for granted that fathers devote the first nine months after birth to their babies insofar as mothers have devoted much time and energy in the nine months preceding the birth. If as a society we begin with the assumption that every paid employee also has, at some point in the life cycle, elderly parents, children, and perhaps ailing partners to care for, we must redesign the demands of employment. Our economic structure currently is built on the invisible, nurturing work of women. If the gender structure is simply deleted from the screen, the expectations that we make of paid workers and the organization of workplaces and schools will need dramatic changes. If we do not presume that women inside the family are responsible for the caregiving and nurturing that we all need, we just might have to integrate the expectation of caring relationships into all aspects of our lives, even in our workplaces (Hays 1996).

But the abolition of our gender structure is considerably more challenging to the status quo than the mere blurring of social roles in our families, and even more challenging than the reorganization of our economy that it would require. Perhaps the most challenging implications of abolishing our gender structure would be to our psyches. We all have much at stake in our gendered identities, beyond our social roles. We not only fill gendered roles, we also do gender in the way we walk and talk and dress and eat and play. Gender, as we do it, is not only about subordination, inequality, and stratification but also about who we are and how we experience our selves and our relationships.

In order to rout out the inequality that is a consequence of gender structure we must challenge what it means to be men and women in the twenty-first century. This may ultimately be liberating for ourselves, our children, and future generations. But the immediate gender vertigo will make us more

From *Gender Vertigo* (New Haven, CT: Yale University Press, 1998), pp. 157–62.

than dizzy; it may even be disorienting. For our clothes, hairstyles, and jewelry are among the few realms in society in which we are free to play, to fantasize, to be creative. Today there are limits to social acceptability in this creativity; ask any man whose inner self dictates that he wear a skirt to the office, or any woman who chooses to shave her head. But there are relatively few men who prefer skirts and women who prefer a bald head. Most of us enjoy playing with our looks, makeup, and clothes in socially acceptable ways. This is gendered play. For although both men and women may enjoy finding the right earrings, women usually wear at least two of them at a time and in both ears; men usually wear none or decorate only one ear. Presentation of self is one of the areas in which each of us has some autonomy and control, and is allowed the pleasure to play even in adulthood – as long as we stay within gendered parameters.

My guess is that at least some of the deeply felt reaction to changing gendered roles in families or in the workplace springs from the fear of going too far, of denying one of the few means of easily accessible, socially acceptable, nonfattening, healthy pleasures available to us: doing gender in ways we enjoy. Consider that this pleasure in doing gender is intertwined with heterosexual sexuality and even the most dedicated heterosexual feminist perceives a threat to happiness if gender itself is eliminated. Only a very foolish feminist theoretician would put these destabilizing aspects of gender at the center of her agenda for social change.

And yet we cannot have inequality unless we have difference, and these gendered means of pleasure are part and parcel of making biological males and females into what appear to be greatly differentiated, gendered men and women. Different enough to be unequal. This is conundrum from which I have yet to find escape. [. . .] There are simply too few ways in our society for people to use and show their creativity; gendered displays of self have become important for these reasons.

REFERENCE

Hays, Sharon. 1996. *The Cultural Contradictions of Motherhood*. New Haven, CT: Yale University Press.

Do you agree with Risman's claim that gender should be "irrelevant to all aspects of our lives"? What would a society where gender is irrelevant look like?

Bibliography

AAUW Educational Foundation. 2001. *Beyond the "Gender Wars": A Conversation about Girls, Boys, and Education.* Washington, DC: AAUW Educational Foundation.

Acker, Joan. 1989. *Doing Comparable Worth: Gender, Class, and Pay Equity.* Philadelphia, PA: Temple University Press.

Acker, Joan. 1990. "Hierarchies, Jobs, and Bodies: A Theory of Gendered Organizations." *Gender & Society* 4: 139–58.

Acker, Joan. 1992a. "Gendering Organizational Theory." In Albert J. Mills and Peta Tancred (eds.), *Gendering Organizational Analysis.* Newbury Park, CA: Sage, pp. 248–60.

Acker, Joan. 1992b. "Gendered Institutions." *Contemporary Sociology* 21: 565–9.

Adler, Patricia A. and Adler, Peter. 1998. *Backboards and Blackboards: College Athletes and Role Engulfment.* New York: Columbia University Press.

Adler, Patricia A., Kless, Steven J. and Adler, Peter. 1992. "Socialization to Gender Roles: Popularity among Elementary School Boys and Girls." *Sociology of Education* 65: 169–87.

Alexander, Gerianne M. and Hines, Melissa. 1994. "Gender Labels and Play Styles: Their Relative Contributions to Children's Selection of Playmates." *Child Development* 65: 869–79.

Allmendinger, Jutta and Hackman, Richard J. 1995. "The More, the Better? A Four-Nation Study of the Inclusion of Women in Symphony Orchestras." *Social Forces* 74: 423–60.

Andersen, Margaret and Collins, Patricia Hill. 1995. *Race, Class, and Gender: An Anthology*, 2nd edition. Belmont, CA: Wadsworth.

Angier, Natalie. 1999. *Woman: An Intimate Geography.* New York: Houghton Mifflin.

Anker, Richard. 1998. *Gender and Jobs: Sex Segregation in Occupations of the World.* Geneva: International Labour Office.

Aries, Elizabeth. 1996. *Men and Women in Interaction.* New York: Oxford University Press.

Astin, A. W. 1993. *What Matters in College? Four Critical Years Revisited*. San Francisco, CA: Jossey-Bass.

Baker, David P. and Perkins Jones, Deborah. 1993. "Creating Gender Equality: Cross-National Gender Stratification and Mathematical Performance." *Sociology of Education* 66: 91–103.

Baker, Janet G. and Fishbein, Harold D. 1998. "The Development of Prejudice towards Gays and Lesbians by Adolescents." *Journal of Homosexuality* 36: 89–100.

Bandura, Albert and Walters, R. H. 1963. *Social Learning and Personality Development*. New York: Holt, Rinehart, and Winston.

Bardwell, Jill R., Cochran, Samuel W. and Walker, Sharon. 1986. "Relationship of Parental Education, Race, and Gender to Sex Role Stereotyping in Five-Year-Old Kindergartners." *Sex Roles* 15: 275–81.

Baron, James N. and Bielby, William T. 1985. "Organizational Barriers to Gender Equality." In Alice Rossi (ed.), *Gender and the Life Course*. Hawthorne, NY: Aldine de Gruyter, pp. 233–51.

Baron, James N. and Newman, Andrew. 1990. "For What it's Worth: Organizations, Occupations, and the Value of Work." *American Sociological Review* 55: 155–75.

Bazzini, Doris G., McIntosh, William D., Smith, Stephen M., Cook, Sabrina and Harris, Caleigh. 1997. "The Aging Woman in Popular Film: Underrepresented, Unattractive, Unfriendly, and Unintelligent." *Sex Roles* 36: 531–43.

Bell, Daniel. 1973. *The Coming of Post-Industrial Society*. New York: Basic Books.

Bellas, Marcia L. 1992. "The Effects of Marital Status and Wives' Employment on the Salaries of Faculty Men: The (House) Wife Bonus." *Gender & Society* 6: 609–22.

Beller, Andrea H. 1982. "Occupational Segregation by Sex: Determinants and Changes." *Journal of Human Resources* 17: 371–92.

Bem, Sandra Lipsitz. 1983. "Gender Schema Theory and Its Implications for Child Development: Raising Gender-aschematic Children in a Gender-schematic Society." *Signs* 8: 598–616.

Bem, Sandra Lipsitz. 1993. *The Lenses of Gender*. New Haven, CT: Yale University Press.

Benenson, Joyce F. 1993. "Greater Preference among Females than Males for Dyadic Interaction." *Child Development* 64: 544–55.

Benenson, Joyce F., Apostoleris, Nicholas H. and Parnass, Jodi. 1997. "Age and Sex Differences in Dyadic and Group Interaction." *Developmental Psychology* 33: 538–43.

Benenson, Joyce F., Atkins-Ford, Shari and Apostoleris, Nicholas H. 1998. "Girls' Assertiveness in the Presence of Boys." *Small Group Research* 29: 198–211.

Berger, Peter L. and Luckmann, Thomas. 1967. *The Social Construction of Reality*. New York: Anchor Books.

Berk, Sarah Fenstermaker. 1985. *The Gender Factory*. New York: Plenum.

Bernard, Jessie. 1972. *The Future of Marriage*. New York: Bantam Books.

Bernard, Jessie. 1973. "My Four Revolutions: An Autobiographical History of the ASA." *American Journal of Society* 78: 773–91.

Bernard, Jessie. 1992. "The Good-Provider Role: Its Rise and Fall." In Michael S. Kimmel and Michael A. Messner (eds.), *Men's Lives*. New York: Macmillan Publishing, pp. 203–21.

Bianchi, Suzanne M., Milkie, Melissa A., Sayer, Liana C. and Robinson, John P. 2000. "Is Anyone Doing the Housework? Trends in the Gender Division of Household Labor." *Social Forces* 79: 191–228.

Bielby, William T. and Baron, James N. 1984. "A Woman's Place is with Other Women: Sex Segregation within Organizations." In Barbara F. Reskin (ed.), *Sex Segregation in the Workplace: Trends, Explanations, Remedies*. Washington, DC: National Academy Press, pp. 27–55.

Bielby, William T. and Baron, James N. 1986. "Men and Women at Work: Sex Segregation and Statistical Discrimination." *American Journal of Sociology* 91: 759–99.

Bielby, William T. and Bielby, Denise B. 1992. "I Will Follow Him: Family Ties, Gender Role Beliefs, and Reluctance to Locate for a Better Job." *American Journal of Sociology* 97: 1241–67.

Birrell, Susan and Cole, Cheryl C. (eds.). 1994. *Women, Sport, and Culture*. Champaign, IL: Human Kinetics Press.

Blackless, Melanie, Charuvastra, Anthony, Derryck, Amanda, Fausto-Sterling, Anne, Lauzanne, Karl, and Lee, Ellen. 2000. "How Sexually Dimorphic are We? Review and Synthesis." *American Journal of Human Biology* 12: 151–66.

Blair, Sampson Lee and Johnson, Michael P. 1992. "Wives' Perceptions of the Fairness of the Division of Household Labor: The Intersection of Housework and Ideology." *Journal of Marriage and the Family* 54: 570–81.

Blair, Sampson Lee and Lichter, D. T. 1991. "Measuring the Division of Household Labor: Gender Segregation of Housework among American Couples." *Journal of Family Issues* 12: 91–113.

Blair-Loy, Mary. 1999. "The Cultural Construction of New Family Schemas: The Case of Female Finance Executives." Unpublished paper.

Blau, Peter and Duncan, Otis Dudley. 1967. *The American Occupational Structure*. New York: John Wiley.

Block, Jeanne H. 1976. "Issues, Problems, and Pitfalls in Assessing Sex Differences: A Critical Review of *The Psychology of Sex Differences*." *Merrill-Palmer Quarterly* 22: 283–308.

Blum, Linda M. 1991. *Between Feminism and Labor: The Significance of the Comparable Worth Movement*. Berkeley, CA: University of California Press.

Blumstein, Philip and Schwartz, Pepper. 1983. *American Couples*. New York: William Morrow.

Booth, Alan, Johnson, David R. and White, Lynn. 1984. "Women, Outside Employment, and Marital Instability." *American Journal of Sociology* 90: 567–83.

Bordo, Susan. 1990. "Feminism, Postmodernism, and Gender Skepticism." In Linda J. Nicholson (ed.), *Feminism/Postmodernism*. New York: Routledge, pp. 133–56.

Boserup, Ester. 1970. *Women's Role in Economic Development*. New York: St. Martin's Press.

Boston, Martha B. and Levy, Gary D. 1991. "Changes and Differences in Preschoolers' Understanding of Gender Scripts." *Cognitive Development* 8: 417–32.

Breedlove, S. Marc. 1994. "Sexual Differentiation of the Human Nervous System." *Annual Review of Psychology* 45: 389–418.

Brines, Julie. 1994. "Economic Dependency and the Division of Labor." *American Journal of Sociology* 100: 652–88.

Brinton, Mary C. 1993. *Women and the Economic Miracle: Gender and Work in Postwar Japan.* Berkeley, CA: University of California Press.

Britton, Dana M. 2000. "The Epistemology of the Gendered Organization." *Gender & Society* 14: 418–34.

Bronstein, Phyllis. 1984. "Differences in Mothers' and Fathers' Behaviors Toward Children: A Cross-Cultural Comparison." *Developmental Psychology* 20: 995–1003.

Budig, Michelle J. 2002. "Male Advantage and the Gender Composition of Jobs: Who Rides the Glass Escalator?" *Social Problems* 49: 258–77.

Budig, Michelle J. and England, Paula. 2001. "The Wage Penalty for Motherhood." *American Sociological Review* 66: 204–25.

Buss, David M. 1995. "Psychological Sex Differences." *American Psychologist* 50: 164–8.

Caldera, Yvonne M., Huston, Aletha C., and O'Brien, Marion. 1989. "Social Interactions and Play Patterns of Parents and Toddlers with Feminine, Masculine, and Neutral Toys." *Child Development* 60: 70–6.

Cancian, Francesa. 1987. *Love in America: Gender and Self-Development.* Cambridge: Cambridge University Press.

Cancian, Francesa. 1989. "Love and the Rise of Capitalism." In Barbara J. Risman and Pepper Schwartz (eds.), *Gender in Intimate Relationships.* Belmont, CA: Wadsworth, pp. 12–25.

Carpenter, Laura M. 1998. "From Girls into Women: Scripts for Sexuality and Romance in *Seventeen* Magazine." *The Journal of Sex Research* 35: 158–68.

Casper, Lynne M. and Bianchi, Suzanne M. 2002. *Continuity and Change in the American Family.* Thousand Oaks, CA: Sage Publications.

Chang, Mariko Lin. 2000. "The Evolution of Sex Segregation Regimes." *American Journal of Sociology* 105: 1658–701.

Charles, Maria. 1992. "Cross-National Variation in Occupational Sex Segregation." *American Sociological Review* 57: 483–502.

Charles, Maria. 1998. "Structure, Culture, and Sex Segregation in Europe." *Research in Social Stratification and Mobility* 16: 89–116.

Chatman, Jennifer A., Polzer, J., Barsade, S., and Neale, M. 1998. "Being Different Yet Feeling Similar: The Influence of Demographic Composition and Organizational Culture on Work Processes and Outcomes." *Administrative Science Quarterly* 43: 749–80.

Chemers, Martin M., Oskamp, Stuart, and Costanzo, Mark A. (eds.). 1995. *Diversity in Organizations: New Perspectives for a Changing Workplace.* Thousand Oaks, CA: Sage Publications.

Chodorow, Nancy. 1978. *The Reproduction of Mothering.* Berkeley, CA: University of California Press.

Chodorow, Nancy. 1995. *The Power of Feelings: Personal Meaning in Psychoanalysis, Gender, and Culture.* New Haven, CT: Yale University Press.

Christen, Yves. 1991. *Sex Differences: Modern Biology and the Unisex Fallacy*. New Brunswick, NJ: Transaction Publishers.

Clearinghouse on Urban Education Digest. 2001. "Gender Differences in Educational Achievement within Racial and Ethnic Groups." 164 (August).

Coakley, Jay J. 1998. *Sport and Society*. New York: McGraw-Hill.

Cohn, Lawrence. 1991. "Sex Differences in the Course of Personality Development: A Meta-Analysis." *Psychological Bulletin* 109: 252–66.

Cole, D. A., Martin, J. M., Peeke, L. A., Seroczynski, A. D., and Fier, J. 1999. "Children's Over- and Underestimation of Academic Competence: A Longitudinal Study of Gender Differences, Depression, and Anxiety." *Child Development* 70: 549–473.

Collins, Patricia Hill. 1998. "On Book Exhibits and New Complexities: Reflections on Sociology as Science." *Contemporary Sociology* 27: 7–11.

Collins, Patricia Hill, Maldonado, Lionel L., Takagi, Dana Y., Thorne, Barrie, Weber, Lynn, and Winant, Howard. 1995. "On West and Fenstermaker's *Doing Difference*." *Gender & Society* 9: 491–505.

Collins, Randall, Chafetz, Janet Saltzman, Blumberg, Rae Lesser, Coltrane, Scott, and Turner, Jonathan H. 1993. "Toward an Integrated Theory of Gender Stratification." *Sociological Perspectives* 36: 185–216.

Coltrane, Scott. 1989. "Household Labor and the Routine Production of Gender." *Social Problems* 36: 473–90.

Coltrane, Scott. 1997. *Family Man: Fatherhood, Housework, and Gender Equity*. New York: Oxford University Press.

Coltrane, Scott. 1998. *Gender and Families*. Thousand Oaks, CA: Pine Forge Press.

Coltrane, Scott and Adams, Michele. 1997. "Work–Family Imagery and Gender Stereotypes: Television and the Reproduction of Difference." *Journal of Vocational Behavior* 50: 323–47.

Connell, R. W. 1995. *Masculinities*. Berkeley, CA: University of California Press.

Correll, Shelley J. 2001. "Gender and the Career Choice Process: The Role of Biased Self-Assessments." *American Journal of Sociology* 106: 1691–730.

Cotter, David A., DeFiore, Joann M., Hermsen, Joan D., Kowalewksi, Brenda Marsteller, and Vanneman, Reeve. 1995. "Occupational Gender Desegregation in the 1980s." *Work and Occupations* 22: 3–21.

Cotter, David A., Hermsen, Joan D., Ovadia, Seth, and Vanneman, Reeve. 2001. "The Glass Ceiling Effect." *Social Forces* 80: 655–82.

Cowan, Ruth Schwartz. 1983. *More Work for Mother*. New York: Basic Books.

Crosby, Faye J. (ed.). 1987. *Spouse, Parent, Worker: On Gender and Multiple Roles*. New Haven, CT: Yale University Press.

Crouter, Ann C., McHale, Susan M., and Bartko, W. Todd. 1993. "Gender as an Organizing Feature in Parent–Child Relationships." *Journal of Social Issues* 49: 161–74.

Dalton, Susan E. and Bielby, Denise D. 2000. "That's Our Kind of Constellation: Lesbian Mothers Negotiate Institutionalized Understandings of Gender within the Family." *Gender & Society* 14: 36–61.

Davis, Nancy J. and Robinson, Robert V. 1991. "Men's and Women's Consciousness of Gender Inequality." *American Sociological Review* 56: 72–84.

Deaux, Kay. 1984. "From Individual Differences to Social Categories: Analysis of a Decade's Research on Gender." *American Psychologist* 39: 105–16.

Deaux, Kay. 1985. "Sex and Gender." *Annual Review of Psychology* 36: 46–92.

Deaux, Kay and Emswiller, T. 1974. "Explanations of Successful Performance on Sex-Linked Tasks: What's Skill for the Male is Luck for the Female." *Journal of Personality and Social Psychology* 29: 80–5.

Deaux, Kay and Major, Brenda. 1990. "A Social-Psychology of Gender." In Deborah L. Rhode (ed.), *Theoretical Perspectives on Sexual Difference*. New Haven, CT: Yale University Press, pp. 89–99.

Demo, David H. and Allen, Katherine R. 1996. "Diversity within Lesbian and Gay Families: Challenges and Implications for Family Theory and Research." *Journal of Social and Personal Relationships* 13: 415–34.

DeRosier, Melissa E., Gillessen, Antonius H. N., and Coie, John D. Dodge. 1994. "Group Social Context and Children's Aggressive Behavior." *Child Development* 65: 1068–79.

DeVault, Marjorie L. 1991. *Feeding the Family: The Social Organization of Caring as Gendered Work*. Chicago, IL: University of Chicago Press.

Dunne, Gillian A. (ed.). 1998. *Living "Difference": Lesbian Perspectives on Work and Family Lives*. New York: Harrington Park Press.

Eagly, Alice H. 1987. *Sex Differences in Social Behavior: A Social Role Interpretation*. Hillsdale, NJ: Lawrence Erlbaum Associates.

Eagly, Alice H. 1995. "The Science and Politics of Comparing Women and Men." *American Psychologist* 50: 145–58.

Eagly, Alice H. and Crowley, Maureen. 1986. "Gender and Helping Behavior: A Meta-Analytic Review of the Social Psychological Literature." *Psychological Bulletin* 100: 283–308.

Eagly, Alice H. and Johnson, Blair T. 1990. "Gender and Leadership Style: A Meta-Analysis." *Psychological Bulletin* 108: 233–56.

Eagly, Alice H. and Steffen, Valerie J. 1986. "Gender and Aggressive Behavior: A Meta-Analytic Review of the Social Psychological Literature." *Psychological Bulletin* 100: 309–30.

Eder, Donna. 1995. *School Talk: Gender and Adolescent Culture*. New Brunswick, NJ: Rutgers University Press.

England, Paula. 1982. "The Failure of Human Capital Theory to Explain Occupational Sex Segregation." *Journal of Human Resources* 17: 358–70.

England, Paula. 1984. "Wage Appreciation and Depreciation: A Test of Neoclassical Economic Explanations of Occupational Sex Segregation." *Social Forces* 62: 726–49.

England, Paula. 1992. *Comparable Worth: Theories and Evidence*. New York: Aldine de Gruyter.

England, Paula. 1998. "What Do We Mean When We Say Something is Gendered?" *Newsletter of the Organizations, Occupations, and Work Section of the American Sociological Association*. Fall: 1.

England, Paula. 2001. "Review of *The Case for Marriage: Why Married People are Happier, Healthier, and Better Off Financially*." *Contemporary Sociology* 30: 564–5.

England, Paula and Farkas, George. 1986. *Households, Employment, and Gender: A Social, Economic, and Demographic View*. New York: Aldine De Gruyter.

England, Paula and Folbre, Nancy. 1999. "The Cost of Caring." *Annals of the American Academy of Political and Social Science* 561: 39–51.

England, Paula, Thompson, Jennifer, and Aman, Carolyn. 2001. "The Sex Gap in Pay and Comparable Worth: An Update." In Ivar Berg and Arne Kalleberg (eds.), *Sourcebook on Labor Markets: Evolving Structures and Processes*. New York: Plenum, pp. 551–6.

Epstein, Cynthia. 1988. *Deceptive Distinctions: Sex, Gender, and the Social Order*. New York: The Russell Sage Foundation.

Erickson, Rebecca J. 1993. "Reconceptualizing Family Work: The Effect of Emotion Work on Perceptions of Marital Quality." *Journal of Marriage and the Family* 55: 888–900.

Etaugh, Claire and Liss, Marsha B. 1992. "Home, School, and Playroom: Training Grounds for Adult Gender Roles." *Sex Roles* 26: 129–47.

Fagot, Beverly I. and Hagan, Richard. 1991. "Observations of Parent Reactions to Sex-Stereotyped Behaviors: Age and Sex Effects." *Child Development* 62: 617–28.

Fagot, Beverly I. and Leinbach, Mary D. 1993. "Gender-Role Development in Young Children: From Discrimination to Labeling." *Developmental Review* 13: 205–24.

Fagot, Beverly I., Leinbach, Mary D., and O'Boyle, Cherie. 1992. "Gender Labeling, Gender Stereotyping, and Parenting Behaviors." *Developmental Psychology* 28: 225–30.

Farley, Reynolds. 1996. *The New American Reality: Who We Are, How We Got Here, Where We Are Going*. New York: Russell Sage Foundation.

Feingold, Alan. 1993. "Cognitive Gender Differences." *Sex Roles* 29: 91–112.

Feingold, Alan. 1994. "Gender Differences in Personality: A Meta-Analysis." *Psychological Bulletin* 116: 429–56.

Ferguson, Ann Arnett. 2001. *Bad Boys: Public Schools in the Making of Black Masculinity*. Ann Arbor, MI: University of Michigan Press.

Ferguson, Kathy E. 1984. *The Feminist Case against Bureaucracy*. Philadelphia, PA: Temple University Press.

Ferree, Myra Marx. 1990. "Beyond Separate Spheres: Feminism and Family Research." *Journal of Marriage and the Family* 52: 866–84.

Floge, Lilianne and Merrill, Deborah M. 1986. "Tokenism Reconsidered: Male Nurses and Female Physicians in a Hospital Setting." *Social Forces* 64: 925–47.

Friedland, Roger and Alford, Robert R. 1991. "Bringing Society Back In: Symbols, Practices, and Institutional Contradictions." In Walter W. Powell and Paul J. DiMaggio (eds.), *The New Institutionalism in Organizational Analysis*. Chicago, IL: University of Chicago Press, pp. 232–65.

Gamst, Frederick C. 1995. "Introduction." In Frederick C. Gamst (ed.), *Meanings of Work: Considerations for the Twenty-First Century*. Albany, NY: State University of New York Press, pp. xi–xxii.

Garfinkel, Harold. 1967. *Studies in Ethnomethodology*. Englewood Cliffs, NJ: Prentice Hall.

Garson, Barbara. 1988. *The Electronic Sweatshop*. New York: Penguin Books.

Gerson, Kathleen. 1986. *Hard Choices: How Women Decide about Work, Career, and Motherhood*. Berkeley, CA: University of California Press.

Gerson, Kathleen. 1993. *No Man's Land: Men's Changing Commitments to Family and Work*. New York: Basic Books.

Gerstel, Naomi and Gallagher, Sally K. 1993. "Kinkeeping and Distress: Gender, Recipients of Care, and Work–Family Conflict." *Journal of Marriage and the Family* 55: 598–607.

Gilligan, Carol. 1982. *In a Different Voice: Psychological Theory and Women's Development*. Cambridge, MA: Harvard University Press.

Gilmore, Sean and Crissman, Alicia. 1997. "Video Games: Analyzing Gender Identity and Violence in this New Virtual Reality." *Studies in Symbolic Interaction* 21: 181–99.

Glass, Jennifer. 1992. "Housewives and Employed Wives: Demographic and Attitudinal Change, 1972–1986." *Journal of Marriage and the Family* 54: 559–69.

Glass, Jennifer L. and Camarigg, Valerie. 1992. "Gender, Parenthood, and Job–Family Compatibility." *American Journal of Sociology* 98: 131–51.

Glenn, Evelyn Nakano. 1992. "From Servitude to Service Work: Historical Continuities in the Racial Division of Paid Reproductive Labor." *Signs* 18: 1–43.

Goffman, Erving. 1977. "The Arrangement between the Sexes." *Theory and Society* 4: 301–31.

Goldscheider, Frances K. and Waite, Linda J. 1991. *New Families, No Families? The Transformation of the American Home*. Berkeley, CA: University of California Press.

Goodwin, Marjorie Harkness. 1990. *He-Said-She-Said: Talk as Social Organization Among Black Children*. Bloomington, IN: Indiana University Press.

Gordon, Joel M. 1996. *Fat and Mean: The Corporate Squeeze of Working Americans and the Myth of Managerial Downsizing*. New York: Free Press.

Gornick, Janet, Meyers, Marcia, and Ross, Katherine E. 1998. "Public Policies and the Employment of Mothers: A Cross-national Study." *Social Science Quarterly* 79: 35–54.

Gose, Ben. 1998. "The Feminization of Veterinary Medicine." *Chronicle of Higher Education* April 24, 1998, pp. A55–A56.

Granovetter, Mark. 1974. *Getting a Job: A Study in Contacts and Careers*. Chicago, IL: University of Chicago Press.

Grant, Linda. 1994. "Helpers, Enforcers, and Go-Betweens: Black Females in Elementary School Classrooms." In Maxine Baca Zinn and Bonnie Thornton Dill (eds.), *Women of Color in US Society*. Philadelphia, PA: Temple University Press, pp. 43–63.

Gutek, Barbara A. and Morasch, B. 1982. "Sex Ratios, Sex Role Spillover, and Sexual Harassment of Women at Work." *Journal of Social Issues* 38: 55–74.

Guttentag, Marcia and Secord, Paul F. 1983. *Too Many Women? The Sex Ratio Question*. Newbury Park, CA: Sage Publications.

Hall, Elaine J. 1993. "Waitering/Waitressing: Engendering the Work of Table Servers." *Gender & Society* 9: 329–46.

Hall, Richard H. 2002. *Organizations: Structures, Processes, and Outcomes*, 8th edition. Upper Saddle River, NJ: Prentice Hall.

Harding, Sandra. 1986. *The Science Question in Feminism.* Ithaca, NY: Cornell University Press.

Hare-Mustin, R. T. and Marecek, M. 1988. "The Meaning of Difference: Gender Theory, Postmodernism, and Psychology." *American Psychologist* 43: 455–64.

Hareven, Tamara K. 1990. "A Complex Relationship: Family Strategies and the Processes of Economic and Social Change." In Roger Friedland and A. F. Robertson (eds.), *Beyond the Marketplace: Rethinking Economy and Society.* New York: Aldine de Gruyter, pp. 215–44.

Hasbrook, Cynthia A. 1999. "Young Children's Social Constructions of Physicality and Gender." In Jay Coakley and Peter Donnelly (eds.), *Inside Sports.* New York: Routledge, pp. 7–16.

Hawkesworth, Mary. 1997. "Confounding Gender." *Signs* 22: 649–713.

Henson, Kevin D. and Rogers, Jackie Krasas. 2001. "'Why Marcia You've Changed!' Male Clerical Temporary Workers Doing Masculinity in a Feminized Occupation." *Gender & Society* 15: 218–38.

Hirschfeld, Lawrence A. 1996. *Race in the Making: Cognition, Culture, and the Child's Construction of Human Kinds.* Cambridge, MA: MIT Press.

Hochschild, Arlie. 1979. "Emotion Work, Feeling Rules, and Social Structure." *American Journal of Sociology* 85: 551–75.

Hochschild, Arlie Russell. 1983. *The Managed Heart: The Commercialization of Human Feeling.* Berkeley, CA: University of California.

Hochschild, Arlie 1989. *The Second Shift: Working Parents and the Revolution at Home.* New York: Viking Penguin.

Hochschild, Arlie. 1997. *The Time Bind.* New York: Metropolitan Books.

Hochschild, Jennifer L. 1995. *Facing Up to the American Dream: Race, Class, and the Soul of the Nation.* Princeton, NJ: Princeton University Press.

Hodson, Randy and Sullivan, Teresa A. 1990. *The Social Organization of Work.* Belmont, CA: Wadsworth.

Hoff Sommers, Christina. 2000. *The War against Boys: How Misguided Feminism is Harming Our Young Men.* New York: Touchstone Books.

Holland, Dorothy C. and Eisenhart, Margaret A. 1990. *Educated in Romance: Women, Achievement and College Culture.* Chicago, IL: University of Chicago Press.

Hollander, Jocelyn A. and Howard, Judith A. 2000. "Social Psychological Theories on Social Inequalities." *Social Psychology Quarterly* 63: 338–51.

Howard, Judith. 2000. "Social Psychology of Identities." *Annual Review of Sociology* 26: 367–93.

Hoyenga, Katherine Blick and Hoyenga, Kermit T. 1993. *Gender-Related Differences: Origins and Outcomes.* Boston, MA: Allyn and Bacon.

Hyde, Jane Shibley and Plant, Elizabeth Ashby. 1995. "Magnitude of Psychological Gender Differences." *American Psychologist* 50: 159–61.

Jackman, Mary R. 1994. *The Velvet Glove: Paternalism and Conflict in Gender, Class, and Race Relations.* Berkeley, CA: University of California Press.

Jacobs, Jerry. 1989. *Revolving Doors: Sex Segregation and Women's Careers.* Stanford, CA: Stanford University Press.

Jacobs, Jerry A. 1999. "The Sex Segregation of Occupations: Prospects for the 21st Century." In Gary N. Powell (ed.), *Handbook of Gender and Work.* Thousand Oaks, CA: Sage, pp. 125–41.

Jacobs, Jerry A. and Lim, Suet T. 1992. "Trends in Occupational and Industrial Occupation by Sex in 56 Countries, 1960–80." *Work and Occupations* 19: 450–86.

Jencks, Christopher. 1992. *Rethinking Social Policy: Race, Poverty, and the Underclass*. Cambridge, MA: Harvard University Press.

Jepperson, Ronald L. 1991. "Institutions, Institutional Effects, and Institutionalism." In Walter W. Powell and Paul J. DiMaggio (eds.), *The New Institutionalism in Organizational Analysis*. Chicago, IL: University of Chicago Press, pp. 143–63.

Johnson, Miriam M. 1988. *Strong Mothers, Weak Wives: The Search for Gender Equity*. Berkeley, CA: University of California Press.

Johnston, William B. and Packer, Arnold E. 1987. *Workforce 2000*. Indianapolis, IN: The Hudson Institute.

Jones, Jacqueline. 1987. *Labor of Love, Labor of Sorrow: Black Women, Work, and the Family from Slavery to the Present*. New York: Vintage Books.

Kane, Emily. 1992. "Race, Gender, and Attitudes toward Gender Stratification." *Social Psychology Quarterly* 55: 311–20.

Kane, Emily W. 2000. "Racial and Ethnic Variations in Gender-Related Attitudes." *Annual Review of Sociology* 26: 419–39.

Kanter, Rosabeth Moss. 1977. *Men and Women of the Corporation*. New York: Basic Books.

Keister, Lisa A. and Moller, Stephanie. 2000. "Wealth Inequality in the United States." *Annual Review of Sociology* 26: 63–81.

Kennelly, Ivy, Merz, Sabine N., and Lorber, Judith. 2001. "Comment: What is Gender?" *American Sociological Review* 66: 598–604.

Kessler, Suzanne J. 1990. "The Medical Construction of Gender." *Signs* 16: 3–26.

Kessler, Suzanne J. 1998. *Lessons from the Intersexed*. New Brunswick, NJ: Rutgers University Press.

Kessler, Suzanne J. and McKenna, Wendy. 1978. *Gender: An Ethnomethodological Approach*. Chicago, IL: University of Chicago Press.

Kimmel, Michael S. 2000. *The Gendered Society*. New York: Oxford University Press.

Kimmel, Michael S. and Messner, Michael A. (eds.). 1989. *Men's Lives*. New York: Macmillan.

King, Mary C. 1992. "Occupational Segregation by Race and Sex, 1940–88." *Monthly Labor Review* 115: 30–6.

Kluegel, James R. and Smith, Eliot R. 1986. *Beliefs about Inequality: Americans' Views of What Is and What Ought to Be*. New York: Aldine de Gruyter.

Kohlberg, Lawrence A. 1966. "A Cognitive-Developmental Analysis of Children's Sex Role Concepts and Attitudes." In E. E. Maccoby (ed.), *The Development of Sex Differences*. Stanford, CA: Stanford University Press, pp. 82–172.

Kurdek, Lawrence. 1995. "Lesbian and Gay Couples." In Anthony R. D'Augelli and Charlotte J. Patterson (eds.), *Lesbian, Gay, and Bisexual Identities over the Lifespan*. New York: Oxford University Press, pp. 243–61.

Landers, Melissa A. and Fine, Gary Alan. 1996. "Learning Life's Lessons in Tee Ball: The Reinforcement of Gender and Status in Kindergarten Sport." *Sociology of Sport Journal* 13: 87–93.

Landry, Bart. 2000. *Black Working Wives: Pioneers of the American Family Revolution.* Berkeley, CA: University of California Press.

Larson, Reed and Richards, Maryse H., 1994. *Divergent Realities: The Emotional Lives of Mothers, Fathers, and Adolescents.* New York: Basic Books.

Larson, Reed W., Richards, Maryse H., and Perry-Jenkins, Maureen. 1994. "Divergent Worlds: The Daily Emotional Experience of Mothers and Fathers in the Domestic and Public Spheres." *Journal of Personality and Social Psychology* 76: 1034–46.

Leaper, Campbell. 1994. "Exploring the Consequences of Gender Segregation on Social Relationships." *New Directions for Child Development* 65: 67–86.

Lee, Sharon and Fernandez, Marilyn. 1998. "Trends in Asian American Racial/Ethnic Intermarriage: A Comparison of 1980 and 1990 Census Data." *Sociological Perspectives* 41: 323–42.

Lefkowitz, Joel. 1994. "Sex-Related Differences in Job Attitudes and Dispositional Variables: Now You See Them, . . ." *Academy of Management Journal* 37: 323–49.

Lemert, Charles. 1997. *Social Things: An Introduction to the Sociological Life.* New York: Rowman and Littlefield.

Lenski, Gerhard, Nolan, Patrick, and Lenski, Jean. 1995. *Human Societies: An Introduction to Macrosociology,* 7th edition. New York: McGraw-Hill.

Lesko, Nancy (ed.). 2000. *Masculinities at School.* Thousand Oaks, CA: Sage.

Lieberson, Stanley. 2000. *A Matter of Taste: How Names, Fashions, and Culture Change.* New Haven, CT: Yale University Press.

Lieberson, Stanley, Dumais, Susan and Baumann, Shyon. 2000. "The Instability of Androgynous Names: The Symbolic Maintenance of Gender Boundaries." *American Journal of Sociology* 105: 1249–87.

Lin, Nan. 1999. "Social Networks and Status Attainment." *Annual Review of Sociology* 25: 467–87.

Lippe, Tanja van der and Dijk, Liset van (eds.). 2001. *Women's Employment in a Comparative Perspective.* New York: Aldine De Gruyter.

Lorber, Judith. 1994. *Paradoxes of Gender.* New Haven, CT: Yale University Press.

Lytton, Hugh and Romney, David M. 1991. "Parents' Differential Socialization of Boys and Girls: A Meta-Analysis." *Psychological Bulletin* 109: 267–96.

Maccoby, Eleanor E. 1992. "The Role of Parents in the Socialization of Children: An Historical Overview." *Developmental Psychology* 28: 1006–17.

Maccoby, Eleanor E. 1998. *The Two Sexes: Growing Up Apart, Coming Together.* Cambridge, MA: Harvard University Press.

Maccoby, Eleanor E. and Jacklin, Carol. 1974. *The Psychology of Sex Differences.* Stanford, CA: Stanford University Press.

Maccoby, Eleanor E., Snow, M. E., and Jacklin, C. N. 1984. "Children's Dispositions and Mother–Child Interaction at 12 and 18 Months: A Short-Term Longitudinal Study." *Developmental Psychology* 20: 459–72.

Macdonald, Cameron Lynne and Sirianni, Carmen. 1996. "The Service Society and the Changing Experience of Work." In Cameron Lynne Macdonald and Carmen Sirianni (eds.), *Working in the Service Society.* Philadelphia, PA: Temple University Press, pp. 1–26.

Mandel, Laurie and Shakeshaft, Charol. 2000. "Heterosexism in Middle Schools." In Nancy Lesko (ed.), *Masculinities at School*. Thousand Oaks, CA: Sage, pp. 75–104.

Marini, Margaret Mooney. 1989. "Sex Differences in Earnings in the United States." *Annual Review of Sociology* 15: 343–80.

Marini, Margaret Mooney and Shu, X. 1998. "Gender-Related Change in the Occupational Aspirations of Youth." *Sociology of Education* 71: 43–67.

Marsden, Peter V. 1987. "Core Discussion Networks of Americans." *American Sociological Review* 52: 122–31.

Martin, Carol Lynn. 1993. "New Directions for Investigating Children's Gender Knowledge." *Developmental Review* 13: 184–204.

Martin, Carol Lynn, Eisenbud, Lisa and Rose, Hilary. 1995. "Children's Gender-Based Reasoning about Toys." *Child Development* 66: 1453–71.

Martin, Karin A. 1998. "Becoming a Gendered Body: Practices of Preschools." *American Sociological Review* 63: 494–511.

Massey, Douglas S. and Denton, Nancy A. 1993. *American Apartheid: Segregation and the Making of the Underclass*. Cambridge, MA: Harvard University Press.

Mauldin, Teresa and Meeks, Carol B. 1990. "Sex Differences in Children's Time Use." *Sex Roles* 22: 537–54.

McMahon, Martha. 1995. *Engendering Motherhood: Identity and Self-Transformation in Women's Lives*. Toronto: Guilford Press.

McPherson, J. Miller, Popielarz, Pamela A. and Drobnic, Sonja. 1992. "Social Networks and Organizational Dynamics." *American Sociological Review* 57: 153–70.

McPherson, J. Miller and Smith-Lovin, Lynn. 1986. "Sex Segregation in Voluntary Associations." *American Sociological Review* 51: 61–79.

Messner, Michael A. 1992. *Power at Play: Sports and the Problem of Masculinity*. Boston, MA: Beacon Press.

Messner, Michael A. and Sabo, Donald F. (eds.). 1990. *Sport, Men, and the Gender Order: Critical Feminist Perspectives*. Champaign, IL: Human Kinetics Publishers.

Messner, Michael A., Duncan, Margaret C. and Jensen, Kerry. 1992. "Separating the Men from the Girls: The Gendered Language of Televised Sports." *Gender & Society* 7: 121–37.

Milkie, Melissa A. 1999. "Social Comparisons, Reflected Appraisals, and Mass Media: The Impact of Pervasive Beauty Images on Black and White Girls' Self-Concepts." *Social Psychology Quarterly* 62: 190–210.

Milkman, Ruth. 1987. *Gender at Work: The Dynamics of Job Segregation by Sex During World War II*. Urbana, IL: University of Illinois Press.

Mischel, Walter. 1970. "Sex-Typing and Socialization." In Paul H. Mussen (ed.), *Carmichael's Manual of Child Psychology*, vol. 2, 3rd edition. New York: John Wiley, pp. 3–72.

Mishel, Lawrence, Bernstein, Jared, and Schmitt, John. 2001. *The State of Working America*. Ithaca, NY: Cornell University Press.

Molloy, Beth L. and Herzberger, Sharon D. 1998. "Body Image and Self-Esteem: A Comparison of African-American and Caucasian Women." *Sex Roles* 38: 631–43.

Moore, Gwen. 1990. "Structural Determinants of Men's and Women's Personal Networks." *American Sociological Review* 55: 726–35.

Munch, Alison, Miller, McPherson, and Smith-Lovin, Lynn. 1998. "Gender, Children, and Social Contact: The Effects of Childrearing for Men and Women." *American Sociological Review* 62: 509–20.

Murphy, Raymond. 1988. *Social Closure: The Theory of Monopolization and Exclusion.* Oxford: Clarendon Press.

Nieva, Veronica F. and Gutek, Barbara A. 1981. *Women and Work: A Psychological Perspective.* New York: Praeger Publishers.

Oliver, Mary Beth and Hyde, Janet Shibley. 1993. "Gender Differences in Sexuality: A Meta-Analysis." *Psychological Bulletin* 114: 29–51.

Oppenheimer, Valerie Kincade. 1994. "Women's Rising Employment and the Future of the Family in Industrialized Societies." *Population and Development Review* 20: 293–342.

Orfield, Gary. 2001. *Schools More Separate: Consequences of a Decade of Resegregation.* Report prepared for The Civil Rights Project. Cambridge, MA: Harvard University.

Padavic, Irene and Reskin, Barbara. 2002. *Women and Men at Work.* Thousand Oaks, CA: Pine Forge Press.

Parsons, Talcott. 1964. *Essays in Sociological Theory.* New York: The Free Press.

Parsons, Talcott and Bales, Robert F. 1955. *Family, Socialization and Interaction Process.* New York: The Free Press.

Patterson, Charlotte J. 1995. "Lesbian Mothers, Gay Fathers, and their Children." In Anthony R. D'Augelli and Charlotte J. Patterson (eds.), *Lesbian, Gay, and Bisexual Identities over the Lifespan: Psychological Perspectives.* New York: Oxford University Press, pp. 262–90.

Piaget, Jean. 1932. *The Moral Judgment of the Child.* London: Routledge & Kegan Paul.

Pierce, Jennifer. 1995. *Gender Trials: Emotional Lives in Contemporary Law Firms.* Berkeley, CA: University of California Press.

Polachek, Solomon. 1979. "Occupational Segregation among Women: Theory, Evidence, and a Prognosis." In Cynthia Lloyd (ed.), *Women in the Labor Market.* New York: Columbia University Press, pp. 137–57.

Pomerleau, A., Bolduc, D., Malcuit, G., and Cosette, L. 1990. "Pink or Blue: Environmental Stereotypes in the First Two Years of Life." *Sex Roles* 22: 359–67.

Popielarz, Pamela. 1999. "(In)Voluntary Association: A Multilevel Analysis of Gender Segregation." *Gender & Society* 13: 234–50.

Portes, Alejandro. 1998. "Social Capital: Its Origins and Applications in Modern Sociology." *Annual Review of Sociology* 24: 1–24.

Powell, Gary N. 1993. *Women and Men in Management,* 2nd edition. Newbury Park, CA: Sage.

Press, Angela. 1991. *Women Watching Television: Gender, Class, and Generation in the American Television Experience.* Philadelphia, PA: University of Pennsylvania Press.

Provenzo, Eugene F. 1991. *Video Kids: Making Sense of Nintendo.* Cambridge, MA: Harvard University Press.

Raag, Tarja and Rackliff, Christine L. 1998. "Preschoolers' Awareness of Social Expectations of Gender: Relationships to Toy Choices." *Sex Roles* 38: 685–700.

Raymond, Diane. 1994. "Homophobia, Identity, and the Meanings of Desire: Reflections on the Cultural Construction of Gay and Lesbian Adolescent Sexuality." In Janice M. Irvine (ed.), *Sexual Cultures and the Construction of Adolescent Identities*. Philadelphia, PA: Temple University Press, pp. 115–50.

Reskin, Barbara F. 1993. "Sex Segregation in the Workplace." *Annual Review of Sociology* 19: 241–70.

Reskin, Barbara F. and Hartmann, Heidi I. 1986. *Women's Work, Men's Work: Sex Segregation on the Job*. Washington, DC: National Academy Press.

Reskin Barbara and Padavic, Irene. 1994. *Women and Men at Work*. Thousand Oaks, CA: Pine Forge Press.

Reskin, Barbara F. and Roos, Patricia A. 1990. *Job Queues, Gender Queues: Explaining Women's Inroads into Male Occupations*. Philadelphia, PA: Temple University Press.

Reskin, Barbara F., McBrier, Debra B., and Kmec, Julie A. 1999. "The Determinants and Consequences of Workplace Sex and Race Composition." *Annual Review of Sociology* 25: 335–61.

Ridgeway, Cecilia L. 1993. "Gender, Status, and the Social Psychology of Expectations." In Paula England (ed.), *Theory on Gender/Gender on Feminism*. New York: Aldine de Gruyter, pp. 175–98.

Ridgeway, Cecilia L. 1997. "Interaction and the Conservation of Gender Inequality." *American Sociological Review* 62: 218–35.

Ridgeway, Cecilia L. and Diekama, David. 1992. "Are Gender Differences Status Differences?" In Cecilia L. Ridgeway (ed.), *Gender, Interaction, and Inequality*. New York: Springer-Verlag, pp. 157–80.

Ridgeway, Cecilia L. and Smith-Lovin, Lynn. 1999. "The Gender System and Interaction." *Annual Review of Sociology* 25: 191–216.

Risman, Barbara J. 1998. *Gender Vertigo*. New Haven, CT: Yale University Press.

Risman, Barbara J. 2000. "Calling the Bluff of Value-free Science." *American Sociological Review* 66: 605–11.

Robinson, John P. and Godbey, Geoffrey. 1997. *Time for Life: The Surprising Ways Americans Use Their Time*. State College, PA: Pennsylvania State University Press.

Roos, Patricia A. 1985. *Gender and Work: A Comparative Analysis of Industrial Societies*. Albany, NY: State University of New York Press.

Roos, Patricia A. and Gatta, Mary Lizabeth. 1999. In Gary N. Powell (ed.), *Handbook of Gender and Work*. Thousand Oaks, CA: Sage, pp. 95–123.

Rosenthal, Carolyn J. 1985. "Kinkeeping in the Familial Division of Labor." *Journal of Marriage and the Family* 47: 965–74.

Ross, Catherine E., Mirowsky, J., and Huber, J. 1983. "Dividing Work, Sharing Work, and In-Between: Marriage Patterns and Depression." *American Sociological Review* 48: 809–23.

Ross, Hildy and Taylor, Heather. 1989. "Do Boys Prefer Daddy or His Physical Style of Play?" *Sex Roles* 20: 23–33.

Ross, L. 1977. "The Intuitive Psychologist and His Shortcomings: Distortions in the Attribution Process." In L. Berkowitz (ed.), *Advances in Experimental Social Psychology*. New York: Academic Press, pp. 174–221.

Rossi, Alice S. 1977. "A Biosocial Perspective on Parenting." *Daedalus* 106: 1–31.

Rothman, Robert A. 2002. *Inequality and Stratification: Race, Class, and Gender*, 4th edition. Upper Saddle River, NJ: Prentice Hall.

Rotolo, Thomas and Wharton, Amy S. 2003. "Living Across Institutions: Exploring Sex-Based Homophily in Occupations and Voluntary Groups." *Sociological Perspectives* 46: 59–82.

Rowe, Reba and Snizek, William E. 1995. "Gender Differences in Work Values." *Work and Occupations* 22: 215–29.

Rubin, Jeffrey Z., Provenzano, Frank J., and Luria, Zella. 1974. " 'The Eye of the Beholder': Parents' Views on Sex of Newborns." *American Journal of Orthopsychiatry* 44: 512–18.

Ryan, Joan. 1995. *Little Girls in Pretty Boxes*. New York: Warner Books.

Sadker, Myra and Sadker, David. 1994. *Failing at Fairness: How Our Schools Cheat Girls*. New York: Simon & Schuster.

Shelton, Beth Anne. 1992. *Women, Men, and Time: Gender Differences in Paid Work, Housework, and Leisure*. Westport, CT: Greenwood Press.

Shelton, Beth Anne and John, Daphne. 1996. "The Division of Household Labor." *Annual Review of Sociology* 22: 299–322.

Shinagawa, Larry Hajime and Jang, Michael. 1998. *Atlas of American Diversity*. Walnut Creek, CA: Altamira Press.

Siegal, Michael. 1987. "Are Sons and Daughters Treated More Differently by Fathers than by Mothers?" *Developmental Review* 7: 183–209.

Signorella, Margaret L., Bigler, Rebecca S., and Liben, Lynn S. 1993. "Developmental Differences in Children's Gender Schemata about Others: A Meta-Analytic Review. *Developmental Review* 13: 147–83.

Skelton, Christine. 2001. *Schooling the Boys: Masculinities and Primary Education*. Philadelphia, PA: Open University Press.

Skolnick, Arlene S. 2001. "The State of the American Family." In Susan J. Ferguson (ed.), *Shifting the Center: Understanding Contemporary Families*. Mountain View, CA: Mayfield, pp. 41–53.

Smith, Dorothy. 1974. "Women's Perspective as a Radical Critique of Sociology." *Sociological Inquiry* 44: 7–13.

Smith, Ryan and Elliott, James R. 2002. "Does Ethnic Concentration Influence Employers' Access to Authority? An Examination of Contemporary Urban Labor Markets." *Social Forces* 81: 255–80.

Smith, Tom W. 1985. "Working Wives and Women's Rights: The Connection Between the Employment Status of Wives and the Feminist Attitudes of Husbands." *Sex Roles* 12: 501–8.

Smith-Lovin, Lynn and McPherson, J. Miller. 1993. "You Are Who You Know: A Network Approach to Gender." In Paula England (ed.), *Theory on Gender/Feminism on Theory*. New York: Aldine de Gruyter, pp. 223–51.

Spain, Daphne and Bianchi, Suzanne M. 1996. *Balancing Act: Motherhood, Marriage and Employment Among American Women*. New York: Russell Sage Foundation.

Spelman, Elizabeth V. 1988. *Inessential Woman*. Boston, MA: Beacon Press.

Spence, Janet T. 1984. "Masculinity, Femininity, and Gender-related Traits: a Conceptual Analysis and Critique of Current Research." In B. A. Maher and W. B.

Maher (eds.), *Progress in Experimental Personality Research*, vol. 13. New York: Academic Press, pp. 1–97.

Spence, Janet T., Deaux, Kay and Helmreich, Robert L. 1985. "Sex Roles in Contemporary American Society." In Gardner Lindzey and Elliot Aronson (eds.), *Handbook of Social Psychology*, vol. 2. New York: Random House, pp. 149–78.

Stacey, Judith. 1996. *In the Name of the Family: Rethinking Family Values in the Postmodern Age*. Boston, MA: Beacon Press.

Stacey, Judith and Thorne, Barrie. 1985. "The Missing Feminist Revolution in Sociology." *Social Problems* 32: 301–16.

Stack, Carol V. 1974. *All Our Kin*. New York: Harper & Row.

Steinberg, Ronnie J. and Haignere, Lois. 1987. "Equitable Compensation: Methodological Criteria for Comparable Worth." In Christine Bose and Glenna Spitze (eds.), *Ingredients for Women's Employment Policy*. Albany, NY: State University of New York Press.

Stern, Marilyn and Karraker, Katherine Hildebrandt. 1989. "Sex Stereotyping of Infants: A Review of Gender Labeling Studies." *Sex Roles* 20: 501–22.

Stetsenko, Anna, Little, Todd D., Gordeeva, Tamara, Grasshof, Matthias, and Oettingen, Gabrielle. 2000. "Gender Effects in Children's Beliefs about School Performance: A Cross-Cultural Study." *Child Development* 71: 517–27.

Stockard, Jean and Johnson, Miriam M. 1992. *Sex and Gender in Society*. Englewood Cliffs, NJ: Prentice Hall.

Stone, Linda and McKee, Nancy P. 1999. *Gender and Culture in America*. Upper Saddle River, NJ: Prentice Hall.

Stroeher, S. K. 1994. "Sixteen Kindergarteners' Gender-Related Views of Careers." *The Elementary School Journal* 95: 95–103.

Sutton, Robert I. 1991. "Maintaining Norms about Expressed Emotions: The Case of Bill Collectors." *Administrative Science Quarterly* 36: 245–68

Tannen, Deborah. 1990. *You Just Don't Understand: Women and Men in Conversation*. New York: Ballantine Books.

Tannen, Deborah. 1994. *Talking from 9 to 5*. New York: William Morrow.

Tanner, Nancy and Zihlman, Adrienne. 1976. "Women in Evolution. Part I: Innovation and Selection in Human Origins." *Signs* 1: 585–608.

Thomas, W. I. 1966. *W. I. Thomas on Social Organization and Social Personality*, ed. Morris Janowitz. Chicago, IL: University of Chicago.

Thompson, Linda. 1993. "Conceptualizing Gender in Marriage: The Case of Marital Care." *Journal of Marriage and the Family* 55: 557–69.

Thorne, Barrie. 1982. "Feminist Rethinking of the Family: An Overview." In Barrie Thorne and Marilyn Yalom (eds.), *Rethinking the Family: Some Feminist Questions*. New York: Longman, pp. 1–24.

Thorne, Barrie. 1993. *Gender Play: Girls and Boys in School*. New Brunswick, NJ: Rutgers University Press.

Thorne, Barrie. 1995. "Symposium: On West and Fenstermaker's 'Doing Difference.'" *Gender & Society* 9: 497–9.

Tilly, Charles. 1998. *Durable Inequality*. Berkeley, CA: University of California Press.

Tilly Louise A. and Scott, Joan W. 1978. *Women, Work and Family*. New York: Holt, Rinehart and Winston.

Tomaskovic-Devey, Donald. 1993. *Gender and Racial Inequality at Work*. Ithaca, NY: ILR Press.

Tomaskovic-Devey, Donald, Kalleberg, Arne L. and Cook, Cynthia R. 1996. "Gender Differences and Organizational Commitment." In Arne L. Kalleberg, David Knoke, Peter V. Marsden, and Joe L. Spaeth (eds.), *Organizations in America*. Thousand Oaks, CA: Sage, pp. 302–23.

Tomaskovic-Devey, Donald, Kalleberg, Arne L., and Marsden, Peter V. 1996. "Organizational Patterns of Gender Segregation." In Arne L. Kalleberg, David Knoke, Peter V. Marsden, and Joe L. Spaeth (eds.), *Organizations in America*. Thousand Oaks, CA: Sage, pp. 276–301.

Tsui, Anne S. and Gutek, Barbara A. 1999. *Demographic Differences in Organizations*. New York: Lexington Books.

Tsui, Anne S., Egan, Terri D., and O'Reilly III, Charles A. 1992. "Being Different: Relational Demography and Organizational Attachment." *Administrative Science Quarterly* 37: 549–79.

Turner, J. C. 1987. *Rediscovering the Social Group: A Self-Categorization Theory*. New York: Basil Blackwell.

Turner, Stephanie S. 1999. "Intersex Identities: Locating New Intersections of Sex and Gender." *Gender & Society* 13: 457–79.

Tzeng, Jessie and Mare, Robert D. 1995. "Labor Market and Socioeconomic Effects on Marital Stability." *Social Science Research* 24: 329–51.

Udry, J. Richard. 2000. "Biological Limits of Gender Construction." *American Sociological Review* 65: 443–57.

United States Department of Education. 1997. *Statistical Abstract of the United States*. Washington, DC: US Government Printing Office.

United States Department of Education, National Center for Education Statistics. 1999. *National Study of Postsecondary Faculty*. Washington, DC: US Government Printing Office.

United States Department of Education. 2001. *Digest of Educational Statistics*. Washington, DC: US Government Printing Office.

Voyer, Daniel, Voyer, Susan, and Bryden, M. P. 1995. "Magnitude of Sex Differences in Spatial Abilities: A Meta-Analysis and Consideration of Critical Variables." *Psychological Bulletin* 117: 250–70.

Waite, Linda J. and Gallagher, Maggie. 2000. *The Case for Marriage*. New York: Doubleday.

Weber, Max. 1946. "Bureaucracy." In H. H. Gerth and C. Wright Mills (eds.), *Max Weber: Essays in Sociology*. New York: Oxford University Press, pp. 196–244.

Weber, Max. 1994. "Open and Closed Relationships." In David B. Grusky (ed.), *Social Stratification in Sociological Perspective*. Boulder, CO: Westview Press, pp. 126–9.

Weiler, Jeanne Drysdale. 2000. *Codes and Contradictions: Race, Gender Identity, and Schooling*. Albany, NY: SUNY Press.

Weisner, Thomas S., Garnier, Helen, and Loucky, James. 1994. "Domestic Tasks, Gender Egalitarian Values and Children's Gender Typing in Conventional and Nonconventional Families." *Sex Roles* 30: 23–54.

Wells, Thomas. 1999. "Changes in Occupational Sex Segregation during the 1980s and 1990s." *Social Science Quarterly* 80: 370–80.

Welsh, Sandy. 1999. "Gender and Sexual Harassment." *Annual Review of Sociology* 25: 169–90.

West, Candace and Fenstermaker, Sarah. 1995. "Doing Difference." *Gender & Society* 9: 8–37.

West, Candace and Fenstermaker, Sarah. 1993. "Power, Inequality and the Accomplishment of Gender: An Ethnomethodological View." In Paula England (ed.), *Theory on Gender/Feminism on Theory*. New York: Aldine De Gruyter, pp. 151–74.

West, Candace and Zimmerman, Don H. 1987. "Doing Gender." *Gender & Society* 1: 125–51.

Wharton, Amy S. and Baron, James N. 1987. "So Happy Together? The Impact of Gender Segregation on Men at Work." *American Sociological Review* 52: 574–87.

Wharton, Amy S. and Baron, James N. 1991. "Satisfaction? The Psychological Impact of Gender Segregation on Women at Work." *Sociological Quarterly* 32: 365–87.

Whiting, Beatrice B. and Edwards, Carolyn P. 1988. *Children of Different Worlds: The Formation of Social Behavior*. Cambridge, MA: Harvard University Press.

Whyte, William Foote. 1946. "The Social Structure of the Restaurant." *American Journal of Sociology* 54: 302–10.

Wilkie, Jane Riblett. 1993. "Changes in US Men's Attitudes toward the Family Provider Role, 1972–1989." *Gender & Society* 7: 261–79.

Williams, Christine. 1989. *Gender Differences at Work: Women and Men in Nontraditional Occupations*. Berkeley, CA: University of California Press.

Williams, Christine. 1995. *Still a Man's World*. Berkeley, CA: University of California.

Williams, Christine L., Giuffre, Patti A. and Dellinger, Kirsten. 1999. "Sexuality in the Workplace." *Annual Review of Sociology* 25: 73–93.

Williams, Joan. 2000. *Unbending Gender: Why Work and Family Conflict and What to Do About It*. New York: Oxford University Press.

Williams, Katherine Y. and O'Reilly III, Charles A. 1998. "Demography and Diversity in Organizations: A Review of 40 Years of Research." *Research in Organizational Behavior* 20: 77–140.

Wilson, William Julius. 1996. *When Work Disappears: The World of the New Urban Poor*. New York: Alfred A. Knopf.

Zhao, Yilu. 2002. "The Feminization of Veterinary Medicine." *The New York Times*, Sunday, June 9.

Index

NB: Page numbers in *italics* denote tables

LIVERPOOL JOHN MOORES UNIVERSITY
Aldham Roberts L.R.C.
TEL. 051 231 3701/3634